JAPAN SINCE 1980

This book tells the story of the performance of Japan's economic and political institutions starting in the late 1970s through late 2007. The authors explain how Japan's flawed response to new economic, political, and technological forces, requiring more open markets and political institutions, ushered in almost fifteen years of economic and financial distress and lost economic and financial development potential from 1990 to 2005. Japan's impressive economic performance in the 1980s in fact masked an "accident waiting to happen": the burst of the bubble in equity and real estate prices in 1990 and 1991. Japan's iron triangle of politicians, bureaucrats, and client industries, combined with a flawed financial liberalization process and policy errors by the Bank of Japan and the Ministry of Finance, brought Japan to an abyss of deflation, recession, and insolvency by the late 1990s. The turning point was the election of Koizumi as prime minister in 2001. Koizumi took advantage of important institutional changes in Japan's electoral system and policy making and implemented many changes in economic policy. The book explores Koizumi's economic reform, new developments in Japanese people's socioeconomic conditions, the politics and economy after Koizumi, and the economic and political challenges facing Japan in the new century.

Thomas F. Cargill is a professor of economics at the University of Nevada, Reno. He studies financial and central bank policy in Japan and the United States. Professor Cargill is coauthor of *The Political Economy of Japanese Monetary Policy* (1997), *Financial Policy and Central Banking in Japan* (2000), and *Postal Savings and Fiscal Investment in Japan* (2003). He has published in *Journal of Comparative Economics, Journal of Economic History, Journal of Political Economy*, and *Monetary and Economic Studies*.

Takayuki Sakamoto is a professor of political science at the Department of Policy Studies, the University of Kitakyushu, Japan. He studies comparative political economy of industrialized democracies. Professor Sakamoto is the author of *Economic Policy and Performance in Industrial Democracies* (2008) and *Building Policy Legitimacy in Japan* (1999). His articles have appeared in *Comparative Political Studies, European Journal of Political Research*, and *Party Politics*.

THE WORLD
Since 1980

This new series is designed to examine politics, economics, and social change in important countries and regions over the past two and a half decades. No prior background knowledge of a given country will be required by readers. The books are written by leading social scientists.

Volumes published

Brazil Since 1980; Francisco Vidal Luna and Herbert S. Klein
Israel Since 1980; Guy Ben-Porat, Yagil Levy, Shlomo Mizrahi,
    Ayre Naor, and Erez Tzfadia
Mexico Since 1980; Stephen Haber, Herbert S. Klein, Noel Maurer,
    and Kevin J. Middlebrook
The United States Since 1980; Dean Baker

Volumes in preparation

Britain Since 1980; Roger Middleton
China Since 1980; Ross Garnaut
France Since 1980; Timothy Smith
India Since 1980; Sumit Ganguly
Russia Since 1980; Steven Rosefielde and Stefan Hedlund

JAPAN
Since 1980

Thomas F. Cargill
University of Nevada, Reno

Takayuki Sakamoto
University of Kitakyushu, Japan

CAMBRIDGE
UNIVERSITY PRESS

CAMBRIDGE UNIVERSITY PRESS

Cambridge, New York, Melbourne, Madrid, Cape Town, Singapore, São Paulo, Delhi

Cambridge University Press

32 Avenue of the Americas, New York, NY 10013-2473, USA

www.cambridge.org
Information on this title: www.cambridge.org/9780521672726

First published 2008

Printed in the United States of America

A catalog record for this publication is available from the British Library.

Library of Congress Cataloging in Publication Data

Cargill, Thomas F.
Japan since 1980 / Thomas F. Cargill, Takayuki Sakamoto.
    p.   cm. – (The world since 1980)
Includes bibliographical references and index.
ISBN 978-0-521-85672-0 (hardcover : alk. paper) – ISBN 978-0-521-67272-6
(pbk. : alk. paper)
1. Japan – Economic conditions – 1989–   2. Japan – Economic conditions – 1945–1989.
3. Japan – Economic policy – 1989–   I. Sakamoto, Takayuki, 1963–   II. Title.
HC462.95.C37   2008
330.952–dc22   2008027115

ISBN   978-0-521-85672-0 hardback
ISBN   978-0-521-67272-6 paperback

Contents

Preface

The beginning of the new century witnessed a major turning point in Japan's economic and political performance and institutional design. Starting from a flawed financial liberalization process in the 1980s and the collapse of equity and land prices in the early 1990s, followed by a decade of economic and political distress in the 1990s, Japan started a transition toward more aggressive market reforms after Prime Minister Junichiro Koizumi came to power in 2001. By 2005, there were signs that the Japanese economy and financial system had finally commenced a sustainable recovery. Japan's economic and political institutions have also undergone significant redesign.

The book is part of a new series of books by Cambridge University Press and focuses on Japan's economic, political, and social development since 1980; hence, the title of this book – *Japan Since 1980*. Clearly the date of 1980 is somewhat arbitrary, especially when applied to more than one country. Nonetheless, important institutional changes took place in many developed and developing countries in the past three decades, with 1980 as a loose pivotal year. This is certainly the case for Japan.

It was not an easy task to provide an overview of Japan's economic and political performance and institutional development over the past three decades. At a minimum, it required the collaboration of an economist and political scientist to tell the story properly. Our collaboration on this book essentially started when Cargill and Sakamoto met and participated in a conference at Southern Methodist University in 2004. The collaboration has been successful; each has learned from the other, and the book reflects a political-economy perspective of Japan's development since 1980. The story also had to be told in such a way so as not to get bogged down in detailed discussion of economic and political institutions and events that would be of interest only to the specialist. We have made every effort to present the story in as clear a manner as possible so that the reader can obtain an overview of Japan's economic and political development during the past three decades.

The book is not merely a narrative of events but adopts a framework and point of view consistent with a wide range of research published in the specialist literature in economics and political science. Many examples of this research are cited in the book. We also made abundant use of information provided by Japanese newspapers and government ministries and agencies. The new institutional design of Japan's economy and political system is emerging, and Japan appears to have turned the corner on the severest of the economic distress of the past.

However, Japan continues to face serious economic and political challenges – the demographic challenges from a declining and aging population, the need to make the economy efficient and productive to survive and prosper in today's globalized economy, and the need to enhance the government's policy-making capabilities to generate policy innovations necessary to meet these demographic and economic challenges. The challenges are indeed formidable; however, we are cautiously optimistic that Japan will meet the new challenges with relative success. Although its path will not lead it to a Western set of economic and political institutions, Japan will continue to become more open economically and politically. Japan will remain one of the most important countries in the world for some time to come.

Cargill would like to thank students at the University of Nevada, Reno (UNR), his home institution, and the University of Hawaii at Manoa where he has been fortunate to teach during the summer for a number of years. Much of the material in this book was used in these courses. In fall 2007 at UNR, much of the manuscript was used in a class on Japan. He expresses appreciation to Susanna Powers, his graduate assistant, for reading the entire manuscript, preparing the index and for other contributions and, finally, expresses appreciation to Mary Cargill for her support.

Sakamoto would like to thank his enthusiastic students for providing useful feedback on different parts of the book used in his classes in political science. He also gives special thanks to Chad Sheinbein, who provided valuable research assistance. Sakamoto would like to express gratitude to Barbara and Miku Sakamoto for their support.

Both of us would like to thank our editor, Scott Parris, for his encouragement and guidance in preparing the manuscript. We appreciate the reviews of the initial proposal and, especially, the two detailed reviews of the draft manuscript. The reviewers made a large number of suggestions that significantly improved the book. Of course, we are responsible for any errors.

Abbreviations

BIS	Bank for International Settlements
BOJ	Bank of Japan
CEFP	Council on Economic and Fiscal Policy
CGP	Clean Government Party (also *Komeito*)
DIC	Deposit Insurance Corporation
DP	Democratic Party of Japan (formally DPJ in English)
DSP	Democratic Socialist Party
FDIC	Federal Deposit Insurance Corporation
FILP	Fiscal Investment and Loan Program
FSA	Financial Services Agency
GDP	Gross Domestic Product
HGP	High Growth Period
IMF	International Monetary Fund
JCP	Japanese Communist Party
JNP	Japan New Party
JSP	Japan Socialist Party (same as SDP)
LDP	Liberal Democratic Party
LP	Liberal Party
MITI	Ministry of International Trade and Industry
MMD	multimember district (an electoral system)
MOF	Ministry of Finance
NFP	New Frontier Party
OECD	Organization for Economic Cooperation and Development

PCA	Prompt Corrective Action
PR	proportional representation (an electoral system)
PSS	Postal Savings System
QEP	Quantitative Easing Policy
SDP	Social Democratic Party of Japan (formally SDPJ in English, the same as JSP)
SMD	single-member district (an electoral system)
ZIRP	Zero-Interest-Rate Policy

1

Introduction and Overview

Introduction

The evolution and transition of Japan's economic and political institutions during the entire post–World War II period is remarkable for two reasons. First, Japan completed reindustrialization and reestablished prewar economic growth trends in record time. By the 1970s, Japan emerged as the second largest economy in the world. Japan remains a major component of the world economy with one of the world's higher standards of living for its population.[1] Second, following the completion of reindustrialization, Japan's economic and political development exhibited wide fluctuations in performance. After a short but turbulent period of economic distress in the early 1970s, Japan achieved impressive economic, financial, and political stability from 1975 to 1989. The perception of Japan's economic invincibility became widespread during this period. Starting in 1990, however, Japan experienced intense economic, financial, and political distress. The economy and financial system continued to decline or stagnate until 2005. Despite economic recovery by the mid-2000s, Japan continues to face lingering economic and political problems.

---

[1] World Bank estimates of GDP, gross national income, and population can be found at http://www.worldbank.org, Quick Reference Tables. World Bank GDP rankings for 2006 in terms of Purchasing Power Parity (PPP) indicate that Japan is now the fourth largest economy in the world after the United States, China, and India. The 2006 data show Japan only slightly smaller than India but significantly smaller than the United States or China. PPP takes into account differences in price levels between countries so that an international dollar has the same purchasing power over GDP as a U.S. dollar has over GDP in the United States. In terms of 2006 real GDP adjusted for market exchange rates, Japan remains the second largest economy in the world.

The record of Japan's economic performance since the early 1970s
and how Japan has adapted to internal and external forces of change
have offered a number of important insights into the development
process in general.[2] Japan has become a major case study and has influenced economic and political institutions in many countries as they
either tried to emulate Japan's economic success or learn from Japan's
failures.

The general outline of Japan's postwar development can best be
understood by dividing the postwar period into four distinct periods.
The first period, from 1945 to 1950, is one of *establishing economic
stability*. During this period, Japan focused on stabilizing its economic
and political institutions following the end of World War II. Serious
efforts to stabilize the economy commenced in 1949 with the Dodge
Line austerity program designed to reduce inflation, balance the budget, redesign the Bank of Japan (BOJ) to render it less susceptible to
pressure to expand the money supply, and establish a fixed-exchange
rate at ¥360 to $1.00. The second period, from 1950 to 1970, is one of
reindustrialization and *relative political stabilization*. Japan achieved reindustrialization in record time because of the combined effect of the
Dodge Line policies, the stimulative impact of the Korean War starting
in June 1950, and the process of political stabilization starting in 1955
when the Liberal Democratic Party (LDP) assumed power. The period
from 1950 to 1970 is frequently referred to as the High Growth Period
(HGP) because annual real GDP growth averaged about 10 percent[3]
with moderate inflation of about 5 percent. This is a relatively low
inflation rate for such a rapid pace of real output growth. The third
period, from 1970 to 1980, is one of *new environment* during which

[2] There is an immense literature on Japan's pre- and postwar economic development, some
of which will be cited in subsequent chapters; however, a general overview of economic
development through the late 1980s is provided by Ito (1992) and Yamamura and Yasuba
(1987). Hoshi and Patrick (2000) provide a number of perspectives on the "lost decade" of
the 1990s. Cargill, Hutchison, and Ito (1997 and 2000) review Japan's postwar financial and
monetary development.

[3] Some observers regard 1955 rather than 1950 as the start of the HGP because the size of
the economy did not achieve the prewar peak until about 1955. The starting year of 1950
used in this discussion is based on three considerations; first, the Dodge Line established a
"takeoff" position for the Japanese economy; second, the start of the Korean War in June
1950 significantly stimulated the Japanese economy as Japan was used as a base of operations
by the United States and allies; and, third, real GNP started rapid growth after 1949 (Ito,
1992, pp. 44–45). According to data cited in Ito (1992, p. 45), the average growth of real
GDP from 1953 to 1970 was approximately 9.4 percent.

Japan's economic institutions came into conflict with a new set of economic, political, and technological forces. These forces set into motion a transition toward a "new" Japan that differs from the "old" Japan. The fourth period, starting around 1980, is one of *transition* toward a more market-directed economy and transition in the political regime. The transition continues to the present and is the subject of this study.

The wide swings in economic and political performance render the fourth period remarkable. In the 1980s, Japan seemed invincible in terms of economic, financial, and political stability, whereas in the 1990s and the beginning of the new century, Japan seemed unable to do anything right. The distress by the late 1990s illustrated to all but a few that the "old" Japan was no longer viable. Japan needed to adapt its economic and political institutions to a new environment and, in the process, the old social contract between the government and the population began to unravel.

These four periods – economic stabilization, reindustrialization and relative political stability, new environment, and transition – are pedagogical perspectives to conceptualize the main shifts and time periods of Japan's economic and political performance since the end of World War II. The starting and ending points are not precise, but they are close enough to identify the major shifts in economic, financial, and political institutions in Japan. The transition period is the most significant because it represents a dramatic shift in how Japan operates. The first three periods are collectively referred to as the pretransition stages of postwar Japan.

The pretransition stages of postwar Japan have been discussed extensively from both an economic and political perspective; however, it is important to summarize the highlights of the events leading up to the fourth period – the transition of Japan since 1980. The following is a brief summary of postwar Japan up to 1980.

The Pretransition Period: Developments up to 1980

Many of Japan's economic and political institutions in the postwar period up to 1980 continued to develop along trends established in the prewar period. The trends, however, were modified by the war experience and the Allied Occupation of Japan that lasted from 1945 to 1952.

Establishing Stability, 1945–1950

The immediate objective of the postwar government was to shift from wartime to peacetime production, absorb large numbers of returning military, and stabilize an economy marked by hyperinflation, unemployment, and government deficits. Japan's economic stabilization policies commenced under the guidance of a competent and strong bureaucracy. Economic and financial instability was addressed in 1949 by a series of polices collectively referred to as the Dodge Line, named after Joseph Dodge, who served as economic advisor to the Allied Occupation. The Dodge Line austerity policies would have generated significant economic cost in Japan in the short run; however, the start of the Korean War in June 1950 stimulated the Japanese economy so that Japan was able to establish a "takeoff" platform for reindustrialization and avoid the recession that normally would be expected from implementing the Dodge Line policies.

Democratization and the establishment of a new and stable government was the primary political objective of this period. Japan became fully democratic with free elections, free party competition, and universal suffrage after the new constitution came into effect in 1947. The constitution deprived the emperor of political power, and he became a symbol of state. Japan also was demilitarized completely.

Reindustrialization and Political Stabilization, 1950–1970

By 1950, the economy stabilized. The next two decades would witness a reindustrialization process in record time, accompanied by economic and political stability. This performance was achieved with a set of economic and political institutions that in many respects were a continuation of prewar trends. The bureaucracy was an important influence over the economy. The politicians would set a broad, general course for the nation, whereas bureaucrats crafted and implemented the economic policy to achieve the goal of economic recovery and growth. Japan developed a set of economic institutions designed to limit risk and bankruptcy through mutual support systems, nontransparency, long-term "customer relationships" rather than short-term "market-relationships," and relied on mercantilist trade policy. These clearly were a continuation of trends established in the prewar period.

Figures 1.1–1.5 provide an overview of Japan's economic performance for a major part of the postwar in terms of real and nominal

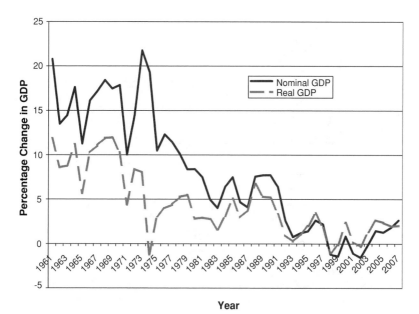

Figure 1.1. Annual Percentage Changes in Nominal and Real GDP, 1961 to 2007.
Source: The OECD *Economic Outlook* (various years). *Note:* The values for 2006–07
are projections.

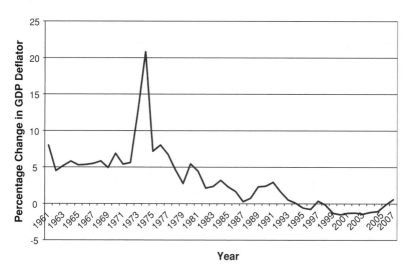

Figure 1.2. Annual Percentage Changes in GDP Deflator, 1961 to 2007. *Source:* The
OECD *Economic Outlook* (various years). *Note:* The values for 2006–07 are projections.

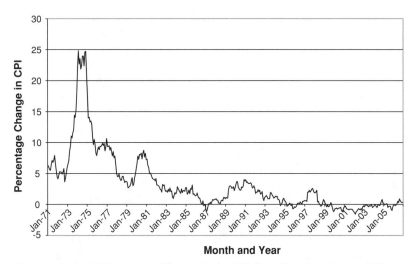

Figure 1.3. Annual Percentage Changes in the CPI from Year Ago, January 1971 to December 2006. *Source:* Ministry of Internal Affairs and Communications, Statistics Bureau, Consumer Price Index, http://www.stat.go.jp/english/data/cpi/index.htm.

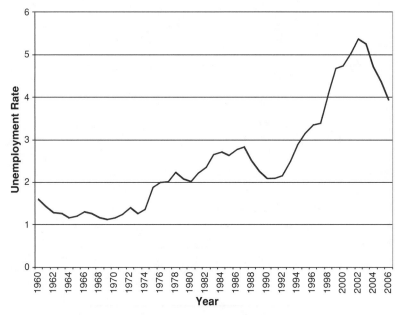

Figure 1.4. Unemployment Rate, 1960 to 2007. *Source:* The OECD *Economic Outlook* (various years). *Note:* The values for 2006–07 are projections.

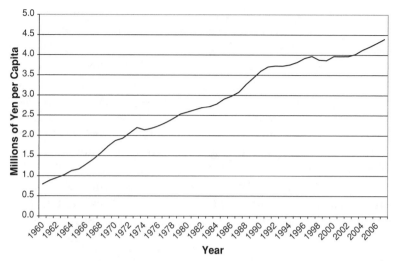

Figure 1.5. Real GDP per Capita, 1960 to 2007. *Source:* 1960–1979: GDP from Figure 1.1 and population from Ministry of Internal Affairs and Communications, Historical Statistics of Japan, Population; http://www.stat.go.jp/english/data/chouki/02.htm; 1980–2007: International Monetary Fund, World Economic Outlook Database, Japan, http://www.imf.org/external/pubs/ft/weo/2007/01/data/index.aspx. *Note:* The values for 2006–2007 are estimates.

GDP growth, GDP deflator and CPI inflation, unemployment rate and standard of living measured by real GDP per capita. The macroeconomic performance, the rise in the standard of living, and the relative political stability exhibited by the 1960s vindicated Japan's approach. The political system started its transition to a stable system in 1955, when two conservative parties merged to form the LDP, and the left and right wings of socialist parties merged to become the Japan Socialist Party (JSP). The new party system built around the two parties formed the basis of the so-called 1955-System, which lasted until 1993. In the 1955-System, the LDP controlled the Japanese government without interruption, with the JSP as the distant second largest party. Other small center-left opposition parties usually allied themselves with the JSP[4] in the earlier periods; however, from the end of the 1970s to 1993, they cooperated with the LDP more frequently.

[4] The JSP later changed its name to the Social Democratic Party of Japan (SDP); hence, JSP is appropriate when referring to its origin while SDP is appropriate for references to later periods.

The general contours of Japan's industrial goals and approaches to achieving those goals did not experience wide shifts during the HGP, because of the LDP's one-party rule, the absence of political divisions affecting policy, and stable management by a bureaucracy staffed with permanent officials. In many ways, the industrial goals were a continuation of prewar objectives of first catching up with Western countries in economic development and then achieving superiority with Western countries, minus the goal of achieving military superiority to the West. This industrial objective had first been adopted around the time of the Meiji Restoration in 1868, when the country realized that it lagged far behind the West in industrialization and militarization after two and a half centuries of isolationist policy by the Edo government, which had ruled Japan between 1603 and 1867 (Tokugawa Period).

New Environment, 1970–1980

Three events impacted Japan in the 1970s that would induce and influence Japan's transition after 1980. First, the economic stability of the previous two decades ended with a short but turbulent period in the early 1970s of high inflation, referred to as "wild inflation." An unprecedented oil price shock in 1973, combined with several previous years of expansionary monetary policy, drove up inflation rates on a monthly basis to 30 percent per annum, adversely affecting economic growth. Japan weathered the oil shock reasonably well, and by 1975 the economy stabilized; however, the 1973 oil shock and another oil crisis in 1979 lowered Japan's natural growth path.

Second, Japan's reindustrialization process was completed by the late 1960s. The resulting decline in the rate of domestic investment spending, combined with higher energy prices, reduced the 10 percent growth rate of the HGP to the 3 to 5 percent range. Slower growth would have important impacts on Japan. Slower growth initiated financial liberalization, reduced revenue growth and contributed to government deficits, and began to alter the implicit social contract between the government and Japanese households. Japanese households had been willing to forgo access to the financial system as a source of funds (consumer and mortgage credit), place their substantial savings in government controlled low-interest financial assets, and support a producer-oriented public policy in exchange for high rates of real income growth and economic security. Although households continued to have faith that the government would guarantee economic security, the slower growth environment began to weaken a major pillar of the social contract that emerged after World War II – high and secure economic growth.

Third, Japan found itself in a new operating environment as the world started experiencing new economic, political, and technological developments in the 1970s. In varying degrees, these developments induced liberalization or "neoliberal" policies in a wide range of developed and developing economies.

The new economic environment was characterized by higher energy prices, uncertain supplies of energy, high and uncertain inflation rates, collapse of the fixed exchange rate system in 1973, and financial disruptions caused by government efforts to impose interest rate controls and other limits on the flow of funds. The new economic environment set into motion a financial liberalization process that eventually would affect most of Japan's economic and political institutions because it clashed with Japan's rigidly controlled, internationally isolated, and regulated economic and financial system.

The new political environment was characterized by a general shift in attitudes in industrial democracies away from collectivist approaches to managing the economy such as that adopted by Japan toward market-directed resource allocation systems as in the United States. This in no way is meant to imply that the United States was a model of individualism, but of all of the major industrialized economies during this time, the United States relied less on collectivist approaches to managing the economy than any major country. The collectivist approach had been found wanting in many places by the 1980s and, as a result, a new political attitude emerged that emphasized open and transparent markets, less government interference, and more open and democratic political institutions. The pace and extent of liberalization varied from country to country and the process was more often driven by market innovations rather than government innovations. In fact, it was market innovations especially in the financial sector that forced governments to change regulations. The process was well under way in the United States by the 1970s and reinforced by the election of President Ronald Reagan in 1980. Margaret Thatcher's election as prime minister in 1979 was a turning point in the United Kingdom. Japan was not immune. Japan experienced increasing demands from the United States, the United Kingdom, and Europe to cease its mercantilist policies, open its real and financial sectors to the rest of the world, and in general adopt a more market-oriented set of economic institutions.

The new technological environment was characterized by advances in computer and telecommunication technology, making it increasingly difficult for governments to impose binding constraints over the financial system or to regulate the inflow and outflow of capital. The international financial system was becoming increasingly flexible, and the collapse of the fixed exchange rate system made it difficult for export-oriented countries such as Japan to remain isolated from the international financial system.

The new economic, political, and technological environment, combined with slower long-run growth potential, set the stage for the transition of Japan's economic and political institutions, which continues to the present day. The transition after 1980 started with limited financial liberalization, which appeared successful in the 1980s. Flaws in the process, combined with policy errors by the BOJ and the Ministry of Finance (MOF), brought Japan to an abyss of deflation, recession, and the insolvency of its banking system in the late 1990s. As a result, the nature and extent of the transition changed dramatically.

The Transition since 1980 in Broad Perspective

The past three decades have witnessed major changes in Japan's economic and political institutions. Although Japan has and will continue to develop its own model of the market and democracy conditioned by its culture, history, and perception of its place in the world, the newly evolving economic and political institutions will continue to become more open, competitive, transparent, and responsive to a different set of socioeconomic interests than in the past. The ongoing transition has and will affect the social contract between the government and its citizens.

The transition in broad perspective can be considered in terms of four periods defined by Japan's economic and financial performance, response of the government to the new operating environment, policy outcomes of that response, and the extent to which Japan's economic and political institutions changed. The transition is decomposed into phases defined both in terms of time sequence and policy outcomes.

The High-Water Mark of Japanese Economy, 1980–1985

The designation of this period as the "high-water" mark of the transition is a result of the apparent success that Japan achieved in adapting to the new environment and achieving a high degree of economic and political stability in sharp contrast to other countries' experiences. Much of the world came to admire Japan's economic and political institutions because Japan seemed to have achieved economic, financial, and political stability, whereas many industrialized economies were dealing with high rates of inflation, unemployment, and financial disruptions.

The period started with Japan avoiding the inflation-disinflation process typical of virtually every industrial economy in response to the second set of oil price shocks in 1979–1980. The typical response in most countries was to inflate the economy by central bank policy to offset the adverse effects of higher prices on real GDP. This policy was based on the traditional Phillips curve long-run trade-off between inflation and employment in which higher employment could be purchased with higher inflation. The Phillips curve policy was fundamentally flawed, however. The attempt by central banks in other industrial economies to offset the recessionary pressures of the oil crisis and maintain employment failed, and the high inflation required central banks subsequently to disinflate the economy, which intensified the economic distress. These countries ended up with "stagflation" – higher inflation and lower employment (higher unemployment). Japan not only avoided stagflation and its associated economic disruptions, but, more remarkably, the BOJ continued to follow a price stabilization policy while at the same time being one of the world's most formally dependent central banks. This performance earned the BOJ the reputation as a "model central bank" in terms of price stabilization policy outcomes and its credibility as a price-stabilizing central bank. This performance and reputation contradicted the conventional wisdom that formally dependent central banks were more likely to generate inflation than formally independent central banks such as the Federal Reserve System.

It was not just Japan's economic policy success that drew world attention. Japan also appeared to be engaged in a successful financial liberalization process on both the domestic and international front. Long recognized as critical to the functioning of the entire economy, the financial system was designed to transfer the large savings of the household sector to the corporate sector. The Japanese financial system that reached maturity in the 1970s was rigidly regulated, administratively controlled, internationally isolated, and relied on the transfer of funds through private and public bank channels, as opposed to relying on money and capital markets. In fact, corporate governance was intimately tied to the financial system relying on a set of company groups or *keiretsu*, centered on a large financial institution, usually one of the large city banks. This system also was known as the main bank system.

Japan's transition starting in the second half of the 1970s focused almost entirely on the financial system[5] by permitting financial institutions to become more market-oriented in how they evaluated credit, monitored credit, and priced credit; by commencing a policy of interest rate liberalization; by relaxing constraints on the inflow and outflow of capital; by permitting money and capital market to develop; and by permitting greater access to the domestic financial system by foreign financial institutions. The pace of reform was slow and incremental but, by the early 1980s, Japanese financial markets and institutions were more competitive, more diversified, and more open to international competition than previously.

Japan's financial transition outcomes stood in sharp contrast to the experiences of other countries, especially the United States and parts of Europe. These countries were dealing with high rates of inflation and unemployment, and financial disruptions ranging from banking problems in a large number of countries to the collapse of the savings and loan industry in the United States. Japan had not only become the second largest economy in the world and appeared to be a "model of financial liberalization" with a "model central bank" that maintained price stability but also emerged as a major financial power in the world by the mid-1980s. In 1985, Japan became the largest creditor nation in the world, Japanese banks were the largest in the world, and Japanese financial institutions appeared sound and stable.

---

[5]   The financial reforms started in 1976 increased in pace so that by the early 1980s, Japan was officially committed to liberalizing its financial system, including allowing foreign financial institutions to play a meaningful role in the allocation of credit. In 1976, the MOF officially recognized a short-term market in repurchase agreements based on government bonds (*gensaki* market) and in 1978 permitted banks to issue large certificates of deposits (CDs). The MOF made a series of administrative decisions starting in 1978 that relaxed controls over the government bond market and permitted secondary markets in government bonds to be established.

Japan's financial liberalization process was impressive, considering the starting point; however, the reforms paled in comparison to the changes needed to render Japan's financial system open, competitive, and transparent. As a result, developed countries continued to pressure Japan to increase the pace and extent of financial liberalization and extend liberalization to the nonfinancial sectors of the economy by eliminating trade barriers, restructuring corporate governance, and reforming labor markets. In hindsight, the apparent stability of the financial transition was misleading for two reasons.

First, the transition toward more open and competitive institutions was confined to specific and narrow components of the financial system. Nor did policy makers comprehend the far-ranging effects on economic and political institutions that even limited financial liberalization would generate. Increased emphasis on financial innovation, competition, and greater presence of foreign financial institutions would require a changed view of Japan's labor practices of "lifetime" employment and the seniority-based wage system. The entrance of foreign financial institutions and new financial services and assets would require higher labor productivity and incentives to innovate not constrained by lifetime employment or seniority wages.

Second, financial liberalization policy was fundamentally flawed and masked growing conflicts that made the financial system and general economy susceptible to any shock. In this regard, the successful price stabilization policy of the BOJ played an important role. Price stability narrowed the gap between regulated and unregulated interest rates and, hence, made it easier for Japan to pursue a slow and gradual financial liberalization process that essentially left the old regime in place and limited any manifestation of the growing conflicts. In addition, the BOJ's policy successes contributed to overconfidence in the ability of monetary policy to achieve economic stabilization that increased the probability of policy error.

An Accident Waiting to Happen, 1985–1990

The end of the "high-water" period began in 1985 at the very height of Japanese economic and political stability, when the BOJ, with the support of the MOF, conducted a monetary policy focused on external rather than internal conditions. This policy was designed to redress trade imbalance between the United States and Japan agreed to by the Group of Five (G5), known as the September 1985 Plaza Accord.[6] The policy first focused on depreciating the dollar (appreciating the yen) to reduce the large U.S. current account deficit. But because the dollar started to decline more rapidly than desired, the BOJ shifted to an expansionary monetary policy to defend the dollar and stem yen appreciation. The easy monetary policy also was rationalized as a countercyclical response to Japan's recession induced by the rapid yen appreciation and its negative effects on exports. The government was not willing to use fiscal policy (increased spending) for economic stimulus because it had been pursuing fiscal austerity since 1980 to reduce the budget deficit. As a result, the Japanese government placed the burden of economic stimulus on the BOJ's monetary policy. Money and credit expanded after 1985.

Although the second half of the 1980s appeared to be a continuation of the first half in terms of macroeconomic performance and continued financial liberalization, the shift toward expansionary monetary policy after 1985 combined with a flawed financial liberalization process led to the "bubble" in equity and real estate prices. Equity and real estate prices by 1988 exhibited all of the characteristics of an unsustainable asset bubble. The flawed financial liberalization process, combined with a set of political institutions wedded to the old regime, turned Japan into an "accident waiting to happen." Any shock to the system would generate economic and financial distress. The collapse of asset prices in 1990 and 1991 provided the shock.

The "burst of the bubble economy" commenced in 1989 when the BOJ raised the discount rate in May 1989 over concern about asset price inflation and an increase in the general inflation rate. The immediate effect was to slow asset inflation and economic growth. But by 1990 and 1991, asset prices collapsed, and subsequent events revealed a fundamentally weak financial system and set the stage for a long period of intense economic distress. It is common to refer to Japan's economic performance during the 1990s as Japan's "lost decade"; however, since the economic distress continued into the new century, it might be just as appropriate to refer to Japan's economic stagnation over the 1990–2005 period as Japan's "lost decade and half."

---

[6] The Plaza Accord was signed September 22, 1985, at the Plaza Hotel in New York City by the G5 – France, West Germany, Japan, the United States, and the United Kingdom. The decision was made to coordinate exchange market interventions to depreciate the dollar against the yen and the German mark.

Japan's economic bureaucracy and politicians were wedded to the old regime of mutual support and nontransparency and, at the same time, maintained high confidence in their ability to manage the economy. Policies that emerged from this condition failed to reverse the economic and financial distress, which ultimately led to a redesign of Japan's economic and political institutions.

Economic, Financial, and Political Distress, 1990 to 2001

The 1990s begin with the collapses of asset prices, disinflation, and recession. At the start, policy makers and the public were not particularly concerned. In the past, Japan's recessions were relatively short and not severe. Inflation had been contained successfully since 1975. Although misconceived, the asset bubble had increased the wealth of a large number of households. The public remained passive and continued to have faith that Japan's economy would prosper, and continued to anticipate an increase in the standard of living in a relatively risk-free socioeconomic environment. In sum, the slowdown after 1989 was viewed as only temporary by both the public and the government. Japan would again regain the momentum of the 1980s under the current political-economic regime.

This attitude changed as the decade progressed. Economic and financial distress continued and intensified after a brief recovery in 1995–1996. The near collapse of the economy in 1998 and major solvency problems in the financial system forced Japan to acknowledge that the set of economic and political institutions that had served Japan since the end of World War II were incompatible with the new environment and, hence, had to be changed. Public perceptions of how the Japanese economy worked and public expectations of their future standard of living changed radically near the end of the 1990s. Continued economic and financial distress dashed the public's confidence in their economic security based on low unemployment and lifetime employment. The failure of government to end the crisis dashed the public's confidence in the ability of the government to manage the economy. A series of corruption scandals involving the MOF and the BOJ further shook the public's confidence in the economic bureaucracy. The public also started to lose trust in the social security pensions and health care systems provided by either the government or their employers, because of their rising costs as a result of the significant aging of the population – the public expected increased future contributions and premiums and reduced benefits.

The economic and financial distress reversed a record of four decades of stability, growth, and development. Japan's economy exhibited either negative or very low positive growth in the 1990s. Starting in late 1997 and throughout 1998, Japan came close to collapse. Prices started falling in 1995, and deflation continued to at least 2007. The unemployment rate increased. Unemployment doubled to around 5 percent compared to the pre-1990 period. The 1990s is referred to as Japan's "lost decade" because of the lost economic and financial development potential. The economic and financial distress was matched by great political instability.

Japanese politics under LDP rule had remained relatively static from the mid-1950s to the late 1980s. But in the late 1980s, Japanese politics and policy making started undergoing changes that were gradual but altered the nature of the postwar economic-political regime. In 1989, the LDP lost its majority in the upper house election for the first time since 1955. More important, the LDP lost control of government in 1993 for the first time in its history when it lost its majority in the lower house election. Just before the 1993 election, two groups of LDP politicians left the party to form two new conservative parties, and, as a result, the LDP was unable to win the majority in the lower house. The LDP was replaced by a non-LDP eight-party coalition government. From the early 1990s on, political parties split, merged, or were created on a large scale. Many politicians switched party affiliation in efforts to ensure their reelection and improve the prospects of being in a party that could win control of government. In this environment, it almost appeared that responding to the economic crisis was secondary in politicians' priorities, as they were preoccupied with their own political survival. The LDP returned to power in 1994, but because of decline of the LDP's electoral strength, the Japanese government has since been ruled by coalition governments most of the time.

Important electoral reform took place in 1994. The multimember district system (MMD) was replaced with a mixed member system combining single-member districts (SMD) and proportional representation (PR). This reform initiated large-scale party realignment and changed the structure of party competition. Electoral reform also changed the power relationship between party leadership and member politicians. Previously, the intraparty factions in the LDP retained significant power vis-à-vis party leadership, including the party president (prime minister) because the factions controlled the LDP presidential election, post assignments, individual candidate nomination and endorsement, and financial resources. Electoral reform indirectly redistributed power from the factions to party leadership by introducing a new party subsidy system in which government subsidies were given to political parties that were controlled by party leadership. This power shift became conspicuous under the Koizumi administration (2001–2006), when Junichiro Koizumi significantly reduced the power of the factions by depriving them of their power of cabinet post assignments and policy-making control.

Another political change induced partly by electoral reform took place after Koizumi came to power, when policy competition came to play a larger role in intra-LDP competition as well as in interparty competition. The role of public opinion became increasingly important in policy competition within the LDP and across political parties, because the new electoral system made politicians more sensitive to public opinion, as will be explained in Chapter 7. Political parties started judging the legitimacy of different policies by the public support that they enjoyed. Public opinion likewise came to constrain the power of the bureaucracy, because public support became important in policy making and implementation and politicians came to pay more attention to public opinion.

Koizumi – The Unconventional Politician, April 2001– September 2006

The public wanted change by the end of the 1990s, and time was ripe for the emergence of strong and effective leadership that could make policy outside the box of the LDP's conventional distributive politics. Prime Minister Koizumi's succession of power could not have come at a more opportune time. Koizumi was elected prime minister by the LDP in April 2001 after a campaign against former Prime Minister Hashimoto, a traditional LDP leader. Koizumi ended his tenure as prime minister at the end of September 2006. During this period, Japan was to experience significant changes in politics and the economy.

Koizumi was considered unconventional. First, although he was an LDP politician, he set out to destroy what he called the "old" LDP that was at the center of Japan's interest-based iron triangle of the LDP, bureaucracy, and business, and that was largely unresponsive to the general public. His mutinous approach to his own LDP was possible because he had always been outside the mainstream factions and been a loner and thus did not have as high stake in the party as regular senior LDP politicians.

Second, under the slogans of "There will be no economic recovery without structural reform" and "Structural reform without sanctuary," Koizumi advocated more aggressive reforms to solve the economic and financial distress than did his predecessors. Koizumi wanted a faster resolution of the huge nonperforming loan problem in the banking system, more drastic restructuring of "zombie" corporations and banks, and more deregulation and privatization to increase the efficiency and competitiveness of the Japanese economy. In this respect, he departed from the approach adopted by all previous LDP administrations – gradual reform while protecting and minimizing losses to client industries and sectors. Liberalization policy shifted from rhetoric to a more realistic possibility.[7] Koizumi brought leadership based on public support to resolve Japan's economic and financial distress.

Third, Koizumi advocated privatization of the Postal Savings System (PSS) and restructuring of the Fiscal Investment and Loan Program (FILP) budget, thus reducing the role of the government in the financial system in an effort to improve Japan's resource allocation efficiency. The PSS and FILP were long overdue for reform. But reform lagged because of the close relationships among post offices, the LDP, the government ministries and FILP agencies, local governments, and socioeconomic interests that benefited from the two related programs. As long as these institutions remained part of government and represented a large part of the financial system, Japan would not achieve resource allocation efficiency and would not develop a modern financial system capable of meeting future economic challenges.

Postal deposits accounted for 35 percent of total savings deposits in Japan. Postal deposits provided the main source of funding for the FILP budget, and the FILP budget represented about 10 percent of GDP at the time that Koizumi became prime minister. In fact, Koizumi's effort to privatize the PSS brought him into direct conflict in 2005 with the LDP politicians and factions that drew votes from postmasters, and

---

[7] It should be noted, however, that Koizumi was not the first one to conceive many of these structural changes, as policies such as the redesign of the banking system and government financial intermediation were tried in the late 1990s. Koizumi built on these existing initiatives and carried them out decisively by providing strong leadership.

government ministries wanting to secure budgets and employment by preserving the FILP agencies that received resources from the FILP and provided employment for retired bureaucrats. When his privatization bill was rejected by the upper house, Koizumi dissolved the lower house in August 2005, called a "snap" election, and single-handedly punished the LDP politicians who had voted against his privatization bill by denying them party nomination in the election. The gamble paid off. The public gave Koizumi a historical, overwhelming popular mandate that legitimized his privatization bill. Even though the eventual privatization plan contained many flaws, the fact that any significant change was accomplished is a direct result of Koizumi's leadership.

Koizumi's opposition to the "old" LDP with its relationship with the bureaucracy and client industries, his emphasis on structural change as a necessary condition for economic recovery, and his opposition to government ministries set a new precedent in Japan. The iron triangle of the LDP, the bureaucracy, and their client industries had long dominated Japanese politics and policy making. Koizumi resolutely overrode the bureaucracy's intense opposition to many of his reforms and, as a result, the power of the bureaucracy in economic policy making declined. Elected government leaders (i.e., politicians) increased their power against bureaucrats. He also overrode policy opposition by the LDP's powerful *zoku* (tribal) politicians and factions who specialize in a specific policy area.

The most significant aspect of the Koizumi period is the prime ministerial leadership that Koizumi brought to economic policy making. He had a political style that was different from previous prime ministers. The assertive policy-making style exercised by Koizumi will remain as a precedent for successive administrations, although whether or not future prime ministers can successfully take advantage of the precedent and exercise strong leadership will depend on the political skills and audacity of individual prime ministers. If successfully exercised, prime ministerial power can limit the power of the bureaucracy. Meanwhile, the relative power of the bureaucracy will depend on how willing the prime minister is to counter the bureaucracy or to accommodate and cooperate with it.[8] Japanese politicians are now more susceptive to public opinion, giving at least slightly more political power to the public.

---

[8] Prime Minister Fukuda at the time of this writing is more accommodating to the bureaucracy than Koizumi.

The end of the Koizumi period in 2006 coincided with economic and financial recovery that had first begun in 2003 and appeared reasonably sustained by 2006. The end of the Koizumi period thus ends Japan's "lost decade and half" of unrealized economic and financial potential. Much has changed in Japan's economic and political institutions. The Japanese economic-political regime is not likely to revert completely back to the old patron-client distributive politics that existed during the LDP's one-party dominance (1955–1993). The new regime, however, will not be a wholesale break with the old one – the new system will be a gradual evolution of the old system. There is uncertainty about whether successive Japanese governments can maintain the course of market reform and the prime minister's policy-making initiative with presidential-style strong leadership initiated by Koizumi. Koizumi was able to achieve significant reforms because he was willing to clash with his own LDP and ignore the long-established norms and procedures of consensual decision making in the LDP. He enjoyed enormous public support. This public support allowed Koizumi to remain in power and push for reform despite an LDP establishment that wanted him replaced with a more traditional politician. These favorable conditions for political leadership will be difficult for Koizumi's successors to replicate, especially if Japan continues to recover and the "lost decade-and-half" fades in the memory of the public.

Beyond September 2006

The LDP elected Shinzo Abe to replace Koizumi in September 2006. Abe was the first prime minister who was born after the war and represented the new generation of political leaders. He tried to maintain the reform momentum established by Koizumi. But in his efforts to distinguish himself from his predecessor and realize his conservative ideals, Abe advanced nationalistic agendas, including the promotion of patriotism, nationalism, and tradition, and the revision of the Japanese constitution. However, the Japanese public was more interested in improvements in their economic and financial conditions, and Abe's nationalistic agendas did not appeal to them. His failure to appeal to the public, the lack of Koizumi's charisma and political skills, and a series of scandals in his administration resulted in a major loss for the LDP in the July 2007 upper house elections. It was one of the LDP's most devastating electoral defeats since 1955. Although Abe resisted resignation, he eventually resigned on September 12, 2007. Subsequently, Yasuo Fukuda was elected president of the LDP and, hence, Japan's new prime minister in late September.

It is debatable whether the substance of Koizumi's reform efforts matched the rhetoric. But there is no doubt he introduced significant change to Japan's economic and political institutions and was able to achieve this because of generally high public support throughout his five-year term in office. Abe was a serious disappointment. Currently, Prime Minister Fukuda has had severe difficulty passing his government bills in the Diet because the upper house is now controlled by the majority opposition parties as a result of the 2007 election. Many cases of bureaucratic mismanagement revealed during his administration have also exacerbated his legislative difficulty. At the time of this writing, it also appears that he and his LDP will likely face grim prospects in the next lower house election, which will need to take place no later than October 2009.

Japan faces challenges at the beginning of this new century. First, Japan needs economic and social policy innovations and strong political leadership to generate them in order for the country to respond effectively to socioeconomic problems, such as dramatic demographic changes in progress, the growing unequal distribution of wealth, and the collapse of the old social contract. Japan's population is declining and becoming "grayer." Without continued efforts to improve productivity of labor and capital, the standard of living will decline. Despite the recovery of Japan's economy starting in 2005, there is increasing evidence the rural economies, small and medium businesses, and traditional sectors are not experiencing the expansion. Despite the expanding economy and tighter labor markets, wages have not increased, whereas corporate profits have expanded. There is more uncertainty and insecurity on the part of the average Japanese than in the past.

Second, Japan cannot assume that it has completely recovered from fifteen years of lost economic potential. The recovery at this point is not robust and is overly dependent on the export sector. Real GDP continues to increase at a rate of only 1 to 2 percent. Although some claim that deflation has ended, the measured rate of price change shows either slightly declining prices or small positive price increases. This should be no comfort to policy makers, given the well-known upward bias in the price index. A small positive measured inflation rate is, in reality, slight deflation. In July 2006, the BOJ indicated that it would end an unprecedented policy that had brought short-term interest rates to zero for almost seven years. The BOJ increased interest rates in July 2006 and February 2007 as the economy expanded. There is, however, a concern that the BOJ is adopting an exit policy too soon. Thus, the recovery that started under Koizumi may not be as sustainable as claimed by the government.

Third, the public and policy makers supported deregulation and liberalization during the Koizumi administration, partly because of the obvious failure of the old regime in the 1990s. However, interest in further significant reform is waning. In Japan, a view has emerged among the public, media, and politicians that liberal market reform has gone too far and has caused negative economic consequences, including economic disparities among different economic sectors and segments of the population. This view emerged toward the end of the Koizumi administration and increasingly will be a constraint on further reform. Most politicians and observers believe that economic disparities were one of the major causes of the LDP's devastating defeat in the 2007 upper house election. Politicians – whether LDP or otherwise – are likely to find it difficult to resist pressures to slow down the pace of reform and pressures to increase spending to deal with the growing social problems that have emerged as Japan moves toward a freer and more competitive structure.

Fourth, Japan also faces external challenges. Criticism of Japan's "checkbook" diplomacy during the 1991 Iraq War induced Japan to project itself into world affairs to an extent that sharply breaks with over five decades of limiting world involvement to trade. The North Korean missile and nuclear threats are a concern to Japan. Japan is also concerned about the rise of China's economic and military power in Asia. Furthermore, Japan needs to meet the economic challenges posed by newly emerging economies in Asia and elsewhere. This confirms the need for Japan continuously to improve the productivity and competitiveness of the economy.

Outline of the Study

The objective of this study is to provide a detailed narrative of the transition of Japan's economic and political institutions since 1980. The specific commencement date of the transition is somewhat arbitrary; however, 1980 is a reasonable starting point, because the 1970s represented a period of new economic, political, and technological forces and shocks that stimulated institutional change in Japan, and the first half of the 1980s represented a concerted effort from Japan's perspective to liberalize parts of the financial system.

This study offers four innovations in reviewing Japan's transition during the past three decades.

First, the study emphasizes the economic and political aspects of the transition. It is neither an economic nor political review of Japan's transition, but it offers a perspective incorporating both elements. Economists have a tendency to play down political factors, whereas political scientists have a tendency to play down the underlying economic issues. Both perspectives are important, and this study makes a concerted attempt to tell the story from a political-economy perspective.

Second, the complex story of institutional redesign in Japan is developed in terms of a straightforward six-part chronological framework: (1) the pretransition base in terms of existing economic and political institutions and their implied social contract between the government and citizens (pretransition period); (2) the impact of new economic, political, and technological forces on Japan and Japan's apparent success in adapting its financial system to these new forces (1980 to 1985); (3) the buildup of financial stress, asset price inflation, and collapse of asset prices (1985 to 1990); (4) economic, financial, and political distress (1990s); (5) a new form of policy making, followed by economic and financial recovery (2001 to 2006); and (6) unraveling of the old social contract between the government and the public and the public's changed life expectation.

Third, the study posits a specific line of causation; that is, the study is more than a mere telling of events. The sequence starts from the financial system and then progresses to the rest of Japan's economic institutions and eventually Japan's political institutions. That is, the existing political-economic regime came into conflict with new forces in the economy and technology; the old regime generated limited and flawed financial liberalization; flawed financial liberalization and the nonadaptive regime caused and intensified economic distress; the new forces and economic distress caused political distress; and economic and political distress eventually led to a meaningful shift toward market-oriented institutions and more responsive government.

Fourth, the study traces the most important political and economic events during the past three decades, such as electoral reform, market reforms by Koizumi, political changes, PSS and FILP reform, and BOJ policy with sufficient detail to highlight the main lines of the story. The study is intended for the nonexpert to gain an appreciation of the political economy of Japan since 1980 in one reading. A brief summary of the study follows.

Chapter 2 outlines the pretransition set of economic and political institutions as of the late 1970s and early 1980s. This discussion provides a point of reference to understand how Japan's economic and political institutions have evolved in the last three decades. The discussion specially focuses on Japan's financial system, labor markets, corporate governance, and political institutions.

Chapter 3 discusses Japan's response to the new economic, political, and technology forces during the first half of the 1980s. The response was limited to only certain segments of the financial system with little effort to reform corporate, labor market, regulatory, and political institutions or adopt an economy-wide perspective to reform. The transition toward markets was more rhetoric than substance, and although Japan adopted an official policy of financial liberalization, this policy was more a passive response to external pressure and specific internal pressures than a rethinking of the existing regime.

Chapter 4 discusses how a flawed and incomplete financial reform process combined with policy errors by the BOJ and MOF generated conditions for a bubble economy from 1985 to 1990. The aftermath of the asset inflation and the collapse of asset prices eventually forced Japan to reevaluate its economic and political institutions.

Chapter 5 discusses Japan's "lost decade" of the 1990s. The banking debacle manifested the clearest structural problem of the old regime, and the regulatory response to the banking problems revealed the failure of the old political institutions in the new environment. The dominance of the LDP began to unravel, as did the dominance of the MOF and the reputation of economic bureaucracies, especially the MOF and the BOJ. At the end of the decade, Japan's economic and political institutions began a transition toward more open markets and democracy, which accelerated after Koizumi became prime minister in April 2001.

Chapter 6 focuses on various factors that account for the long period of distress in Japan with special focus on BOJ policy. BOJ policy was a drag on the economy throughout the 1990s and through the first years of the new century. There were issues of basic misunderstanding about how to measure the effects of monetary policy as well as a variety of political issues that constrained BOJ policy.

Chapter 7 discusses the transition of the political system in the 1990s up to 2006. In the late 1980s and the early 1990s, Japan's politics were characterized by the LDP's one-party rule; the iron triangle relationship between politicians, the bureaucracy, and their client industries; and the relatively small influence of public opinion. But from 1993 on, Japanese politics experienced a series of changes, including the split of the LDP and its fall from power in 1993, emergence of successive coalition governments, electoral reform, large-scale party realignment, reform of the government bureaucracy, central bank reform, and the inauguration of the reform-minded Koizumi administration. These events, in tandem with economic and financial developments, altered many aspects of Japanese politics and economic policy making.

Chapter 8 discusses fiscal policy and government financial intermediation during the 1990s, both of which limited Japan's ability to deal with the economic and financial distress in the 1990s and first part of the new century. Like central bank policy, the Japanese government made a series of fiscal policy errors. In the 1990s, the LDP government implemented a series of Keynesian economic stimulus packages designed to pull the economy out of recession, but to no avail. The LDP government in 1997 turned to fiscal austerity or fiscal contraction in an effort to reduce large deficit and debt. This action pushed the fragile economy into an even deeper recession and deflation. The government likewise allocated resources inefficiently by using FILP and PSS and contributed to the economic and financial distress.

Chapter 9 continues the review of the fiscal program in Chapter 8 by analyzing the Koizumi administration's market reforms and fiscal consolidation. It examines Koizumi's efforts at deficit reduction and market reforms, including fiscal retrenchment, postal privatization, restructuring of government financial institutions, FILP budget reduction, privatization of Japan Highway Corporations, closure and privatization of public corporations, and administrative reform.

Chapter 10 discusses Japan's recent changes in corporate governance, labor practices, and citizens' social and economic life. The economic problems of the 1990s and 2000s had an impact not only on the Japanese government's economic policy, politics, and political outcomes but also on broader aspects of Japanese society and life. The social contract between the government and the average citizen has been altered. Japan now faces a host of social issues, the most important of which is increases in job insecurity and income inequality.

Chapter 11 brings the story to a close and discusses how Japanese politics are likely to change in the coming decade and how this will impact economic policy, the nature of the economic system, and economic outcomes. The chapter closes with some thoughts on the direction in which Japan's politics and economy are likely to go in the next decade.

2

Economic and Political Institutions in the 1970s

Introduction

Japan emerged from World War II in 1945 as a devastated nation with much of its infrastructure destroyed, hyperinflation fueled by government deficits and rapid monetary growth, political institutions in disarray, and a deep pessimism about the ability of Japan's economic and political institutions to provide economic growth and political stability in the future. The prewar economic and political institutions had embodied Japan's view of how the world functioned and had served Japan up to World War II but were found wanting in the postwar environment.[1] This was an especially difficult attitudinal change on Japan's part, considering the overall impressive performance of the Japanese economy since the start of modernization in the 1870s.

The modernization effort itself was the outcome of the political decision manifested by the Meiji Restoration of 1868 to develop a set of economic and political institutions to first achieve industrial and military parity with the West and then surpass the West. These institutions over time incorporated a social contract between the government and its citizens, in which the government was given authority to manage the economy in exchange for economic security. The institutions that evolved after the Meiji Restoration built on a series of

---

[1] Kuznets (1971) and Ohkawa and Rosovsky (1973) provide comprehensive information on Japan's industrial development focusing on the period after the Meiji Restoration in 1868. Various aspects of Japan's institutional evolution can be found in Aoki (1988 and 2001), whereas Lincoln (2001) discusses how Japan's financial institutions incorporated Japanese culture, especially the tendency toward risk-aversion and nonmarket transactions. Freedman (2006) provides a concise overview of Japan's development emphasizing the importance of risk-aversion and collectivist institutions. Patrick and Rosovsky (1976) provide a detailed overview of Japan's economic and political institutions in the postwar period before 1980.

favorable conditions established during the Tokugawa period (1603–1867), such as a road system, centralized government, strong work ethic, and relatively high level of education. The policy outcomes of the Meiji Restoration were impressive by any standard. Japan achieved a record of industrial development matched by few countries of the world from the start of modernization through the 1930s.

These achievements, however, paled in comparison to the devastation of World War II and the loss of faith in those institutions to provide security to the Japanese people. The second half of the 1940s was a period of extreme economic, financial, and political distress, which was gradually resolved by the Allied Occupation's efforts to democratize and demilitarize Japan, culminating in the foundation of a full-fledged democratic political system; by the Dodge Line policies to stabilize the economy; by the stimulative effect on the economy generated by the Korean War from June 1950 to 1953; by a competent bureaucracy; and eventually by the rise of a party system in 1955 centering around the two largest parties – the LDP and the Social Democratic Party of Japan (SDP) – which would become a foundation of the so-called 1955-System. These developments established a foundation for Japan's reindustrialization and ultimate emergence as the second largest economy in the world by the 1970s. Although economic growth slowed to a range of 3 to 5 percent in the 1970s, Japan continued to exhibit impressive macroeconomic performance compared to the other industrialized economies.

The objective of this chapter is to outline Japan's political and economic institutions and the social contract implicitly formed between the government and the public, as they existed in the 1970s.[2] The decade of the 1970s is used in this study as the reference period, because these institutions were the main pillars of the old or pre-transition Japanese regime up to 1980 and had reached maturity in the 1970s. It was widely accepted inside and outside Japan that these institutions were responsible for Japan's impressive postwar economic

---

[2] This study makes frequent positive references to Japan's economic performance and political stability during much of the postwar period. But these references are not intended to suggest an absence of economic and social issues that plagued Japan. Not all workers and firms benefited, and the government decision-making process placed a low value on the concerns of the household sector. Even though Japan's institutions provided an impressive economic growth record and political stability through the 1980s, they weakened Japan's ability to adjust to the changes in its external environment.

growth through the 1970s. This chapter is not intended to detail the historical evolution of these institutions but, more modestly, to outline the most important characteristics of these institutions as of the 1970s and to provide a point of reference for Japan's transition after 1980.

This point of reference is important for two reasons. First, specific characteristics of the economic and political institutions led Japan to adopt an unsuccessful response to the new economic, political, and technology forces that emerged in the 1970s. Japan's "bubble" economy in the second half of the 1980s and the almost fifteen years of economic distress in the 1990s and first few years of the new century can be traced to Japan's unwillingness to depart from key elements of the old regime. Second, the juxtaposition of the newly evolving economic and political institutions in the first decade of the new century with the old set of institutions provides a perspective on how much Japan has changed and how a new social contract is emerging.

Economic and Political Institutions: Is Japan Special?

There is a tendency to view the evolution of economic and political institutions in terms of two perspectives. The first perspective regards these institutions in the narrow sense of existing to allocate limited resources among competing ends (economic institutions) and to determine social rankings of different social policies based on individual rankings (political institutions). This is the "one size fits all" view and, in the extreme, is the Marxian view that the means of production defines culture, attitudes, religion, and even political institutions. The second perspective regards these institutions as the reflection of a complex set of forces summarized by a country's history and culture and that each country's set of institutions cannot be understood independent of the culture and history of that country. This is the "one size fits only one country" view and, in the extreme, is the Hegelian view that ideas and concepts determine the means of production and political institutions.

The problem with the first perspective is that it ignores the obvious observation that although economic and political issues of any country may be directed toward solving the same set of problems, these institutions do not evolve in a vacuum. A country's economic and political institutions are not independent of that country's history, culture, and national goals. The problem with the second perspective is that it seeks to explain too much with culture and ends up being a tautology with no ability to generalize and ignores the fact that every society faces the same set of economic and political problems.

In Japan's case, the second perspective has tended to dominate and often provides a misunderstanding of Japanese economic and political institutions that they are "unique" and "different" and not easily understood by standard analytical tools derived from Western thinking.[3] This is a common perspective held by the Japanese themselves and by many outside observers. This adherence to "uniqueness" has been one reason that Japan in the 1980s failed to learn important lessons from the financial disruptions in many industrialized economies. Japanese policy makers viewed issues such as moral hazard and market-regulatory conflict as unique to Western-oriented economies; hence, these types of problems were not applicable to Japan because of its unique economic and political intuitions.

This study regards both perspectives as offering insights into Japan's economic and political institutions but places more weight on the first consideration. That is, this study plays down the view that Japan is "different" or "special" because of its culture. Japan is no more special than the United States or other Western countries in that Japan faces the same economic and political issues and problems. Japan is no more special than the United States or other Western countries in that, as in Japan, culture, history and national aspirations influence the economic and political institutions of these countries.

At the same time, however, Japan's economic and political institutions appear to be more sensitive to risk-aversion and accepting of collectivism. Its risk-aversion and collectivism in turn render Japanese economic and political institutions resistant to change, and when change does occur, it is usually in response to a change in the external environment. Every society incorporates these attitudes in varying degrees, but in Japan's case, these attitudes play a larger role in shaping economic and political institutions. Japan perceives itself as having fewer degrees of freedom than other countries in making economic and political decisions because of a limited resource base, limited land areas that can be utilized for production and living, and Japan's susceptibility to natural disasters such as earthquakes and violent weather.

---

[3] For a view that recognizes Japan's uniqueness in explaining its politics and economy, see, for example, Johnson (1982) and van Wolferen (1989).

This in turn has provided incentives to develop institutions based on mutual support, insularity, and aversion to risk and change.

Freedman (2006) suggests that Japan can be viewed as an extended clan that protects its members. This is a reasonably accurate description of postwar Japan before the economic crises and market reform of the 1990s and 2000s. This is also reminiscent of the famous American institutionalist John R. Commons. Commons (1934) defined an institution as collective control over individual action designed to confront competitive challenges and assure each member of the institution a place at the economic table. Commons used his concept of institutions and institutional evolution to explain the development of labor unions in the United States. A labor union is an institution designed to control individual action for the benefit of the collective group, and its institutional design would evolve over time in response to increasing competition starting at the local level and eventually involving the world. Commons's concept of an institution fits Japan well. Japan evolved a set of institutions designed to control individual action to ensure individuals a place at the economic table in a low-risk environment as it competed against the rest of the world.

The point is that if there is anything special about Japan compared to other countries, it is a resistance to change, aversion to risk, and collectivism in economics and politics. At the same time, it is hard to attribute these characteristics to some special cultural characteristic of Japan that itself cannot be traced to some objective element in Japanese history and geography. Thus, Japanese institutions are special only to the extent they incorporate risk aversion to a greater extent than Western countries. Beyond this, Japan's institutions share far more similarities with Western economic and political institutions than differences.

In the following discussion, Japan's institutions as they existed in the 1970s are bifurcated into economic and political institutions. Economic institutions are designed to allocate resources in terms of what is produced, how it is produced, and the distribution of the outcome of the production process. Of the many economic institutions, the following represent some of the most important to understanding Japan's pretransition regime: the financial system, corporate governance, and labor market institutions consisting of lifetime employment, wage coordination and restraint, company welfare, and life expectation view. Political institutions delineate how policy decisions are made in society and how they influence the distribution of societal resources.

Of the many political institutions, the following represent some of the most important to understanding pretransition Japan: LDP dominance, the bureaucracy, the iron triangle, and the constrained policy making power of the prime minister.

Two points are important to bear in mind. First, separating Japan's institutions into economic and political does not imply an absence of feedback relationships. In fact, the two sets of institutions are closely related as they are in any country. The bifurcation is a pedagogical device to enhance an understanding of the various components of a political-economic regime and its transition. Second, of all the economic and political institutions in Japan, it is important to keep in mind that only the financial system responded to the forces of change in the late 1970s and early 1980s, and even the financial reform was limited. Few, if any, other important institutions in Japan responded to the new economic, political, and technological environment before the 1990s. Particularly, labor markets, corporate governance, and political institutions resisted meaningful change until the 1990s.

The Financial System

The institutionalization of the savings and investment process is the fundamental foundation of economic development. The financial system is the collection of financial institutions and markets designed to transfer funds from those with excess funds, after their spending needs have been satisfied, to those whose funds are not sufficient to meet their spending needs. In its broadest sense, the financial system not only includes private institutions and markets but also government regulatory and central banking institutions. The regulatory and central banking institutions exist to limit systemic risk, ensure that the private institutions and markets function smoothly, and ensure price stability.

Japanese financial system institutions as they existed in the 1970s can best be understood from three perspectives:[4] first, the evolution of the financial system from 1868 to World War II; second, the financial

---

[4] The Japanese financial system is discussed from a variety of perspectives by Aoki and Patrick (1994), Calder (1990), Cargill, Hutchison, and Ito (1997 and 2000), Cargill and Royama (1988), Cargill and Yoshino (2003), Hoshi and Kashyap (2001), Hamada and Horiuchi (1987), Suzuki (1980 and 1987), and Teranishi (2007).

system as of the 1970s; and, third, the influence that Japan's financial system had on financial systems throughout much of Asia. The third point is interesting in light of the tendency of many observers to attribute much of the rapid economic growth experienced throughout Asia in the 1980s as due in part to the type of institutionalization of the savings-investment process modeled after Japan (World Bank, 1993).

Pretransition Financial Regime, 1868 to World War II

Japan's financial system developed in response to the new policy of industrialization brought about by the Meiji Restoration of 1868. Before the Meiji Restoration, the financial system was barely sufficient to support the monetary needs of an agrarian and internationally isolated economy. There was no organized banking system or organized financial markets. In some cases, merchants acted as banks, issuing their own promises to pay that functioned as money. Coins issued by the central government were the main form of money. This monetary system was rapidly transformed once the political decision was made to modernize Japan's industry and military. Japan began in the 1870s to develop a modern financial system that borrowed heavily from the financial systems of Belgium, the United Kingdom, and the United States.

The detailed development of Japan's financial system up through World War II has been reviewed in many places. The key elements of the financial system can be summarized by considering the objective of the financial system, the structure of the financial system, and the role of government in the financial system.

The objective of the Japanese financial system was to support the industrial and military goals of the government; hence, the financial system was an instrument of industrial policy. The system was designed to encourage a high saving rate among households, limit access to consumer and mortgage credit, and transfer the savings to the industrial sector.

This objective was met by a financial structure based on intermediation or indirect finance; that is, funds were transferred from the household to the business sector through private banks and government institutions with little reliance on open securities markets or international finance. Inflows and outflows of capital to and from Japan were regulated. Securities markets developed along with banking for a few decades, but by the 1930s, Japan transferred the majority of funds through banks.[5] Even at the start of financial modernization, however, banks played a key role in the securities markets through underwriting securities and providing funding to purchase securities.

The private banking system started in 1872 with the establishment of a national banking system modeled after the U.S. national banking system. The system evolved over time so that by the start of the twentieth century, the banking system consisted of a small number of large well-capitalized banks and a large number of small but poorly capitalized banks. As a result of a banking panic in 1927, the government began a policy of bank concentration and consolidation that would come to characterize the postwar banking system. Banks, specialized in terms of types of loans and clients, were frequently under the influence of the large *zaibatsu* (conglomerates) and did not play a meaningful role in corporate governance. According to Hoshi and Kashyap (2001), corporate governance was under the control of shareholders and not banks; however, shareholdings were concentrated.

Government played a significant role in the financial system. The MOF was responsible for explicit government regulation and supervision of the financial system, but explicit regulation and supervision did not become a major feature of the Japanese financial system until the 1927 bank panic and war mobilization in the 1930s. The BOJ was established in 1882, modeled after the Belgium central bank, and assigned responsibility for managing the nation's currency system and providing other central bank functions. The BOJ was administered by the MOF. In 1875, a national system of post offices modeled on the U.K. postal system was established, providing mail and postal deposit services and, after 1912, life insurance services. The MOF assumed responsibility for managing postal and life insurance funds and allocated those funds to targeted sectors of the economy. This relationship elevated government financial intermediation to the second most important channel of funding that would evolve in the postwar period into the FILP.

---

[5] Hoshi and Kashyap (2001) argue that Japan's postwar bank-focused financial system was not a long-term development, but was based on developments in the 1930s as the government increased its influence over the allocation of credit in preparation for war. They argue that securities markets were active before the 1930s; however, it is debatable as to whether these were Western-type securities markets or that these markets were not bank-influenced. Other perspectives on the issue are provided by Lincoln (2001), Teranishi (2007), Ishii (2007), and Okazaki (2007).

Pretransition Financial Regime, 1945–1980

Once economic, financial, and political stability was achieved after the war, Japan's financial system reached maturity in the 1950s and 1960s. The financial system of the 1970s reflected a continuation of prewar trends. The financial system remained an instrument of industrial policy, based on bank finance; government played a significant role in the allocation of funds; and the system remained internationally isolated. The Allied Occupation, however, did have some impact on the development of the financial system. The occupation imposed a Glass-Steagall type rule to prevent banks from functioning as investment banks; however, in the absence of a variable money and capital market, this was largely redundant. In addition, banks were already permitted to hold up to 5 percent of a corporation's outstanding shares to solidify the relationship between the bank and the corporation. More important, the occupation disbanded the prewar *zaibatsu*, which had limited the role of banks in corporate governance; however, corporations reestablished the *zaibatsu* system in the form of the less rigid *keiretsu* or company group structure organized around a financial institution, usually one of the large city banks. In this system, banks came to play an important role in corporate governance compared to the prewar period.

There were four changes in the institutional design of the financial system in the postwar period worth noting.

First, to provide support for rebuilding Japan's infrastructure, a number of government banks, enterprises, and corporations were established and became important components of the FILP, which in turn became an important part of the formation of the national budget. Postal savings deposits and life insurance premiums were the major source of funds for the FILP.

Second, the financial system became more bank-focused, specialized, and concentrated. The private banking system consisted of a small number of very large banks (city banks, foreign exchange bank, long-term credit banks, and trust banks), a larger number of regional banks, and a very large number of small specialized credit cooperatives. City banks and regional banks focused on short-term business loans, whereas long-term credit and trust banks focused on longer-term loans. These banks, combined with the government financial institutions, constituted the center of Japan's postwar financial system.

The large number of small cooperatives dealt with specific sectors of the economy such as agriculture, forestry, fisheries, and so on.

Third, the shift toward bank finance was completed so that by 1975 securities markets played no meaningful role in the flow of funds. In the postwar *keiretsu* system, banks and other financial institutions played a major role in corporate governance because of the importance of bank financing. The *keiretsu* system was also known as the main bank system in which a bank (or other financial institution) assumed a leadership role in the company group. The main bank[6] was not necessarily the primary source of credit but, more important than providing credit, the main bank had access to information about the company group that was valuable to other lenders in the absence of a meaningful financial disclosure framework.

Fourth, the financial system came under the direct control of the government via a system of credit allocation policies, interest rate restrictions, limited competition between financial institutions, restrictions on foreign financial institutions, and restrictions on the inflow and outflow of capital. As of 1975, Japan's financial system was the most regulated, isolated, and administratively controlled financial system of the industrialized economies.[7]

The pretransition Japanese regime was organized on fundamentally different principles than Western financial regimes such as the United States. It was based on the view the financial regime was part of an overall industrial policy under the direction of a central government authority. Banks established a "customer relationship" perspective with their borrowers emphasizing long-term multidimensional relationships that often resulted in credit allocation, evaluation, and monitoring that could not always be justified by economic fundamentals. A major objective was to limit risk and prevent bankruptcy

---

[6] The main bank system is extensively discussed in Aoki and Patrick (1994).

[7] The MOF, the BOJ, and the former Ministry of Posts and Telecommunications regulated all but two interest rates. The MOF in the mid-1960s permitted an "unofficial" market in repurchase agreements based on government bonds to operate, called the *gensaki* market, without explicit interest rate regulations. The interbank or call market also did not operate with an explicit regulation over interest rates. However, in both the *gensaki* and call market, administrative guidance often was used to influence those interest rates.

Money and capital markets played a minor role in corporate financing, and even though corporations obtained about 15 percent of their funds from securities, these securities were purchased by financial institutions without significant secondary markets; that is, bonds frequently were held to maturity and equities were used more as a means to establish relationships between firms and banks through an extensive system of cross-shareholding rather than as a source of long-term capital.

among the most important firms in the economy through a system of mutual support among financial institutions, business firms, and politicians. The emphasis was on sustained, stable, and low-risk economic growth. Market forces were not absent in the Japanese regime; however, government regulation in the form of interest rate controls and credit allocation were pervasive. The system was characterized by nontransparency to assist in limiting bankruptcy and enhance the ability of banks, regulatory authorities, and politicians to ensure the mutual support nature of the system. The BOJ lacked independence and often assisted in maintaining a policy of "no failures of financial institutions or markets" through their lender of last resort services. The system of mutual support was often summarized by the phrase "convoy system" in which the weaker were protected by the strong as in a convoy of merchant ships being protected by more powerful warships in submarine infested waters.

Asian Financial System and Japan

The set of financial institutions developed by Japan as of the 1970s significantly influenced the institutionalization of the savings-investment process throughout much of Asia. Asian financial systems in varying degrees were based on the Japanese model for three reasons.

First, Japan was the first Asian country to industrialize and, by the end of the nineteenth century, Japan embarked on an effort to expand its influence in Asia in competition with the United States and Great Britain. The expansion of influence continued and accelerated through the end of World War II. As a result, many postwar Asian countries inherited Japanese economic and financial institutions. Korea and Taiwan more than any other Asian country emerged from World War II with Japanese economic and financial institutions, although important elements of Japanese finance could be found in many other Asian countries.

Second, although it is a gross simplification to refer to Asian culture and attitude as homogenous, given the considerable heterogeneity one can find in individual Asian countries, there are common elements that support the type of financial regime that emerged in Japan after the Meiji Restoration and reached full development in the postwar period. Asian economic and financial institutions in general emphasize a collectivist as opposed to an individual perspective; minimization of risk and bankruptcy; long-term "customer" relationships between lenders (primarily banks) and borrowers (primarily business firms) as a method of evaluating and monitoring risk; and nontransparency. That is, Asian financial systems reflect an emphasis on mutual support rather than individual self-interest and an emphasis on risk minimization rather than a process of Schumpeterian "creative destruction."[8] Asian financial systems are generally adverse to open money and capital markets and prefer bank-focused regimes rather than mixed intermediation-direct financial regimes. Money and capital markets stand at the opposite end of the Asian model. They are based on individual decision making in the context of competitive and transparent markets in which risk is evaluated and monitored through decisions to buy and sell by large numbers of market participants. Although designed to manage risk, they are inherently based on the concept of creative destruction.

Third, Japan's prewar and postwar record of economic growth and financial stability is impressive by any standard and Asian countries wishing to duplicate Japan's record, readily adopted Japanese economic and financial institutions. Japan achieved an impressive industrialization process in the second half of the nineteenth century to World War II and then, after the devastation of the war, Japan achieved an equally remarkable reindustrialization process by the end of the 1960s. The early 1970s were a turbulent time for Japan; however, Japan was able to reestablish sustained and noninflationary growth after 1975 that continued to 1990.

Corporate Governance

Corporate governance refers to who in the corporation is responsible for decision making and what incentives influence the decision-making process. In most cases, corporations are ultimately sensitive to the owners or shareholders; however, Japanese corporations were not responsive to shareholders. Despite the capitalization of the Tokyo

[8] The phrase "creative destruction" was coined by Schumpeter (1942) in chapter 7 of *Capitalism, Socialism, and Democracy*. Since then, it has become a standard part of the vocabulary of political economy. In the "creative destruction" view of the market, competition destroys industries and firms that are no longer competitive but, in the process, creates new industries and firms enhancing economic potential for all. Should these new industries and firms become complacent, they likewise will be replaced by new competitors as the process continues to support economic growth, increase productivity, and raise the standard of living.

Stock market in the pretransition period, equities were primarily used to solidify relationships between corporations within a company grouping and/or the main bank in the company group.[9] The relationship between the large corporations was defined by the *keiretsu* or main bank system and cross-shareholding by Japanese companies. Japanese corporations were interwoven into extensive, dense, and tight networks of corporate and transactional relationships based on long-term and multidimensional relationships (see, for instance, Lincoln, 2001). Intragroup transactions were more important than intergroup transactions. Enhancing the value of equity and paying dividends to equity holders had very low priority relative to supporting the members of the *keiretsu*. Equity was more a solidifying factor rather than a means to raise capital from investors that imposed a responsibility on the corporation to be responsive to those investors.

Rather than relying on equity as a source of funding, each corporate group was organized around a main bank or other large financial institution. The main bank did not necessarily provide all of the credit needs of the corporate members. More often, the main bank served in a leadership role to assist in obtaining loans from other private lenders and government banks. The main bank had access to inside information in a system that limited public access to meaningful information about company operations and performance. The lack of a meaningful financial disclosure system and the inside knowledge of the main bank elevated the large banks to the center of corporate governance. As a result, Japan's corporate finance system was bank-based (as in Germany), in contrast to equity-market based as in the United States. The MOF held significant control over these main banks, hence facilitating the Japanese government's implementation of industrial policy and its strategic resource allocation in the postwar period.

Crossholding of equity permitted stable long-term relationships with group companies, prevented hostile takeovers, and provided for shared business risks. Cross-shareholding permitted companies to plan and conduct business with a long-term view without excessive concern for short-term profits or stock price movements normally important to shareholders, as these mutually held shares were owned by group companies for long periods. Japanese companies were able to

---

[9] Corporate governance from a historical perspective is discussed in Hoshi and Kashyap (2001). Tett's (2003) analysis of the rise and fall of the Long Term Credit Bank provides insight into corporate decision making and how it contributed to the economic problems of the 1990s.

engage in long-term investments and innovations that would be more difficult if short-term profit maximization was the objective. Hence, in this corporate governance system, the interests of regular market shareholders were downplayed, market shareholders had little influence on corporate management and activities, and management decisions were more responsive to the main bank or other group companies.

This set of corporate governance institutions denied Japanese corporations an effective monitoring mechanism on their decisions and activities normally provided by outside shareholders and the market. The lack of market-determined corporate governance meant that under certain conditions such as the "bubble" economy in the second half of the 1980s, corporations were prone to make speculative investments and, as in the "burst" of the bubble economy in the 1990s, prolong economic distress because of an unwillingness to penalize poor performance. The lack of an effective shareholder influence guaranteed that low profit and nonproductive companies would continue operating. The close relationship between corporations and banks also made it extremely difficult for foreign companies to penetrate the Japanese markets, and, for that matter, made it difficult for domestic firms not part of a company group to establish profitable operations.

Labor Market Institutions

Postwar Japan developed its own labor-corporate system consisting of a set of labor practices, corporate governance, and labor-employer relations. The system formed a component of the social contract between the government and the citizens, and influenced how the national economy worked and performed, how workers and their family related to their employers (companies), and how they formed their life expectations. Some features of the labor-corporate system were generally conducive to Japan's economic success up to the end of the 1980s – lifetime employment, cooperative relationships between labor and employers, employees' and employers' investments in company-specific job training, wage coordination and restraint, and company welfare. These features, however, were not sustainable, as the international and domestic economic conditions changed and as the magnitude of the economic crisis in the 1990s overwhelmed the capacity of the labor-corporate system to make adjustments without changing its features.

Lifetime Employment

Japanese corporations provided employees with lifetime employment, although temporary and part-time workers did not have this benefit, nor did workers who were employed by a large number of small businesses.[10] There is no reliable estimate of the percentage of Japanese workers given lifetime employment in the private sector, but it was estimated to be around 25 percent of the workforce, most of which was concentrated in the export sector. Public employees had lifetime employment, including national and local government workers, teachers, police officers, and firefighters.

The number of employees operating under explicit lifetime employment understates the institution of lifetime employment. Even for employees who were not given lifetime employment, the implicit understanding was that employees would keep their jobs in the absence of extremely poor performance, criminal actions, or antisocial behavior. It was understood by both workers and employers that companies would do everything they could to avoid layoffs. In addition, legal worker protection was strong in Japan. It made employers' recourse to layoffs difficult. It was only during the severe economic distress of the 1990s that Japanese firms started to lay off workers as exhibited by the sharp increase in the unemployment rate in the decade. Even then, companies were obligated not to make layoffs, unless it was evident that they would go bankrupt or suffer other severe consequences. Before the 1990s, Japanese firms almost never resorted to layoffs and would resort to other adjustments in the face of a slowdown. This did not imply that labor adjustments were not made; for example, firms could reduce redundant employees by transferring them to group companies or to their subsidiaries and subcontractors.

With lifetime employment, Japanese workers and employers viewed themselves as part of a family, in which employees devoted themselves to their companies and worked hard, and companies in return took care of salaries, health care, pensions, and other welfare benefits not only for the workers but also for their spouses and children before and

---

[10] Lifetime employment usually meant guaranteed employment to age sixty or, in some cases, to higher ages. Retirees would then either be rehired by their companies at lower wages or enter the labor market in a less secure environment, if they did not go straight into retirement. The government now encourages continued employment for retirees, because of population aging and the decline of the labor force. Japanese corporations are generally very supportive of the government policy.

after retirement. The claimed benefits of the lifetime system included fostering workers' devotion and loyalty to their companies, developing and maintaining work motivation, and enhancing workers' productivity.[11] Lifetime employment contributed to increased productivity by giving both employees and employers an incentive to invest in workers' acquisition of company-specific skills and knowledge (Hall and Soskice, 2001). Japanese employers were able to invest in the provision of job training, because they knew that their workers would stay with them and did not have to worry about losing the returns on their investment in job training. Workers, likewise, knew that they could keep their jobs and get wage increases and promotions, as long as they upgraded their knowledge and skills through training provided by their employers.

Enterprise unionism was another feature of Japan's labor market that helped to develop cooperative relationships between workers and corporations. Enterprise unionism meant that each firm had its own labor union. Workers identified their economic position with their companies' performance and combined with enterprise unionism, workers had a strong incentive to cooperate with their employers. Their cooperative relationship created a stable economic environment that encouraged investment in new technology and high productivity. The cooperative relationship avoided the large losses associated with labor disputes and strikes.

Wage Coordination and Restraint

In 1975, corporations and labor unions established an informal but highly institutionalized system of wage coordination and wage restraint. Wages were essentially set for the entire economy once every spring, and the bonus system was used to make adjustments at the end of the year to ensure that previously set wages were consistent with economic performance. Wage restraint that ensured wage increases below or no higher than productivity gains increased corporate profits, increased corporate investment spending, restrained inflation, kept the unemployment rate low, and ensured that the Japanese economy remained competitive in international trade.

---

[11] The negative side of lifetime employment was that workers had no choice but to work hard for their employers, because Japan had a very small, if any, job market for non–new graduates and mid- or senior-level workers as a result of the wide practice of lifetime employment. That is, if workers were fired, it would be difficult for them to find new employment.

Wages were determined formally by negotiations between individual companies and their enterprise unions. However, to centralize the process, a small number of major firms and unions in four industries (steel, shipbuilding, automobiles, and electronics) set wage rates that, for all practice purposes, acted as a "wage leader" for other sectors of the economy including the public sector (Sako, 1997). These negotiations took place every spring and were known as the "spring offensive."

Wage restraint was one of the prices paid by workers for both explicit and implicit lifetime employment. As long as the economy grew at a rapid rate in real terms, the system of wage coordination ensured that the majority of workers would receive increased real wages over time. Extensive consultation and negotiation took place both within and between employers and unions before wage settlements. This informal wage coordination was possible partly because the unions in the export sector understood that their industries' performance hinged on international competitiveness and wage restraint was necessary to maintain their price competitiveness. These trade-sector unions dominated other unions and assumed leadership in wage bargaining and restraint.

The power of Japanese unions, by international standards, was limited. Despite the high level of wage coordination, Japan's union membership was low, and the level of centralization of union organizations was also low. The lack of centralized and aggressive unions contributed to wage restraint, limited labor disputes, and prevented dissatisfied workers from making high wage demands.

Company Welfare

Japan's labor market practices and corporate governance helped shape its welfare system. Japan's welfare regime is a mixture of residualism and a conservative ideology exemplified by self-help, paternalistic social support, and employment-related welfare (e.g., Esping-Andersen, 1997). It is residual because the Japanese government's welfare spending is minimal and among the lowest of all OECD countries. Japan's public welfare system is based strictly on means-tests because of the traditional belief that support for the aged and poor should be provided by family. Strong social stigma attached to receiving welfare also limits takeup rates in Japan. The company welfare system provided welfare benefits for company employees, and government was responsible for those not covered by the system, such as the self-employed and workers of small companies.

In the early 1970s, Japan's conservative LDP government initiated an expansion of welfare programs in response to rising electoral support for leftist parties and the declining LDP vote. However, the government immediately turned to retrenchment when the first oil shock and the onset of slow economic growth convinced the government and large corporations of the need to curb government spending (Shinkawa, 1993). Private-sector unions supported retrenchment and the maintenance of the residual welfare state because their workers' welfare was provided mainly by their companies. As a result, private-sector unions did not have interest in a universal public welfare system. Enterprise unionism encouraged union members to associate themselves with management and to identify their sense of economic well-being with company performance.

The result was a dualistic structure of welfare recipients. Government employees and employees of big corporations were entitled to generous company welfare, whereas small business employees and the self-employed received less welfare support and were forced to rely on government welfare. Public-sector unions, which favored government provided welfare, were not sufficiently powerful to offset labor's cooperation with employers and the conservative government.

Thus, Japan minimized public welfare spending for most of the postwar period, partly because company employees had generous private welfare benefits from their companies and low-wage workers were not well organized or did not have political power, and because those less fortunate workers followed the wage increase norm set by big business employers and unions. This made it possible for the governing LDP to maintain power without catering to company workers, while generously disbursing government resources to those not covered by company welfare, such as farmers and workers at small and medium businesses.

Life Expectation View

Japan's labor-corporate system played a major role in forming life expectations for the average Japanese citizen. Japan traditionally has been a conservative society in terms of gender equality, with a male-breadwinner model. Husbands were expected to provide for their family and wives served as homemakers taking care of the children. This model fit well with Japan's company welfare system – men devoted themselves to their companies and the companies provided income and welfare for their employees' entire family. A highly meritocratic nature of Japanese society also informed married parents that as long as their children studied hard and attended good universities, their children would have a comfortable life as they matured.

This belief was supported by Japan's rapid economic growth. The financial and material lives of Japanese households continued to improve before the 1990s. Wives stayed home and took care of their children's education. In order to get into a good school, children needed to pass competitive entrance examinations. The competition and their belief in the life benefits of high education led many parents to send their children to "cram schools" in the evening after their regular school and during summer and winter breaks. The objective was to provide their children with a base to secure a job at a large corporation or government agency with welfare benefits and lifetime employment. Families maintained these expectations of life, because lifetime employment guaranteed husbands would keep their jobs until retirement. After retirement, families anticipated financially secure lives because of company pensions and the tradition of children caring for their parents.

As decades passed, there were naturally new developments and movements that modified their life expectations. The idea became slightly stronger over time that men and women should be equal at work and home. Many Japanese also came to believe that stable income and security supported by lifetime employment were not the only important things in life. The quality of life became important, and jobs that would not force workers to sacrifice their spouses, children, and themselves became more desirable. Despite these developments, however, the Japanese public by and large kept their conventional life expectations views until the early 1990s. The public believed that the economy would continue to grow reliably and people's lives would continue to improve economically. Even in the context of recession and decline in asset prices in the early 1990s, the majority of Japanese believed this to be only a temporary interruption to a postwar record of economic growth and security. These expectations and hopes were dashed, however, when Japan's economic recessions were protracted and the conditions worsened. The public also faced new problems that were not visible or problematic during rapid economic growth and the bubble economy. The aging of the population and the growing costs of health care and social security generated increasing uncertainty about the future. In the course of the lost decade of the 1990s, the Japanese people were forced to adjust their life expectations.

LDP Dominance

The LDP dominated Japanese politics from 1955 until 1993. It controlled the government for thirty-eight years without interruption, despite Japan's democracy with periodic, free elections that are usually expected to create alternation of parties in power.[12] It was sometimes alleged that LDP dominance contributed to Japan's economic growth by providing economic policy stability with few policy swings, thus creating a stable economic environment. Corporations were more willing to make long-term investments, as they had few concerns that a different government would assume power in the future and reverse economic policy.

The LDP's one-party rule collapsed in 1993, and Japanese politics went into a state of flux as a result of the electoral reform movement and the LDP's split. From 1993, large-scale party realignment has taken place, and multiparty coalition governments have become the norm to date. But the LDP's dominance has continued because it has remained the largest party and the major governing party in all successive coalition governments from 1994 on.

The LDP was able to maintain power for several reasons. First, the LDP was very adept at cultivating and mobilizing votes. Individual LDP politicians created and maintained large networks of supporters called *koenkai* (supporters' associations). Japan's MMD system allowed a candidate to win a seat with a smaller percentage of votes than under the SMD system. As a result, *koenkai* supporters provided LDP politicians with relatively reliable votes (Ishikawa and Hirose, 1989).

The LDP also effectively organized and mobilized client industries and sectors, including agriculture, construction, distribution, transportation, small and medium-sized businesses, postmasters, and doctors. The LDP used clientelistic distributive politics to maintain electoral support (Hirose, 1981). The LDP was particularly strong in rural

[12] For the description of the LDP's internal politics and one-party dominance, see Fukui (1970), Calder (1988), Sato and Matsuzaki (1986), Curtis (1988, 1999), Richardson (1997), and Pempel (1990, 1998).

areas, and conducted large-scale redistribution of wealth from urban areas to rural areas in the form of government subsidies and grants to local governments and industries, public works projects, and subsidies to farmers. Furthermore, the LDP was adept at incorporating new policy positions and even the opposition parties' policy agendas to broaden its electoral bases and maintain its electoral strength (Calder, 1988).

Second, intense electoral competition between LDP candidates themselves (and intraparty factions) in the same districts under the MMD also assisted vote mobilization for the LDP as a whole and strengthened its electoral power.[13] Under Japan's MMD system, two to six representatives were elected from each district. The LDP's intraparty factions fiercely competed with each other for seats in the same districts to expand their size and increase their power within the party.

Third, Japan achieved rapid reindustrialization and economic prosperity under LDP rule. In the face of constant improvements in economic conditions and the standard of living, voters had little reason to vote the LDP out. In a related point, Japan's opposition parties failed to present themselves to voters as viable, competent alternative governing parties to the LDP. As a result, even when corruption and money scandals plagued the LDP, not enough voters confidently voted for the opposition parties. This is partly a result of LDP politicians' electoral strength – that is, even when they were found to be implicated in corruption scandals or even arrested, many of them continued to get reelected to the Diet.

Japanese politics under the LDP's one-party dominance was characterized by the following features – a policy making process dominated by the alliance of the LDP, bureaucracy, and the LDP's client industries and sectors, which existed in each policy area; a bureaucracy that was stronger and exerted more policy influence than its counterparts in other Western democracies; the diffusion of policy making power among multiple veto players and the resulting difficulty of policy innovations; and relatedly, the weaker policy-making power of the prime minister due to the multiplicity of veto players.

---

[13] The LDP (or any other party that wished to gain majority control in parliament) had to run multiple candidates in each district, because the simple majority was around 256 and there were only 130 districts. The factions competed with each other for expansion, because their larger size meant larger influence in the selection of the LDP president (which equaled a Japanese prime minister for most of the postwar period), larger numbers of and more important positions in the cabinet, party, and Diet, larger policy influence, and more money.

The Bureaucracy

The bureaucracy in most democracies plays an important role in economic and social policy by providing information and recommendations, and implementing policy.[14] But, usually, elected members of the government in the executive and legislative branches (i.e., politicians) set the policy agenda and make legislation. In the case of central banks, the bureaucracy has monetary policy-making power but, even here, central bank policy is often constrained by the broad economic agenda of politicians.

In Japan, the bureaucracy has traditionally exerted greater influence in policy making than in other democracies.[15] Its power comes from its expertise and capability in policy formulation and implementation. This was particularly true in the early postwar period. The Allied Occupation purged many political leaders but left the bureaucracy intact, because they knew that the Japanese bureaucracy was competent and was needed to manage the wartorn country. In the very early postwar period, the bureaucracy almost dominated policy formulation and implementation. The bureaucracy controlled policy making, policy implementation, and guided Japan's effort at economic reconstruction and growth (Johnson, 1982). Politicians were not powerless toward bureaucrats, because, after all, politicians were the elected officials who were given a mandate by the public to make decisions for the country. But in the early postwar period, politicians' lack of expertise and resources in policy formulation kept them at a disadvantage to take policy control away from competent, resourceful bureaucrats. Over time, politicians increasingly acquired policy expertise and gained policy making power vis-à-vis the bureaucracy.

Observers of Japanese politics have long asked the question of who ruled Japan – bureaucrats or politicians. The answer depends on policy issues and time periods. Politicians wielded more power over policy making and became strong vis-à-vis bureaucrats, if issues were salient enough to them or their client industries and businesses. If a policy pursued by bureaucrats cut into the interest of LDP politicians or their clients, LDP politicians most likely dominated bureaucrats – bureaucrats would be forced to revise the policy to meet politicians' needs

---

[14] The role of the bureaucracy in democracies is discussed in Aberbach and Putnam (1981) and Epstein and O'Halloran (1999).

[15] Johnson (1982) provides one of the best-known accounts of the role of the Japanese bureaucracy in managing the economy and supporting economic growth.

or withdraw it. But bureaucrats most likely gained the upper hand if politicians were inattentive to issues, if issues overwhelmed politicians' policy expertise, or if policy imperatives shown by bureaucrats were persuasive enough to overshadow politicians' narrow interests. Also, on issues where bureaucrats' vested interests were at stake, bureaucrats' resistance to politicians' policy attempts would be formidable, and the politicians might be unable to override bureaucratic opposition.

Bureaucrats gradually lost power vis-à-vis politicians over time, though they still remained powerful. But the late 1990s and the next decade saw a clearer decline of bureaucratic power vis-à-vis politicians. The decline came about partly as a result of bureaucrats' failure to manage the economy and resolve Japan's economic problems in the 1990s, partly because of their repeated corruption scandals, and partly because of politicians' relatively successful attempt to shift policy-making power from the bureaucracy to the cabinet and Diet.

Constrained Policy-Making Power of the Prime Minister

Japan's parliamentary system is almost identical to that of the United Kingdom in terms of formal institutions. The British system concentrates policy-making power in the prime minister and creates executive dominance (Lijphart, 1999). The British prime minister usually has good control over her/his party, which in turn is a majority party in parliament. The majority party's control of parliament gives the prime minister significant policy-making powers, as she/he also controls the legislative branch through her/his control over the majority party. The British SMD electoral system also creates a near-two-party system, which produces single-party majority governments and strengthens the prime minister's policy-making power, because of the absence of a coalition party in the cabinet that might oppose her/his policy. The British unitary system – in which policy-making power is concentrated in the national (as opposed to local) government – further bolsters the prime minister's power in implementing his/her own policies.

The Japanese parliamentary system would thus be anticipated to create executive dominance and a strong prime minister, as in the United Kingdom. However, Japan's system generated weak and dependent prime ministers, because a set of informal rules and practices created multiple veto players with whom prime ministers had to contend in their pursuit of their own policy. Four factors combined to limit the power of Japan's prime ministers.

First, the prime minister (who was normally the LDP president) was dependent on the LDP intraparty factions' support for his office, because factional power balance and coalition determined the LDP presidency. The majority factions had the power to replace the prime minister if they wished to do so; for example, Prime Minister Toshiki Kaifu was replaced by a majority coalition of LDP factions in the early 1990s, and incoming Prime Minister Kiichi Miyazawa was handpicked by the same coalition of factions. As a result, the prime minister had considerable difficulty pushing policy opposed by the LDP and its factions.

Second, the LDP was an effective gatekeeper in the flow of Japanese policy making, which can be summarized by the following sequence: the bureaucracy drafted (most) bills in consultation with the cabinet; the bills were sent to the LDP for review and approval; if the LDP approved them, they were sent to the cabinet for approval; and, finally, if they were approved by the cabinet, they were submitted to the Diet for deliberation and approval.[16] This flow of decision making gave the LDP the power to serve as the gatekeeper and block any prime ministerial policy attempt the party opposed. Because of this practice and the resulting veto power of the LDP, the prime minister needed to build consensus with the LDP. Japan's consensual decision making usually forced the prime minister to make concessions and accommodations to the LDP, which could significantly water down the original policies (Sakamoto, 1999a).

Third, the prime minister's policy making was difficult enough with the strong bureaucracy and the powerful, assertive LDP, but the prime minister also faced the LDP's client industries, businesses, and other socioeconomic groups that provided votes and money for the LDP. What made the prime minister's policy making even more difficult was that in each policy area, there was a tightly bound, powerful alliance of LDP politicians, bureaucrats, and their client industries and groups referred to as the iron triangle. They shared the same interests, looked after each other, and tried to protect their narrow interests, even if it meant going against the prime minister's wishes or national interest.

---

[16] The LDP's review and approval of bills before deliberation in the Diet was an informal practice developed by the LDP government. The practice is not stipulated anywhere in the constitution or laws.

These three actors– politicians, bureaucrats, and their client industries – formed a powerful alliance and cooperated to protect each other because they were in mutually beneficial relationships. Politicians protected their client industries and groups in exchange for votes and money. Politicians protected bureaucrats in individual policy areas in exchange for policy influence and government resources they could access from cooperating with bureaucrats who controlled policy and government resources. Bureaucrats looked after politicians in exchange for the policy favors and protection they could provide in the legislative process. Client industries and groups supported politicians and bureaucrats, because of the many government resources and policy favors they could gain from their support.

Bureaucrats protected industries and businesses under their jurisdiction, because the more industries that they had under jurisdiction, the more regulatory power and budget for bureaucrats. An important component of the relationship between the bureaucracy and industries was the practice of *amakudari* or "descent from heaven." Retired ministry officials would descend from "heaven" (government) to well-compensated positions in private corporations. Likewise, government ministries established many public or quasi-public agencies under their jurisdiction, and these corporations accepted retired government officials in executive positions. Colignon and Usui (2001) demonstrate how *amakudari* provided important networks of cooperation between the three elements of the iron triangle.

If the prime minister tried to pursue a policy that ran counter to the interests of the alliance, the alliance formed a united front against the prime minister and tried to foil or emasculate his policy. The prime minister had difficulty pushing his policy because he was dependent on LDP politicians for his office, on bureaucrats for policy formulation and cooperation, and on client industries and groups for votes and money. The iron triangle elevated the bureaucracy and client industries as effective veto players, weakening the power of the prime minister. Japan's consensual decision making also constrained the power of the prime minister in the face of policy opposition by the iron triangle. This was the reason the LDP government was unable for a long time to carry out the economic restructuring and rationalization of Japan's inefficient and uncompetitive sectors that were the LDP's electoral bases.

Fourth, veto players for prime ministerial policy initiatives were not limited to the LDP, bureaucrats, and client industries and groups. The

LDP maintained the absolute majority in both houses of the Diet for much of the postwar period. Majority control should have made it straightforward for the LDP government to pass its bills in the Diet, because the LDP could override the minority opposition with its majority vote. Despite its majority, however, the LDP had difficulty gaining Diet approval for contested bills, because the opposition parties sometimes successfully stalled Diet deliberations and blocked government bills. As a result, the prime minister faced another veto player after clearing the obstacles of the LDP, bureaucrats, and industries.

A combination of formal and informal rules and practices of the Diet equipped the minority opposition parties with the ability to block LDP bills (Mochizuki, 1982; Sakamoto, 1999a). Japanese laws stipulate that bills that fail to get voted on during the same Diet session in which they are introduced will be shelved. That is, a successful bill requires passage in the same session in which it is introduced. This imposes significant time constraints on the government, given the Diet's short sessions. This provision, combined with other rules, elevates the influence of the opposition parties. The House Management Committee – which decides the schedules of deliberations and votes on bills (the equivalent of the U.S. Steering Committee) – uses unanimity rule in decision making (an informal rule). As a result, when opposition parties opposed government bills, the LDP government sometimes could not proceed with deliberations and votes. Unanimity rule thus gave the opposition parties the power to block government bills or at least delay deliberations. The opposition parties tried to stall deliberations as much as possible to exhaust the time in hopes of shelving bills at the end of a session. The LDP government could potentially pass bills unilaterally by using its majority vote. But when the LDP resorted to this "snap vote," the opposition parties most likely boycotted following Diet deliberations, thereby delaying deliberation on all other bills that the LDP government wanted to pass, endangering their passage. Alternatively, the LDP government could try to carry deliberations on its bills into the next Diet session, but this also requires unanimity support of all parties on the committee. The opposition parties' boycott in response to the LDP's snap vote was often supported by the public and media, in the face of Japan's consensual decision making norm and its strong emotional reaction to the dreadful experience with authoritarian rule during the war.

The prime minister (or the LDP government) was forced to build consensus with the opposition parties when the latter opposed the

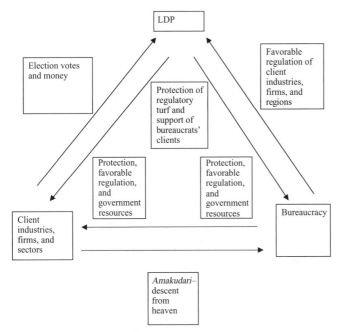

Figure 2.1. The Iron Triangle in Japan.

former's policy proposals, which again added to the time constraints already imposed on the prime minister. In the process, the prime minister was often forced to make policy concessions and accommodations to the opposition parties, potentially compromising the integrity of his policies.

Thus, the prime minister faced multiple veto players in Japan. As a result, he was generally unable to exercise as much power as the British prime minister. The set of Japanese political institutions (rules and practices) diffused policy making power among all these actors, making it difficult for the prime minister to pursue policies in the face of opposition. Japan's consensus decision making and the presence of veto players slowed government policy making and made policy changes difficult and incremental.

The Iron Triangle in Sum

Figure 2.1 illustrates a shorthand way to understand the relationships within the iron triangle of the dominant actors – the LDP, the powerful bureaucracy, and their client industries and sectors. The iron triangle was in large part a feature of the political regime in pretransition Japan. The client industries and firms provided electoral support to the LDP, which in turn delegated policy-making power to the bureaucracy, which in turn provided regulation and favorable policy to protect the client industries and firms. The client industries and firms delegated control to bureaucrats and provided postretirement employment opportunities for bureaucrats via *amakudari*, the bureaucracy mobilized the support of industry and firm for the LDP, and the LDP in turn provided public resources and favorable policy to the client industries.

This regime functioned well enough for much of pretransition Japan to generate economic growth and economic security, social order, and a distribution of income considered more equal than found in many Western economies. The system seemed to function as well after 1980 as Japan began a transition toward a more open and competitive financial system. But in the face of a new environment, the iron triangle did not want to change the beneficial status quo and resisted a policy response necessary for Japan to successfully adapt to the new environment. Thus, the restructuring of Japan's economy required something that would change the dynamics and mechanisms of the political regime. Unfortunately enough, such change did not come fast enough to spare Japan the lost decade of the 1990s.

3

The "High-Water Mark" of the Japanese Economy – A "Model" of Financial Liberalization: 1980 to 1985

Introduction

In the 1970s and 1980s, Japan's economic institutions came into conflict with a new set of economic and technological changes that first emerged in the late 1960s and accelerated by the late 1970s. Japan, however, was not special in this regard. The new environment clashed with the majority of economic institutions throughout the world. Collectivist approaches to managing the economy from the mild welfare state of the United States to the command economies of China, Russia, and Eastern Europe became increasingly incompatible with a new economic and technological environment more consistent with open, transparent, and individualistic solutions to economic and political problems.

The conflict between the new environment and existing institutions throughout much of the world generated a wide variety of market and government innovations from the 1980s on to resolve the conflict. The process differed from country to country but, collectively, it involved the liberalization and internationalization of economic institutions and, in some notable cases, involved dramatic shifts in the political institutions, such as the Soviet Union and East European countries from authoritarian to more representative political regimes in the late 1980s and early 1990s. Liberalization became a widespread phenomenon in the 1980s and continues to the present. Friedman (2000) refers to this process as the "democratization" of technology, finance, and information, and argues that it has made the world "flatter" because there is now a more level playing field among countries (Friedman, 2005). In this new environment, economic and political institutions designed to limit market access, protect markets, or limit

55

the participation of citizens in the political process were increasingly difficult to maintain.

The process, however, has not been smooth. Many countries during the past three decades experienced a wide range of economic and financial distress. There is concern over the costs of the transition from collectivist to individualist structured institutions in the short run and concern that, in the long run, income inequality is the price for more efficient economic institutions. In some parts of the world, such as the Middle East, liberalization has generated a violent reaction. In North Korea, the resistance to any integration with the world has encouraged a policy of nuclear blackmail to support the continuation of its repressive economic and political institutions. Nonetheless, the trend toward liberalization is firmly in place throughout much of the world and not likely reversible. The collapse of the Berlin Wall in November 1989 was the most visible manifestation of the failures of collectivist approaches to managing the economy.

Despite efforts to ignore these forces, Japan was forced to recognize the new environment and adopt an official policy of liberalization starting in the second half of the 1970s. Japan, however, did not fully understand the potent forces of the new environment, nor understand the extent to which its economic and political institutions would need to be redesigned, and overestimated its ability to manage the process. Japan at the start of the process believed it could achieve "*bonsai* liberalization"; that is, Japan accepted liberalization as long as it could be directed and managed like the *bonsai* tree. This resistance to change set the stage for the "bubble" economy of the second half of the 1980s and the "burst" of the bubble economy in the 1990s. However, Japan's response was not special in this regard, as many countries resisted change and, as a result, economic, financial, and sometimes political distress followed.

This chapter focuses on two issues. First, the chapter explains why the financial system in general was the first economic institution to respond to the new forces; that is, the initiation of liberalization frequently focused on financial liberalization policies designed to permit a greater role for market forces in the allocation of credit. As part of this discussion, a general outline or taxonomy of financial liberalization is presented. Second, the chapter then explains how the new forces generated an official policy of financial liberalization in Japan and the outcomes of the liberalization policy through the mid-1980s that earned Japan the status as a "model" of financial liberalization and the BOJ as a "model" central bank.

Financial Liberalization at the Forefront of the Transition

The transition of economic and political institutions in most cases commenced with changes in domestic and international financial institutions, which permitted market forces to play a greater role in the allocation of credit than previously. This is not to claim that the transition has been a linear function with financial liberalization commencing first, and then moving in a predetermined manner to other economic institutions and then to political institutions. There is considerable simultaneity between different economic and political institutions, and the sequence of changes varies from country to country. However, there are four considerations that make it reasonable to regard financial liberalization as the first major manifestation of the transition.

The first two considerations focus on the type of economic changes that took place in the 1970s: the collapse of the Bretton Woods fixed exchange rate system in 1973 and inflationary monetary policy that plagued many countries in the 1970s. The second two considerations focus on the relatively lower transactions cost to change in financial institutions compared to other economic or political institutions and how the transactions cost of change was influenced by advances in computer and telecommunications technology.

Collapse of Bretton Woods

The financial architecture that emerged after the end of World War II emphasized active policy coordination between countries to coordinate domestic and international policies in trade and finance to maintain a system of fixed exchange rates to encourage international trade. Policy coordination was predicated on the view that activist government domestic policy and international cooperation would be able to maintain exchange rates at officially agreed levels. The International Monetary Fund (IMF) was designed to ensure that countries followed policies that maintained agreed fixed exchange rates. If adjustments were required, the adjustments would be agreed to in the context of an international policy framework and would be carried out in an orderly fashion along with domestic reforms to ensure that the imbalances would not likely occur again.

The optimism that governments could coordinate policies and manage market forces reflected the activist approach to managing economic forces that dominated public policy during the first three decades following World War II. The optimism, however, was based on a faulty model of economic behavior that emphasized the inherent instability of markets and tendency for markets to generate suboptimal equilibriums. It also was based on a naive view of the willingness of countries to coordinate policy if coordination required policies that might have adverse effects on certain sectors in their domestic economy.

The collapse of the Bretton Woods system in 1973 occurred because of differing rates of economic activity and rates of inflation between countries and the fundamental unwillingness of governments to subvert domestic policies to international considerations. Inflationary policies in the 1960s and 1970s in many countries caused market exchange rates to deviate from official exchange rates. The system also was hampered by a lack of international liquidity and undue pressure on the United States to both supply dollars to the world for the first decade after the end of World War II and the pressure to retain credibility in the dollar as a "key" international reserve and investment currency.

The fixed exchange rate system required governments to slow the pace of economic activity in the face of persistent current account deficits and to increase the pace of economic activity in the face of persistent current account surplus. However, governments were reluctant to adapt domestic policy to achieve a fixed rate of exchange rate target. Countries experiencing continued deficits found it politically more expedient to adopt a variety of "beggar" thy neighbor policies such as tariffs, quotas, exchange controls, and so on and blame other countries for the imbalances. Some surplus countries were reluctant to increase the pace of economic activity to maintain the fixed exchange rate system out of inflation concerns and, more often, surplus countries were governed by mercantilist tendencies in that they believed current account surpluses contributed to the nation's wealth. The end result was more restrictions on international trade, speculative attacks on the currency of a deficit country in anticipation of devaluation, and pressure on the United States to subvert domestic policy to maintaining the fixed exchange rate.

These trade conflicts were especially intense among Germany, Japan, and the United States. The United States regarded Germany's and Japan's currencies as undervalued given their impressive postwar reindustrialization and economic growth, whereas Germany and Japan argued that the United States needed to reduce the pace of economic growth and inflation. These conflicts led to the August 1971 "Nixon Shock," which was the death knell of the fixed exchange rate system. The Nixon administration unilaterally ended the official convertibility of the dollar into gold and threatened to impose an import surcharge on German and Japanese imports unless they revalued their currencies. This is referred to as a "shock" because the Nixon administration did not consult the international community, especially Japan and Germany, before making the announcement. The IMF attempted to reestablish the fixed exchange rate system; however, by 1973, the Bretton Woods system ended, and most of the world shifted to a flexible exchange rate system.

The failure to maintain a system of exchange rates inconsistent with market forces demonstrated the ineffectiveness of binding regulations on financial markets in general. The collapse of the managed exchange rate system was a precursor to the collapse of policies designed to limit competitive forces in domestic financial markets. High and differing inflation rates among countries in the 1960s and early 1970s played an important role in the collapse of the Bretton Woods system, which, in turn, pressured countries to establish more open domestic financial systems. Countries with meaningful roles in international trade under a flexible exchange rate system require financial assets suitable for international reserve and investment purposes. This requires the establishment of money and capital markets, which, in turn, require greater transparency, and so on.

High inflation rates also brought pressure on countries to remove or relax a number of binding constraints on domestic financial markets because unregulated interest rates responded to inflation whereas government regulated interest rates did not automatically respond to inflation. The wider the gap between unregulated and regulated interest rates, the more intense the disruptions in the financial system and the greater pressure on governments to remove and/or relax constraints on regulated interest rates.

Inflationary Monetary Policy

Central bank policy in the first three decades of the postwar period was greatly influenced by the 1930s Keynesian paradigm that monetary policy was capable of permanently changing the pace of real economic growth, and then in the 1960s by the widespread acceptance of the Phillips curve trade-off between inflation and unemployment, which implied government stabilization policy could purchase higher economic growth and lower unemployment with inflation.[1]

Central bank policy was operationally activist, based on the view that monetary policy could achieve improved real performance in the economy, albeit at the cost of some inflation. Stagflation in the 1970s, however, demonstrated that monetary policy based on the Keynesian paradigm and Phillips curve trade-offs generated only higher rates of inflation and, rather than high economic growth, often generated declines in real GDP and increased unemployment. Theoretical developments in macroeconomics by the late 1970s showed the Keynesian and Phillips curve framework fundamentally flawed and a poor foundation to base monetary policy, which more than likely would generate greater instability and inflation over time. By the late 1970s and early 1980s, much of the economics profession and policy making began to move away from activist policies and, in the case of monetary policy, focus more on long-run price stability.

This revision in views, however, came too late to prevent widespread inflation in many developed and developing countries. In the 1970s and early 1980s, inflation was a major macroeconomic problem throughout much of the world. Inflation affected economic performance in many ways, depending on whether inflation was anticipated or unanticipated. However, the impact on financial markets was especially important for understanding why financial liberalization was the first major manifestation of the transition.

The majority of domestic financial systems in the 1970s imposed a variety of interest rate constraints on lending and deposit taking by financial institutions. These controls were imposed for a variety of reasons and ranged from the imposition of only a few controls as in the United States to the extensive system of interest rate controls in Japan and South Korea. There were fewer attempts, however, to impose interest rate controls on open money and capital markets because of their very nature, but this was largely irrelevant for Japan because Japan until the late 1970s had no meaningful money and capital markets. In the United States, interest rates in money and capital markets were unregulated, and in other places such as Japan and Korea, money and capital market transactions were restricted to only a small part of the flow of funds.

---

[1] These points are discussed in Lacker and Weinberg (2007).

The inflationary central bank policies of the 1960s and 1970s not only contributed to the collapse of the Bretton Woods system but also generated serious conflicts within domestic financial systems. Past and current inflation generated higher inflationary expectations, which adversely affected the relationship between regulated and unregulated interest rates. Financial transactions are forward-looking and the expected future value of money significantly influences the lender-borrower relationship. Unregulated interest rates incorporate inflationary expectations while regulated interest rates do not respond to inflationary expectations. Regulated interest rates are adjusted only a discrete points in time and when they are adjusted, the adjustments are significantly less that what the market would require. In those cases in which some interest rates were regulated and other interest rates were unregulated, inflationary expectations generated wide gaps and induced market innovations. Market participants introduced new financial services and assets to circumvent the binding interest rate controls. These innovations often disrupted the flow of funds and were not available to all participants in the financial system.

The general absence of interest rate controls in money and capital markets permitted these markets to be utilized to generate new financial assets to circumvent interest rate restrictions. In those cases in which money and capital markets were lacking and interest rate controls were more complete, inflationary expectations lowered the real return on holding financial assets, which, in turn, led to other distortions in the economy as households sought ways to earn market interest rates on their holdings of financial assets.

Hence, the gap between regulated and unregulated interest rates caused by inflationary monetary policy interfered with the flow of funds and provided incentives to government either to relax or remove interest rate controls and provided incentives for market participants to find ways to circumvent the interest rate controls, which, in turn, led to further pressure on government to relax or remove interest rate controls.

Low Transactions Cost of Institutional Change in Finance

The transactions cost of institutional redesign plays an important role in the ways that conflicts between existing institutions and a new environment are resolved. The higher the transactions cost of institutional redesign, the longer existing institutions remain in place irrespective of their conflict with the new environment. In the case of corporate governance, labor markets, and especially political institutions, the transactions cost of change tends to be much higher than in the case of financial institutions.

Finance is fungible, and in many cases financial transactions are characterized by a small number of parameters, price, and quantity, making it easier to circumvent regulations. Even in the most repressed economies in which there is little flexibility in business management, labor markets, and political institutions, financial markets illustrate a high degree of adaptability in the face of conflicts between the existing financial system and a new environment. In Korea and Japan, for example, which had the most repressive financial systems among the industrialized economies before 1980, "curb" and various unofficial markets emerged to resolve some of the more significant pressure to liberalize the financial system.

Advances in Computer and Telecommunication Technology

It is difficult to underestimate the impact that advances in computer and telecommunications technology had on institutional change throughout the world. The practical computer was an outcome of the war effort in the United States to build an atomic weapon. In the 1950s and 1960s, mainframe computers became increasingly available to the public and began to revolutionize the ways in which societies conducted business, especially financial transactions. Until the 1970s however, computers were large, expensive, relatively slow, and not user-friendly. The rapid pace of computer technology in the 1970s and 1980s dramatically reduced the size of computers, their expense, and made them increasingly user-friendly.

Advances in computer technology had an especially important impact on financial transactions. Not only did low-cost computing power and computer storage make it possible to achieve improved efficiency in the ways in which financial transactions were conducted, they dramatically lowered the transactions cost of institutional redesign by making it easier to create new financial assets and services to circumvent binding regulations limiting profit. Advances in telecommunications combined with advances in computer technology made it possible to merge domestic and international finance and essentially establish a 24/7 world financial system. Together, they blurred the distinctions among local, national, and international financial markets and eliminated the differences between time zones. In essence, computer and telecommunications technology together contributed greatly to the "democratization" of finance.

Financial Redesign and Financial Liberalization in Broad Perspective

The collapse of the fixed exchange rate system, inflation, the low transactions costs of financial system redesign, and advances in computer and telecommunications technology, combined to ensure that financial systems would most likely be the first to respond to the new environment. That is, the most significant manifestation of liberalization would likely be financial liberalization. This was especially the case in Japan. As a result, the first two decades of Japan's transition focused on financial institutional redesign. We now turn to a general overview of the financial liberalization process.

A country's financial system in the broad sense consists of private financial institutions and markets, government regulatory authorities, the central bank, and, in some cases, parts of the fiscal program of the government. Financial systems are designed for many purposes ranging from serving as instruments of industrial policy to supporting consumer and mortgage credit demands. Irrespective of these differences and differing roles governments impose on their financial system, financial systems share four basic responsibilities: (1) to provide an efficient flow of funds from lenders to borrowers; (2) to provide a stable environment for the flow of funds from lender to borrowers; (3) to provide an adaptable environment responsive to the needs of lenders and borrowers; and (4) to provide a platform for central bank policy to maintain price stability so that the effects of policy are not concentrated in a few sectors and the effects are smoothly and quickly distributed throughout the financial and real sectors of the economy.

The institutionalization of these four basic responsibilities differs from country to country and reflects each country's culture, history, and national policy. Government regulatory agencies and central banks are designed to ensure that, at a minimum, financial institutions achieve these four responsibilities. They do this by providing prudential regulation and supervision over financial institutions and markets; providing lender of last resort services to prevent bank runs; and providing money and credit to meet the needs of the economy without inflation or deflation.

As long as the financial system achieves its basic responsibilities, there is little pressure for institutional redesign; however, if one or more of the basic responsibilities is not being satisfied, redesign takes place. Financial redesign takes place through two channels: first and the most visible are government or regulatory innovations; second, market innovations. Government innovations are manifested by changes in the regulatory parameters of the financial system such as rules defining portfolio diversification powers, rules regulating loan and deposit rates, and rules regulating entry and exit from specific financial markets, and so on. Most often, government innovations are manifested by legislative acts, but administrative rule-making also can play an important role in government innovations. Market innovations are manifested by new financial assets and services introduced by market participants designed to circumvent institutions that limit profit.

The two channels of change are often in conflict. Government regulation is passive and frequently more focused on maintaining the status quo even when there is widespread recognition that institutional redesign of the financial system is necessary. Government regulation is often dominated by "special or client interests," which frequently resist change. Market innovations are more flexible and intended to get around the status quo that limits profit-taking.

Kane (1981) used the concept of the "regulatory-market dialectic" to describe the conflict between these two channels. Government often reacts to innovation by extending regulation to limit innovations. The market in response reinnovates and the government reregulates and so on in a process that ultimately results in regulatory institutional design in line with market innovations. It would not be too bold to claim that most government redesigns of the financial system during the past three decades throughout much of the world were official recognition and acceptance of market innovations that first responded to the failures of the financial system to achieve one or more of its basic responsibilities.

Table 3.1 provides a general taxonomy of financial liberalization[2] that reasonably can be applied to almost any country's efforts to

---

[2] The taxonomy has appeared in various forms in other places; for example, see Cargill (2006).

Table 3.1. Taxonomy of sequence of steps in the financial liberalization process

There is a given prereform institutional design of the financial regime consisting of private financial institutions, markets, government regulatory authorities, and central banking institutions.

↓

The given institutional design conflicts with new economic, political, or technological environment.

↓

The conflicts interfere with the ability of the given financial regime to meet basic responsibilities. The conflicts can be manifested in a variety of ways, ranging from failures of financial institutions to shifts in the allocation of funds among financial institutions.

↓

The resulting financial disruptions and inefficiency stimulate market and regulatory innovations.

↓

Market and regulatory innovations are resisted by various regulatory authorities unwilling to depart from the old regime because they view the transition as a potential loss of regulatory power.

↓

Conflicts between different regulatory authorities influence the transition, as each authority wants to maintain or enhance its regulatory authority as the new system emerges.

↓

Market and regulatory innovations are resisted by various private sectors unwilling to depart from the old regime because they view the transition as a potential loss of property rights and rents enjoyed under the old regime.

↓

Conflicts between different private sectors influence the transition as each sector wants to maintain or enhance its market share as the new system emerges.

↓

The degree of the resistance from the public and private sector determines the timing, the completeness, and the stability of the transition from the old to the new regime.

↓

Financial reform becomes a two-way feedback process between the public and private sectors, in that reform requires institutional redesign of both private and public institutions.

↓

The financial reform process is stable or unstable depending not only on the degree of resistance to redesign from the private and public sector but also on central bank policy, existence and extent of money and capital markets, degree of interface between domestic and international finance, and so on.

redesign its financial system during the past three decade. The basic function of a country's financial system is to provide an orderly and stable flow of funds between lenders and borrowers and a platform for monetary policy. Institutional redesign occurs when the financial regime's basic responsibilities are not achieved. This frequently occurs when the existing regime encounters a new economic, political, or technological environment that conflicts with one or more key elements of the existing financial structure. The reform process itself is a complex interplay between market innovations and government innovations.

The process is seldom smooth, however, because there is considerable resistance to financial reform and conflict between the various participants in the reform process. There is resistance from established groups possessing long-held property rights to regulatory rents embedded in the prereform financial regime. Private banks and depositors regard deposit guarantees as entitlements and hence resist any effort to reduce them or make them more market-sensitive. Regulatory authorities resist reform if they perceive reform as a rejection of past regulatory policies and, more important, if they perceive reform reducing their role or prestige in the new regulatory framework. No country is immune.

Once financial reform becomes an ongoing process, it frequently requires redesign of all of the major components of the financial structure, including government regulatory institutions as well as nonfinancial components such as corporate governance and industrial organization.

Instability and financial disruptions have been notable characteristics of the financial liberalization process in most countries during the past three decades. An IMF study by Lindgren, Garcia and Saal (1996) tabulated 133 significant banking sector problems among the IMF's 188 members from 1980 to 1996. These and other banking problems were manifested by bank failures and insolvency, nationalization of banking systems in some cases, collapse of major sectors of the financial system (savings and loan industry in the United States and *jusen* industry in Japan), financial scandals (Enron in the United States and Daiwa Securities Company in Japan), and asset bubbles and burst of asset bubbles. Overall, it has not been an impressive process, especially given the claimed benefits of a more liberalized financial environment widely expressed in the 1980s.

Two explanations have been offered to account for the lack of a smooth financial liberalization process.

The *Market Failure* view emphasizes the inherent instability in markets caused by rent-seeking activity in a less regulated environment and, hence, places the blame on liberalization itself. That is, providing markets with enhanced portfolio diversification powers allows market participants to assume imprudent levels of risk and increase the market's systemic risk as market participants seek to maximize their own profit. This view emphasizes market failure as the explanation for the lack of a smooth financial transition. The market failure view points to the asset inflation in the second half of the 1980s in Japan, equity price inflation in the United States in the late 1990s, and real estate inflation in United States during the first part of the new century as clear evidence of market failure and what happens when liberalization is carried too far. The policy implication of this view ranges from return to the old-style of controls to a much slower pace of liberalization.

The *Government Failure* view regards liberalization as a positive and inevitable development that enhances economic growth and establishes a "flat world" in which increasing numbers of countries compete on a level basis. The financial disruptions of the past that appear correlated with liberalization are the result of government failure in that government policy exposes the system to systemic risk. The process has been uneven and sometimes disruptive because of government willingness to protect property rights developed under the old regime; willingness to pursue unbalanced rather than comprehensive reform; unwillingness to impose bankruptcy on insolvent financial institutions; unwillingness to reduce government deposit guarantees; and when government action is required to deal with troubled financial institutions, government pursues policies based on forgiveness and forbearance in hope the financial institutions will "work their way out of the problem" if given sufficient time. A significant moral hazard problem emerges because financial institutions are permitted greater asset-liability diversification powers while, at the same time, government continues to guarantee deposits and protect existing financial institutions from competition, which in turn subsidizes risk-taking. As financial institutions encounter problems, government adopts forgiveness and forbearance as the preferred policy for dealing with troubled institutions rather than closing institutions and imposing losses on depositors.

The government failure view, in particular, attributes even the major asset bubbles of the past three decades to government policies. As we will see, the asset inflation in Japan in the second half of the 1980s was a result of the combination of easy monetary policy and a flawed financial liberalization process. Once started, an asset bubble does exhibit market failure or market irrationality; however, poorly designed government policy was the catalysts for the bubble in the first place.

This study takes the position that government failure offers a more reasonable explanation for the financial disruptions of the past three decades. This is not meant to imply that there were no market failures. However, based on many case studies, government failure played a more important role in the financial disruptions than market failure. A complete understanding of the financial disruptions including asset bubbles needs to place significant importance on the role of government policy.

Japan Commences Financial Liberalization

By the 1970s, Japan's economic and political institutions appeared to be successful. Other than the short turbulent period of the early 1970s marked by the first oil price shock and high inflation, the Japanese economy exhibited high rates of real GDP growth with moderate to low inflation from 1950 to the late 1980s. In contrast, during the 1970s and 1980s the majority of other industrial countries experienced a variety of financial disruptions, high inflation, stagflation, and other macroeconomic problems. Japan seemed to avoid the majority of these problems. After the high inflation of the early 1970s, Japan's inflation rate was gradually reduced so that by the late 1970s Japan's price stability stood in sharp contrast to that of most countries. Japan's financial system appeared stable with no bank failures or problem institutions in sharp contrast to the financial distress in most other countries.

The new economic, political, and technological changes that emerged in the 1970s, however, came into conflict with Japan's institutions and set into motion a series of policies to liberalize financial institutions and adopt financial liberalization as official government policy. What were these environmental changes?

Economic Influences

Two major changes in Japan's economic environment occurred in the 1970s: slower economic growth and end of the Bretton Woods fixed exchange rate system. Both changes pressured Japan to liberalize its financial system.

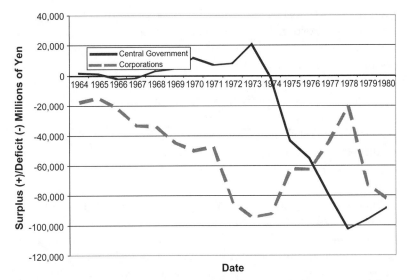

Figure 3.1. Financial Surplus (+) and Deficit (–) of the Central Government and Corporate Sector, 1964 to 1980. *Source:* Ministry of Internal Affairs and Communications, Historical Statistics of Japan, Currency and Flow of Funds, http://www.stat.go.jp/english/data/chouki/04.htm.

Japan's natural or potential growth rate declined in the 1970s because of higher energy prices and because the end of reindustrialization slowed the rate of domestic investment spending. Slower growth impacted corporations, banks, securities companies, and government, and, in one way or another, each became advocates of liberalization for practical reasons.

Corporate investment spending had been financed largely through bank finance, and corporate governance was dominated by bank finance given the prominence of the *keiretsu* system. An important characteristic of the reliance of corporations on bank finance was the system of requiring corporations to maintain large compensating balances with the lending bank. These compensating balances were considered part of the cost of bank borrowing, and as long as demand for bank credit was strong, compensating balance requirements were simply part of the corporate-bank customer relationship. Corporations had no meaningful alternatives to bank finance in most cases because of limited domestic money and capital markets and restrictions on external financing. As the demand for bank credit slowed in a slower investment environment, corporations found themselves with significant amounts of liquidity. Figure 3.1 indicates that, starting in the early 1970s, the corporate sector's flow of funds deficit declined significantly. Corporations then became advocates of a more flexible financial system so as to earn a higher return on their liquidity. They became advocates of expanded investment and borrowing opportunities and fewer controls on inflows and outflows of capital to Japan.

In the slower credit growth environment, banks lost market share. In response, banks sought increased portfolio diversification powers to reestablish market share. They expanded into consumer and mortgage credit, set up subsidiaries known collectively as the *jusen* industry to expand into consumer and mortgage credit, and sought new powers to underwrite securities.

Securities companies played a relatively small role in Japan's financial system because open money and capital markets were undeveloped and most bond issues were handled by banks. The equities market was not viewed as a source of funds. Instead, equities solidified relationships between banks and corporations through extensive crossholding of shares. Securities companies became advocates of liberalization, as they saw an opportunity to provide greater services to a more liquid corporate sector as well as provide greater services to a more internationally open financial system required by flexible exchange rates. The large government deficits in the 1970s (see Figure 3.1) also offered new profit opportunities. The aging of the Japanese population and the need for an expanded set of financial assets to manage retirement funds were also viewed by securities companies as a new profit center that could be realized only if money and capital markets were allowed to expand.

Thus, corporations, banks, and securities companies became demanders of a more open and flexible financial system. Each viewed financial liberalization as a profit opportunity. The government, especially the MOF, as the supplier of financial regulation likewise became a willing supplier of financial liberalization for economic as well as political reasons. The government in the 1950s and 1960s was fiscally conservative running essentially balanced budgets; however, after 1973, the central government deficit increased significantly. Slow growth lowered the growth of tax revenue and government expenditures increased in response to pressure to offset the adverse effects of higher oil prices.

In the past, the central government financed its small deficits through a "captured syndicate" system in which banks and securities companies purchased government debt at below market interest rates.

This system worked well for the MOF because there was no open bond market to sell debt and permitted the MOF to obtain funds at low interest rates. The banks and securities companies participated in the system because the amounts of debt purchased were small, because in the case of banks there was a commitment by the BOJ to purchase the debt after one year at prices guaranteed to ensure no capital loss, and because the MOF was in a position to grant special regulatory favors.

After 1973, the situation changed as the need for deficit financing increased significantly. Banks and securities companies began to resist purchasing large amounts of government debt at below market interest rates and began to exert pressure on the MOF to provide more flexibility in the financial system; that is, to supply liberalization to meet their increased demand for liberalization. In 1976, the MOF officially recognized a repurchase market (*gensaki* market) based on government securities established by securities companies in the 1960s but officially ignored because of its small size. The BOJ announced in 1978 that it would cease purchasing government debt from banks at prices guaranteeing no capital loss. Because of pressure from banks and securities companies, the MOF permitted banks and securities companies to sell debt holdings in an unregulated secondary market. Once a secondary market was established with an unregulated interest rate, pressure to relax interest rate regulations in other parts of the financial system emerged.

Slower economic growth had a profound impact by reducing the size of the corporate deficit and increasing the central government deficit. This set into motion a set of incentives and actions on the part of corporations, banks, securities companies, and the government that started the financial liberalization process in Japan. The end of the fixed exchange rate system added further pressure to liberalize the financial system.

Flexible exchange rate systems require institutions and markets that permit rapid transfer of funds from one currency to another so that exchange rates can adjust to shifts in demand and supply for each country's currency. This requires a money market with short-term and low-risk financial assets denominated in a country's currency that can be used as an international reserve and investment asset. At the end of the Bretton Woods system in 1973, Japan had no such markets and, given Japan's considerable role in world trade, the lack of open money and capital markets made it difficult for Japan to participate in the new flexible exchange rate system.

Political Influences

Although much of the world was in the process of rejecting or reevaluating collectivist approaches to managing the economy, there was no discernable change in Japan's confidence in its collectivist approach to managing the economy. Financial liberalization was viewed merely as a practical issue that required some modification of Japan's financial system, but there was no need to get carried away with liberalization. In fact, other than making some modifications to permit easier financing of government deficits, the government viewed the current set of financial institutions as more than adequate. How could one argue with success? The Japanese economy had grown from the ashes of World War II to become the second largest and one of the most envied countries of the world by the 1980s.

Nonetheless, the general shift toward markets in many countries brought pressure on Japan to liberalize its financial system and permit a greater role for foreign financial institutions, especially securities companies. The political pressures on Japan were based on a revision of views about collectivist versus individualistic economic structures taking place in many places and increasing concerns about Japan's reliance on trade surpluses to drive domestic economic growth.

The reconsideration of the benefits of markets and competition was based on a number of factors. The policy outcomes of government activism fell far short of the promises by the 1970s. Economic distress caused by inflation and stagflation was widespread. The two largest collectivist economies in the world – the Soviet Union and China – faced a number of economic problems that suggested that these command style systems were not sustainable and would eventually adopt market reforms. Economic theory and empirical research demonstrated the limitations of activist government macroeconomic policy and showed that such efforts were likely to increase instability. Stagflation was shown to be the outcome of government efforts to purchase more employment with higher inflation.

Developments in the theory of government decision making showed that government failure was at least as important as market failure and probably more serious. The new view emphasized the importance government attached to maintaining and enhancing power rather than the general welfare of society. Relationships between regulatory authorities as suppliers of regulation and "special" interest as demanders of regulation combined with the government's own emphasis on maintaining and enhancing power often generated policy outcomes adverse to society.

The Great Depression of the 1930s in the United States was a major foundation for government activism in the postwar period and regarded as a case of market failure. Extensive research first initiated by Friedman and Schwartz (1963), however, demonstrated that Federal Reserve policy errors generated the collapse.[3] This reinterpretation of the Great Depression was an important development in the United States and in other Western countries, because the Great Depression had been widely accepted in the postwar period as evidence that the market without extensive and deep government involvement was inherently unstable.

This shift in attitude away from collectivist toward individualistic market structures, however, did not take place in Japan. Japan had never been structured on open, competitive, and transparent markets either in the real or financial sectors, and it was only after the reforms introduced by the Allied Occupation that Japan's political institutions shifted toward democracy. The postwar Japanese economy was essentially collectivist in structure and attitude and, despite the range of economic and financial problems being experienced by much of the world in the 1970s, Japan's economy seemed immune. Nonetheless, the shift in political attitudes outside Japan came to exert pressure on Japan to liberalize.

There was increasing pressure from the United States and Europe to join a worldwide movement toward markets and away from collectivist approaches to allocating resources. There was increasing opinion that Japan's isolated and rigidly regulated economy provided Japan with an unfair competitive advantage in international trade and, hence, there were increasing calls for Japan to end its mercantilist policies. There was a widely held view, especially by the U.S. Treasury, that Japan's administratively controlled financial system gave it an unfair advantage in world trade by undervaluing the yen. This view was incorrect, but it carried considerable political weight.[4]

The U.S. Treasury advanced the view in the late 1970s and early 1980s that Japan's isolated financial system artificially undervalued the yen despite the adoption of flexible exchange rates after 1973. The

---

[3] Cargill and Mayer (1998) show how even at this late date in the debate, many continue to mistakenly regard the Great Depression as an example of market failure.

[4] Frankel (1984) provides a detailed discussion of this debate and illustrates the lack of logic in the U.S. position.

yen had no desirable characteristics of an international reserve or investment asset because Japan lacked money and capital markets and Japan's interest rates were isolated from international forces. Hence, if Japan liberalized its financial system and permitted greater foreign access, the yen would appreciate and reduce trade imbalances. This view was incorrect, however. Financial liberalization in Japan would not have necessarily appreciated the yen. Some policies would lead to yen appreciation, but others would lead to yen depreciation so that, on balance, the effect of financial liberalization on the value of the yen was indeterminate. Nonetheless, the argument had considerable political power and, on the surface, appeared reasonable, at least reasonable enough for political pressure to be brought on Japan.

Technological Influences

Advances in computer and telecommunications technology had profound effects on how countries conducted economic and financial transactions. The growth of the Eurocurrency markets, international banking, financial integration, and interdependence of large numbers of countries were supported by advances in computer and telecommunications technology. Japan participated in these advances and in some cases contributed to their development. To the extent that Japan came under increasing pressure to open its economy to the world, these advances were a catalyst for financial liberalization in Japan. At the same time, they did not play the same role as a foundation for market innovations or as a means to enhance the regulatory-market conflict that they did in other countries, especially the United States.

Computer technology combined with wide and deep money markets in the United States, for example, made it possible to establish money market mutual funds designed to circumvent deposit interest rate ceilings. Money market funds offered market interest rates with little risk that eventually forced the U.S. government to abandon deposit ceilings in 1980. Computer and telecommunications technology made it possible to develop new innovations even for small gaps between regulated and unregulated interest rates.

In Japan's case, this technology did not play the same role because the gap between regulated and unregulated interest rates was much smaller. That is, although technology contributed to Japan's financial liberalization indirectly because it was an important foundation of the internationalization of finance, it did not play a major role in market innovations or market-regulatory conflicts. Not only was the gap much narrower in Japan than elsewhere, Japan lacked the type of money and capital markets that were extensively used in other countries to circumvent government controls over financial institutions.

This is not to imply that market innovations were absent in Japan's liberalization policy. There were several notable innovations, summarized in Cargill and Royama (1988). The *gensaki* market or government bond repurchase market was clearly an innovation by the securities companies to expand their profit opportunities. There is evidence that Japanese banks in the 1970s used foreign correspondent banks to circumvent interest rate ceilings and the BOJ's tight monetary policy, much as U.S. banks used the Eurodollar market for the same purposes. The *sarakin* in the 1960s and 1970s were essentially loanshark type finance companies tolerated by the government because they were viewed as satisfying household demand for consumer loans that could not be satisfied by the mainstream financial system. There are many examples of banks and the PSS using computer technology to package different types of deposits to achieve higher interest and offered an extensive network of cash dispensers to differentiate their institutions.

Financial Liberalization Becomes Official Policy in Japan

Determining the start of financial liberalization in Japan[5] is not as difficult as for other countries because government innovation was the main channel of liberalization policy. Private market innovations were not absent in Japan; however, they played a relatively small role compared to government innovations. Focusing on government innovations removes some complexity in establishing a start date, but even here there is some debate. For example, some might suggest that the decision by the MOF to officially recognize the *gensaki* market in 1976 represents the start of liberalization or, instead, the series of decisions made in 1978 to permit a secondary market in government

---

[5] There is a large volume of material on Japan's financial liberalization process and the following is only a very small sample of that literature. The taxonomy of financial change, the specific influences that induced Japan to commence financial liberalization, and the policy outcomes of the liberalization process are discussed in Cargill (2006), Cargill and Royama (1988), Cargill, Hutchison, and Ito (1997 and 2000), Feldman (1986), and Hoshi and Kashyap (2001). The liberalization process in the United States is discussed in Benston and Kaufman (1997), Cargill and Garcia (1982 and 1985), and Kane (1981). Cargill and Royama (1988) present the liberalization process in Japan and the United States through the mid-1980s from a comparative perspective.

bonds. It seems most appropriate, however, to focus on 1980 as the starting point because the 1949 Foreign Exchange and Trade Control Act was revised in December 1980 and represented a major change in Japan's perspective (Toyo, 2006). Additionally, pressure on Japan to liberalize intensified after 1980, and the number of regulatory changes made by Japan increased significantly after 1980.

The 1980 reform represented a major change in attitude on the part of the government. International isolation had been a major feature of the pretransition institutions and the 1949 Foreign Exchange and Trade Control Act memorized the view that foreign exchange transactions were "prohibited in principle." The 1980 revision changed the intent of the Act to "free in principle unless prohibited." Internationalization in any direction represented a major attitudinal change in Japan, and, hence, any change in institutions to permit greater interaction with the international financial system is a turning point in financial liberalization. The 1980 reform was extended by the 1984 Report of the Joint US-Japan Ad Hoc Group on the Yen-Dollar Relationship, which liberalized the Euro yen market and was an important turning point for increased pressure on Japan to internationalize and liberalize its financial system.

Irrespective of the starting date, financial liberalization by 1980 became a stated policy objective of the Japanese government. What did Japan accomplish? A major theme of this chapter is that the liberalization process, once started, is not necessarily smooth for a variety of reasons. In fact, the process more often than not ends up with considerable economic and financial distress. This was not the case for Japan, however. The liberalization process in the first half of the 1980s was impressive compared to what was occurring in other industrial countries. In the second half of the 1980s, the process again appeared smooth, but in hindsight pressures were accumulating that rendered Japan's financial structure susceptible to shocks and in essence rendered Japan's financial system and economy an "accident waiting to happen." The remainder of this chapter focuses on the positive accomplishments of Japan's liberalization in the 1980s.

Redesign of Japan's Financial System

There are two ways to summarize the many changes to Japan's financial system that commenced after 1980s. First, one can recount each government redesign and administrative decision as provided by Cargill and Royama (1988) and Hoshi and Kashyap (2001); second, one can focus on the broad changes ignoring the details. The focus here is on the broad perspective of Japan's positive accomplishments. The following summary covers the most important accomplishments through the first few years of the new century even though this chapter focuses on the 1980–1985 period. It would be artificial to bifurcate the numerous policy decisions by any given year.

Interest Rate Deregulation

Interest rate deregulation occurred along several lines of development. First, government long-term bond interest rates were liberalized by a series of decisions in the late 1970s so that by the early 1980s, the ask-bid spread narrowed considerably and the difference between the new-issue bond rate and the secondary market rate was small. This was accomplished by the following decisions of the MOF and the BOJ: to offer government bonds at public auction; to permit a secondary market in government bonds; to permit an expanded *gensaki* market; to reduce the amount of time that banks had to hold government bonds when purchased as part of the syndicate system; to eliminate the commitment by the BOJ to repurchased government bonds to ensure no capital loss by banks; and to permit banks to sell government bonds and use government bonds to innovate new types of deposit accounts. Second, a variety of new financial assets were introduced in stages that were not subject to interest rate controls. Restrictions on issuing collateralized and uncollateralized bonds were relaxed so that by the late 1980s a corporate bond market with unregulated interest rates became a feature of Japanese finance. In 1987, commercial paper was permitted. Third, new deposit instruments were introduced such as large CDs (certificates of deposit), MMCs (money market certificates), and large time deposits. These were introduced either with no interest rate regulations (CDs) or with relaxed regulations that were gradually removed. Postal savings deposit rates were increasingly required to be market-sensitive. Regulations limiting the ability of private financial institutions to set loan rates were gradually removed.

As of 1994, interest rate deregulation in Japan was accomplished for all practical purposes. By 1994, domestic interest rates were either market-determined or market-sensitive and from an international perspective, Japan's domestic interest rates reflected the influence of international forces.

Money and Capital Markets

The growth of large CDs, commercial paper, government bonds, and corporate bonds from the late 1970s to the early 1990s significantly changed Japan's financial structure. In fact, CDs became such an important part of the financial system that they were included in the official monetary measure of the BOJ (M2 + CDs). Money and capital markets increasingly were being internationalized and becoming an important source of borrowing and managing financial portfolios. Not only did traditional money and capital markets emerge but also options, futures, and asset-securitized markets emerged over time, so that by the early 1990s, Japan's money and capital markets came to take on the appearance of those in the United States. These markets have continued to grow in variety.

Financial Disclosure

Japan made some efforts toward greater financial disclosure. Before the start of liberalization, there was no meaningful financial disclosure system for two reasons: first, because of the undeveloped money and capital markets, there was no need for a financial disclosure system and, second, most of the lending was conducted by banks in the context of the *keiretsu* system so that financial decisions were made on the basis of information dominated by the main bank or other financial institutions around which the company group was centered. Hence, financial disclosure in Japan had been based on "insider" rather than "outsider" information sources. As money and capital markets began to develop, however, the need for an expanded financial disclosure system to evaluate credit risk arose. In the mid–1980s, several domestic bond rating services were established and over time, several foreign bond rating services were established in Japan. Despite these developments, financial disclosure was not seriously addressed until after the near collapse of the Japanese financial system in the late 1990s.

Intermediation Finance

The most notable changes impacted private bank and nonbank financial institutions. The various types of banks (city, regional, *sogo*, trust, long-term, and *shinkin*) were permitted more flexibility in managing their uses and sources of funds and, hence, were becoming more similar over time. In 1989, *sogo* banks converted to regional banks, which in turn were divided into regional I and regional II banks. Banks other than long-term credit and trust banks previously had been limited to making short-term business loans, but as liberalization progressed, banks increased the maturity of their lending and expanded into consumer and mortgage lending. Banks were especially active in funding the *jusen* industry consisting of seven loan companies. *Jusen* were first established as bank subsidiaries to provide consumer credit and then in the 1980s to provide real estate credit.

Banks were permitted to expand into the securities business. The 1992 Financial Reform Act permitted banks to form subsidiaries that could underwrite corporate securities, and, in turn, securities companies were permitted to establish investment funds and competed with banks for deposits in this regard. The large number of credit-cooperatives adopted more flexible asset and liability portfolios, and especially the agriculture cooperatives became major supplies of funds to the *jusen* industry.

In the 1990s, attention was finally devoted to the insurance industry, which was a major supplier of long-term loans to industry after private and government banks. Reform of the insurance industry lagged reforms in the private banking system. The level of competition and efficiency in the insurance industry was considered low in the 1970s and 1980s. To correct this, the 1940 law governing the insurance business was revised and became effective in 1996. The new law was designed to increase competition and transparency in the insurance industry. Souma and Tsutsui (2005) studied the effects of the new law in the life insurance sector and found evidence of increased competition, but the life insurance industry continues to lag behind developments in the banking system.

Internationalization of Finance

As interest rates became more market-sensitive, Japan's money and capital rates became integrated with international financial markets. Japanese banks expanded their borrowing and lending in the external market. Japanese companies increasingly borrowed in the external market because of fewer restrictions on issuing debt in markets outside Japan. Overall, restrictions across a broad front were relaxed or eliminated on the inflow and outflow of capital. In 1997, all restrictions on foreign exchange transactions from a practical perspective were eliminated.

Government Financial Intermediation

The FILP and PSS continued to expand in the 1980s and 1990s; however, even this fundamental part of the old financial regime was the object of institutional reform. In 1994, the Ministry of Posts and Telecommunications, the then–regulatory authority over the PSS agreed to keep postal deposit rates close to market rates. The PSS had been accused by the BOJ of keeping interest rates higher than private bank deposit rates and changing the ceilings so as to maximize deposit inflow into the PSS. In 1998, a more fundamental change was made when the FILP budget and the PSS were separated. As a result, some FILP agencies would be required effective April 1, 2001, to secure their own funding by issuing securities, and the PSS would be permitted to manage its own portfolio as long as the majority of funds were held in the form of "safe" assets such as government bonds, and so on. In 2003, the PSS was separated from the government and turned into a public corporation called the Japan Post. Starting in 2007, privatization of the PSS commenced.

Government Regulatory Institutions and the BOJ

The MOF had been the major financial regulatory and supervisory authority in Japan from the start of industrialization following the Meiji Restoration. In 1997, a new agency was established to assume these responsibilities. The Financial Services Agency (FSA)[6] became the primary regulatory authority in Japan over the financial system. The BOJ was also the focus of major institutional redesign in 1997. Revision of the BOJ Law provided the Bank with enhanced formal independence and required that the BOJ provide greater transparency in the conduct of monetary policy.

Japan as a Model of Financial Liberalization and Central Bank Policy

Japan commenced an official policy of liberalization in 1976 and, by 1980, the policy was firmly in place and notable institutional change

---

[6] The FSA originally stood for Financial Supervisory Agency; however, now it stands for Financial Services Agency.

occurred. The policy outcomes in the first half of the 1980s were impressive. Japan was able to implement a large number of policies that changed Japan's financial institutions rather dramatically. Interest rate liberalization, internationalization, expanded asset and liability diversification powers for financial institutions, and expanded money and capital markets together generated a financial structure much different from that which existed in the early 1970s.

Japan achieved this transformation without financial disruptions or intense market-regulatory conflicts common to many other industrialized economies. The process was gradual and stable.

Thus, not only was Japan drawing world attention because of its manufacturing and management institutions and their success in Japan's postwar performance, Japan was also regarded as one of the few countries that seemed to have established a stable and smooth financial liberalization process. The record appeared even more remarkable considering the starting place of the financial liberalization process and the fact that Japan had been forced to deal with two major oil price shocks in the 1970s. As one indication of the comparative record, Lindgren, Garcia, and Saal (1996, pp. 21–35) list 133 cases of countries with banking problems starting from 1980 through 1996. Japan's entry as an example of a banking crisis commences only in 1992.

This performance raises the questions as to what accounts for the apparent success in the financial reform process. In this regard, the BOJ's ability to maintain price stability played a major role. The BOJ's success in reducing the high inflation rates of the early 1970s and achieving a low and steady inflation rate provided two major advantages to the Japanese economy. First, price stability and expectations of continued price stability provided a stable background for economic growth and, second, price stability narrowed the gap between regulated and unregulated interest rates. The narrow gap provided fewer incentives for innovation or regulatory-market conflict and provided time for the government to pursue a gradual and incremental financial liberalization policy.

The BOJ's success was the more remarkable because it was considered one of the most dependent central banks in the world at the time. The BOJ Law made it clear the Bank was administered by the MOF. Thus, BOJ policy defied the common wisdom that dependent central banks were more likely to generate inflation than independent central banks.

Hence, BOJ policy not only provided the background for a growing economy in contrast to many other countries at the time by achieving price stability but also provided a stable background for Japan's version of financial liberalization. In terms of price stability outcomes, the BOJ in the 1980s was regarded as a "model" central bank, which in turn provided Japan with the opportunity to pursue a "model" financial liberalization policy.

4

An Accident Waiting to Happen – The Bubble Economy from 1985 to 1990

Introduction

The period from 1980 to 1985 represents the high-water mark of the Japanese economy in terms of financial and central bank policy outcomes. In terms of most economic and financial indicators, Japan's performance outpaced many other industrial countries, especially Japan's ability to achieve stable noninflationary growth in the face of a second set of oil price shocks in 1979 while at the same time adopting a policy of domestic and international financial liberalization. Japan appeared to have successfully adapted to the new economic, political, and technological environment and achieved an impressive record of economic and financial performance. It drew world attention both in terms of Japan's absolute performance and Japan's relative performance to much of the industrialized world.

Japan's state-directed approach to managing the economy combined with a powerful bureaucracy seemed to function in the more liberal and open financial environment as well as it did during the first part of the postwar period. The second half of the 1980s appeared to be a continuation of these trends. But in fact, a slow accumulation of stresses occurred as equity and land prices began to increase in 1985 and 1986 and then began to increase at very rapid rates, which by 1988 reflected a full-blown asset bubble. The asset inflation bubble combined with strong real GDP growth and price stability rationalized the phrase "bubble economy." Despite growing concern by the end of the 1980s over asset inflation, there continued to be widespread optimism both inside and outside Japan about its ability to manage the economy and pursue financial liberalization and internationalization. In hindsight, this view was misplaced. In fact, Japan was becoming an accident waiting to happen, as stresses were accumulating and rendering the entire set of postwar economic and political institutions susceptible to a shock. That shock came in the form of the collapse of asset prices in 1990 and 1991 and ushered in economic, financial, and political distress that lasted for a decade or more.

Japan's Fundamentally Flawed Financial Liberalization Process

Despite an official policy of financial liberalization and despite a number of institutional and regulatory changes (summarized in the last chapter), Japan's liberalization process remained more rhetoric than substance. The key elements of the old financial regime remained firmly in place. The clash between these embedded elements and policies that permitted greater asset diversification powers on the part of financial institutions provided an environment that permitted banks and others to pursue imprudent lending. Imprudent lending played an important part in the asset inflation in the second half of the 1980s. Combined with monetary policy errors after 1985, Japan became an accident waiting to happen.

Six elements of Japan's approach to financial liberalization contributed to the accumulation of stress in the second half of the 1980s. It should be emphasized that the majority of these elements were not unique to Japan, as many countries incorporated the same or similar types of flaws. What differentiated Japan from others, however, was the pervasiveness of the flaws and the interconnectedness of the flaws.

Special Interest-Directed Financial Liberalization

Financial liberalization commenced to resolve specific domestic economic issues and respond to foreign pressure. Financial liberalization on the part of the MOF was motivated by the need to finance large budget deficits, by the pressure brought by banks, securities companies, and corporations for liberalization specific to their needs, and by international pressure. There was never an economy-wide perspective and philosophy of markets over a state-directed economy and, as a result, liberalization was unbalanced and incomplete. Although international pressure was focused on liberalization of both financial and real markets, much of the international pressure on Japan was directed to liberalization of the financial sector in general and the securities markets in particular.

The specific and sometimes contradictory pressures on the MOF to relax the binding constraints on the financial system resulted in a "squeaky wheel" approach to liberalization policy. That is, the MOF supplied liberalization to the most powerful special interest without considering the economy-wide effects of each policy.

Key Elements of the Old Financial Regime Remain in Place

Key elements that defined the old financial regime remained in place despite an official policy of liberalization. There was no effort to enhance transparency either for financial institutions or corporations. Instead, regulatory authorities and banks continued to rely on the system of insider information as the basis for assessing and monitoring risk in the financial system. The close relationship between financial institutions and the MOF and the close relationships between financial institutions and corporations via the *keiretsu* system were regarded as a satisfactory financial disclosure framework. Financial statements provided little meaningful information for anyone outside of the company group to evaluate performance or judge the level of risk-taking. Nontransparency remained a key element of the financial system and, despite criticism from abroad, there was little interest on the part of the MOF to depart from nontransparency.

The policy of "no failures of financial institutions and markets" remained firmly in place. The financial system was stable, so the policy was never tested. But there was little doubt that the government would take whatever means necessary to ensure that financial institutions or markets did not fail. Rather than an explicit deposit insurance system such as the Federal Deposit Insurance Corporation (FDIC) in the United States, deposits in Japan were guaranteed by a general understanding that the Japanese government would use whatever means were required to protect all deposits. Japan established a Deposit Insurance Corporation (DIC) in 1971 with explicit FDIC-styled deposit insurance; however, the DIC played no meaningful role in the financial regulatory or supervisory regime. The DIC had only a small reserve that would be exhausted by the failure of even one regional bank. The DIC had a limited staff of about ten, whose main function was to collect data, ensure that premiums were paid, and generate an annual report. The DIC lacked regulatory power over financial institutions that might be in need of financial assistance.

In fact, the DIC had been established primarily as a political response to complaints by regional banks of increased risk to the banking system because at that time, the MOF permitted city banks greater latitude to expand their branching network. Deposit insurance was never regarded as an institution to limit systemic risk. In fact, the DIC became regarded as more an element of *amakudari*, as the BOJ and the MOF debated between each other in the 1980s as to where the DIC office was to be located.

Japan experienced no explicit financial distress during the 1980 to 1985 period in the form of declared bankruptcy of banks or other financial institutions. However, it was clear that any problem that did emerge would be resolved in the context of the mutual support or "convoy" system directed by the MOF. Led by the MOF, stronger institutions would be required to assist weaker institutions. The MOF would use its regulatory powers, its influence over the discount window of the BOJ, and its ability to require stronger institutions or "white knights" to assist weaker institutions. The flaw in the liberalization process was that Japan would revert to mutual support in the face of any shock.

Reliance on Administrative Guidance to Monitor Risk

The financial regulatory and supervisory regime relied primarily on administrative guidance and insider information to assess and monitor risk in the financial system. This framework was satisfactory when the financial system was rigidly regulated, internationally isolated, and offered few opportunities to assume and manage risk. It was inadequate, however, once restrictions over the inflow and outflow of capital were relaxed and banks along with other financial institutions were permitted greater asset and liability diversification powers. Even though the pace of enhanced asset and liability powers was gradual, each liberalization advance represented a major change in the institutional design of the financial system that permitted greater risk-taking and risk management than previously.

This was especially notable in the *jusen* industry. Organized first as bank subsidiaries offering consumer credit and then shifting into real estate lending, the *jusen* industry became an integral part of the asset inflation in land and real estate prices in the second half of

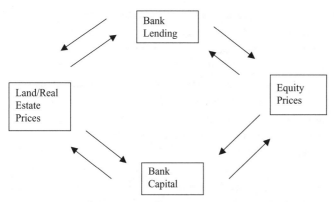

Figure 4.1. Relationship between Bank Lending, Land/Real Estate Prices, Equity Prices, and Bank Capital

the 1980s. The *jusen* industry came to rely about equally on funds provided by banks and credit cooperatives, especially agricultural credit cooperatives. Credit cooperatives at this time were not regulated by the MOF but regulated at the prefecture level. Hence, a major source of funds to the real estate sector evolved without much oversight.

Land Prices – Equity Prices – Bank Capital – Bank Lending and Basel I

Crossholding of equities between corporations and between banks and corporations solidified the relationship between these entities in the *keiretsu* or main bank system. Combined with the widespread practice of collateralizing bank loans with land or real estate established a self-reinforcing relationship among land prices, equity prices, bank capital, and bank lending. The feedback relationship between these elements is illustrated in Figure 4.1.

Capital gains on equities held by banks were regarded as "hidden reserves" or "latent capital." Increased equity prices increased bank capital, which in turn supported increased assets (lending) with a given asset-capital ratio. Because loans were frequently collateralized by real estate, increased real estate prices supported increased bank lending. Hence, increased equity prices and real estate prices supported increased bank lending. This circular relationship came to play an important role in the asset inflation of the second half of the 1980s and was significantly strengthened in 1988 with the Basel I capital asset requirements agreed to by the members of the Bank for International

Settlements (BIS). These requirements were unique because they were the first effort to establish international financial requirements to limit risk and because they were based on risk-adjusted asset measures.

Japan successfully argued that part of the hidden reserves held by banks because of their extensive holdings of corporate shares be included as part of the bank's official capital in computing risk-adjusted capital asset ratios. The final requirement permitted Japanese banks to meet the 8 percent risk-adjusted capital requirement by including 45 percent of the hidden reserves in tier 2 capital.

The relationship among bank capital, equity prices, real estate prices, and bank lending that had been a longtime characteristic of Japan's financial system was thus further institutionalized by the Basel I requirements. This institutionalization ensured that higher equity and real estate prices would generate higher bank lending; higher bank lending would generate higher corporate profits and equity prices; and increased economic activity would generate higher equity and real estate prices, which in turn would increase increased bank lending, and so on.

This flaw was unique to Japan and ensured that asset inflation would increase bank capital and lending, which in turn would support further asset inflation in a self-reinforcing manner. Japanese negotiators thought that they had achieved a major victory in convincing the BIS to permit the inclusion of hidden reserves in meeting the Basel I capital requirements. But, in fact, what they had accomplished was an increasing probability of asset inflation and collapse.

Postal Saving System and Fiscal Investment and Loan Program

Japan's twenty-four thousand post offices not only provided mail services but also represented a major component of the financial system referred to as the PSS. Post offices offered postal deposits, most of which were six-month time deposits, and sold life insurance. Postal deposits represented about 35 percent of total deposits in the nation, whereas postal life insurance represented about a third of all life insurance policies. The PSS was established in 1875 and reached maturity in the early 1950s. It was an official part of the FILP managed by the MOF. The FILP was a flow of funds budget developed in tandem with the government's general revenue-expenditure budget and was often referred to as Japan's second government budget because of its size.

Post offices transferred the majority of postal deposits and life insurance premiums to the MOF's Trust Fund Bureau, which combined these funds with funds from other sources (national welfare and pension premiums and government bonds) and distributed them to government banks and other FILP-financed agencies. The FILP agencies provided subsidized funds to targeted sectors of the economy. The PSS-FILP framework was an important part of the iron triangle of the LDP, bureaucracy, and their client sectors. The PSS and FILP avoided any meaningful reform in the 1980s. In fact, the ratio of the FILP budget to GDP (8–10 percent) continued to increase. The ratio of postal deposits to total deposits (30–35 percent) continued to increase with the only exception being the latter half of the 1980s as postal deposits were shifted to the rapidly rising stock market.

The PSS and FILP avoided reform for four reasons. First, they provided significant advantages to their clients. Post offices relied almost exclusively on *teigaku* time deposits, which provided a no-penalty option to withdraw funds after six months to take advantage of interest rate movements. As a result, *teigaku* deposits offered a higher effective interest rate than any time deposit offered by private banks.[1] Post offices were also more convenient to customers, as their numbers exceeded those of private bank branches in every prefecture for much of the postwar period. Further, funds obtained through the FILP were subsidized, and many borrowers would have been unable to obtain the same level of funding from the private banking system. Second, the FILP as part of the budgeting process was an instrument to maintain and enhance the electoral standing of the LDP government, because local governments and many sectors of the economy were dependent to some degree on funds that the government provided in the FILP budget. Third, the PSS and FILP were so large and pervasive that reform was a daunting process at a minimum. Thus, policy makers were willing to put postal savings and FILP reform on the back burner. Fourth, the PSS and FILP were immensely popular in Japan, criticized only by academics, private banks, and, on occasion, the BOJ.

The PSS and FILP likely had a net positive impact on Japan's reindustrialization in the 1950s and 1960s, especially in rebuilding the infrastructure. However, by the 1980s, the huge role of government

---

[1] The value of the withdrawal option and other features of *teigaku* postal deposits are discussed in Kamada (1993).

financial intermediation increasingly conflicted with efforts to redesign the financial system to become more competitive and open. The PSS enjoyed government-conferred advantages that made it difficult for private banks and insurance companies to compete on an equal footing. For example, the PSS network provided a ready-made subsidized branch system, paid no significant taxes, paid no deposit insurance premiums, had no capital requirements, and faced a far lower regulatory burden. The FILP largely depended on the PSS for funding resulting in substantial misallocation of capital to projects of questionable social value and created systemic risk in the financial system, because PSS investments in these projects were guaranteed by the government. The PSS, with four hundred thousand employees, represented 30 percent of all national government employees and provided a vote mobilization machine for the LDP and some other parties, which in turn protected the PSS and FILP from meaningful reform.

The Bubble Economy in the Second Half of the 1980s – the Beginning of the End

In the second half of the 1980s, asset inflation was evident in many countries. For example, indices of real asset prices for thirteen industrialized countries consisting of equity, residential real estate, and commercial real estate components illustrate a broad-based process of asset inflation in the second half of the 1980s (Borio, Kennedy, and Prowse, 1994). The international character of asset inflation suggested to some that financial liberalization played a role in the financial disruptions of the 1980s. The removal of binding portfolio constraints permitted banks and other depositories to adopt more risky investment and loan portfolios, including the adoption of high loan-to-value ratios:

> In those countries where the asset price boom was most marked in the 1980s (Finland, Sweden, Norway, Japan and the United Kingdom) or where the disruption caused by the downward correction in valuations has caused great concern (Australia and the United States) there is a relatively close correlation between the ratio of private credit to GDP and asset price movements. ... To a large extent, the major expansion of credit during the past decade reflected a relaxation of credit constraints in the financial industry in wake of both market-driven and policy-determined structural developments. (Borio, Kennedy, and Prowse 1994, pp. 27–28)

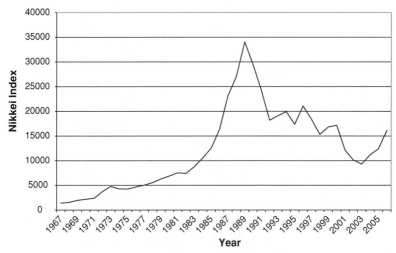

Figure 4.2. Nikkei 225 Stock Price Index, 1967 to 2006. *Source:* European Central Bank, Statistics Data Warehouse, http://sdw.ecb.europa.eu/home.do, Japan.

According to this view, banks, directly or indirectly, provided imprudent levels of credit to real estate and equity markets in an effort to offset declining profit margins and declining market shares and to maintain the franchise value of commercial bank charters supported in the past by a regulated and administratively controlled financial environment.

Japan's asset inflation in the second half of the 1980s stands out in terms of the degree of price increases and the impact the decline in asset prices had on the economy. Figures 4.2 and 4.3 illustrate the magnitude of the asset inflation in equity and real estate prices, respectively. There are two reasons why Japan experienced such a large and disruptive asset inflation process.

First, the financial liberalization process was flawed, incomplete, and, hence, by the mid-1980s, made asset inflation more probable in the context of a newly liberated financial structure than elsewhere. This by itself may not have led to the degree of asset inflation experienced in Japan in the absence of expansionary BOJ policy. However, combined with accommodative monetary policy, asset inflation became highly probable.

Second, BOJ policy accommodated asset inflation inadvertently because of a misreading of the domestic economy, focus on external considerations, and overconfidence in its ability to manage monetary

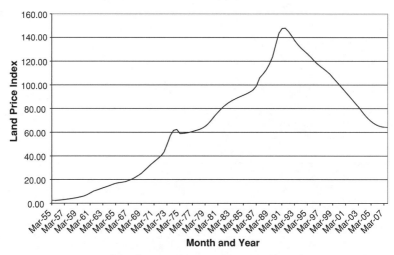

Figure 4.3. Nationwide Urban Land Price Index (Residential, Commercial, and Industrial), 1955 to 2008. *Source:* Japan Real Estate Institute, http://www.reinet.or.jp/e/jreidata/a_shi/index.htm. The authors thank Kaz Fujiki for providing the complete land price index for Japan.

policy. It was a victim of its own successes. BOJ policy also would not have likely generated asset inflation in the absence of a flawed financial liberalization process. Combined with the flawed and incomplete liberalization process, asset inflation became highly probable, however.

Japan's Bubble and Burst of the Bubble à la Minsky

Asset bubbles have occurred through history and represent one of the most significant contradictions to the view that markets are efficient and prices reflect fundamentals. Although the government failure view mentioned in the previous chapter offers important insights into the causes of various financial disruptions during the past three decades, the market failure exhibited by asset bubbles indicates that the market failure view cannot be completely rejected. At the same time, many would argue that the bubble in Japan would not have occurred had there not been government failure in the form of a flawed liberalization process and monetary policy errors.

In 1841, Charles Mackey's *Extraordinary Popular Delusions and the Madness of Crowds* was the first to document bubbles and illustrate the ways in which "irrational exuberance" can dominate a market.

Minsky (1982) has been one of the best-known students of bubbles and offered a taxonomy of bubbles widely accepted. The phases in the four-part model suggested by Minsky are useful to understand the asset inflation process in Japan: displacement, irrational exuberance, speculative excess, and liquidation.

Displacement

The displacement stage represents a change in the economic performance of the economy that deviates from the past and sets up expectations of a "new era." The displacement can be in the form of a change in economic fundamentals such as new technology, new markets, new products, foreign direct investment, and so on. The displacement can also be monetary in origin, such as a sudden increase in money and credit; however, even if the displacement is nonmonetary in origin at some point, credit and monetary accommodation needs to occur for asset inflation to reach bubble proportions. In Japan's case, the displacement was first nonmonetary and then monetary.

Nonmonetary Displacement

There were two sets of economic fundamentals in Japan from the nonmonetary perspective that supported the initial increase in equity and real estate prices.

First, in broad perspective, Japan's economy was becoming more internationalized, and Japan was in the process of redesigning its financial system to become a more integral part of the world economy. Japan had achieved reindustrialization by the late 1960s and after a short but turbulent period of economic instability and inflation in the early 1970s, achieved an impressive record of real GDP growth with price stability. Japan appeared to have successfully adjusted to the new economic, political, and technological environment that emerged in the 1970s. This record suggested a degree of resiliency in Japanese institutions that were better able to adapt to the new environment than those possessed by many other economies; hence, there was reason to believe that the Japanese regime was poised for another period of strong economic growth.

Second, and from a more specific perspective, the displacement affected real estate prices, especially in Tokyo. The initial jump in real estate prices during 1985–1986 was most likely related to changes in fundamentals. Demand for real estate in the Tokyo area, and to some extent the Osaka area, increased as a direct result of liberalization. New access to Japan's financial system by foreign institutions significantly affected Japan's real estate markets in Tokyo and Osaka. In the context of a real estate market with price inelastic supply because of limited land space and an extensive set of regulations protecting "sunshine" and "view" rights, internationalization and financial liberalization increased real estate prices above their historical trend.

Thus, in 1985 and 1986, the initial phase of the asset inflation in equity and real estate prices could be explained by a change in economic fundamentals or a displacement suggesting a new "era" of high corporate profits based on internationalization, which in turn impacted real estate markets, especially in Tokyo and, to a lesser extent, Osaka.

Monetary Displacement

The BOJ shifted to an easy monetary policy in late 1985 and maintained an easy policy until early 1989 for two reasons. First, the BOJ as part of an international policy coordination agreement known as the Plaza Accord in September 1985 intervened in the exchange market to depreciate the dollar. And when the dollar declined too rapidly in the view of the United States, the intervention shifted to stemming dollar depreciation and yen appreciation. The BOJ's policy shift to limit yen appreciation was an effort both to coordinate policy to limit dollar depreciation and offset the adverse effect on Japan's export sector caused by yen appreciation. The BOJ purchased dollar assets and significantly increased high-powered money, which in turn increased the supply of credit and money. The BOJ judged that an expanding money supply could be absorbed by the economy without significant effect on the inflation rate.

Second, the BOJ likely became overconfident in its ability to conduct policy as a result of the impressive record of monetary policy outcomes from the mid-1970s to the late 1980s. The increasing positive world attention to BOJ policy may have contributed to this overconfidence. In hindsight, the BOJ had likely overestimated the degree of productivity increases in the economy, much as the Federal Reserve did in the second half of the 1990s; underestimated the lags in the effect of monetary policy on the price level; and, most important, underestimated the degree of systemic risk that existed in the financial system as a result of the flawed and incomplete liberalization process.

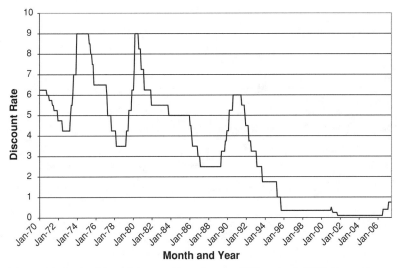

Figure 4.4. Bank of Japan Discount Rate, January 1970 to April 2007. *Source:* Econ-Stats, Interest Rates, Japan, http://www.econstats.com/index.htm.

Figure 4.4 indicates the official discount rate of the BOJ on a monthly basis from January 1970 to May 2007. Starting in 1995, the BOJ began to target the call or interbank interest rate. Its official policy now states that the official discount rate no longer represents a reliable indicator of monetary policy because interest rates were liberalized in 1994. The official discount rate is now regarded as the upper bound on discount loans made to banks at the Bank's discount window. Through 1996, however, the discount rate is one indicator of monetary policy intensions.

Discount rate movements after 1985 are consistent with the view that the BOJ shifted to a very easy monetary policy. The discount rate was lowered from 5.0 percent in January 1986 to 4.5 percent, and then over the next year lowered to 2.5 percent in March 1987, where it remained until May 1989 when the discount rate was raised to 3.25 percent. Figure 4.5 indicates the call rate and also suggests a very easy monetary policy in the second half of the 1980s.

The money supply (M2 + CDs) is regarded by many as a more reliable indicator of the overall intent of monetary policy. Figure 4.6 indicates the monthly annualized percentage change in the money supply from January 1969 to April 2007. The upward trend in monetary growth in the second half of the 1980s is notable. The average monthly growth of money in 1984 was 7.8 percent. However, the

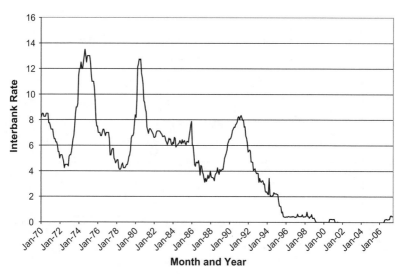

Figure 4.5. Interbank (Call Rate), January 1970 to May 2007. *Source:* Bank of Japan Website, Long Term Time Series, Financial and Economic Statistics, Financial Markets, http://www.boj.or.jp/en/type/stat/dlong/fin_stat/rate/cdab0722.csv.

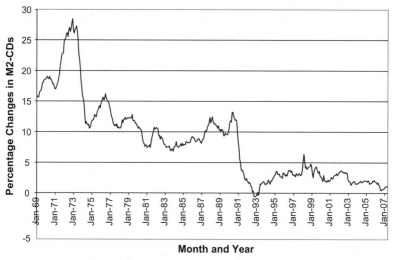

Figure 4.6. M2 + CD Money Supply Percentage Changes from Year Ago, January 1969 to April 2007. *Source:* Bank of Japan Website, Long Term Time Series, Financial and Economic Statistics, Money Stock, http://www.boj.or.jp/en/theme/research/stat/money/index.htm.

average annual growth increased in each year until 1989 – 8.4 percent in 1985, 8.7 percent in 1986, 10.4 percent in 1987, and 11.2 percent in 1988. Money growth averaged 10.3 percent in the first four months of 1989.

Irrational Exuberance

This phase represents the period when asset prices depart from economic fundamentals and when the expectation that the next period's price independent of fundamentals will be higher becomes the driving force of price increases. In blunt terms, this phase is referred to as the "bigger fool" model of asset pricing. An individual understands that he/she is a fool to purchase a share of Sony stock at the current price, but a bigger fool in six months will pay more for the stock simply because prices are expected to continue to increase.

Shiller (2005) provides an excellent review of the rationalizations and psychological motivation used by market participants to justify increasing prices as they become more and more disconnected from economic fundamentals. Cargill, Hutchison, and Ito (1997) discuss why the level of real estate and equity prices in Japan by 1988 and 1989 could not be explained by economic fundamentals. The key element of the irrational exuberance phase is that market participants lose perspective and price expectations are no longer reasonably connected to economic fundamentals.

The irrational exuberance was not only embraced by the public as they were willing to pay higher and higher prices for equities and real estate. It also embraced the financial system. Supported by accommodative monetary policy, banks and other financial institutions commenced a rapid credit expansion that further supported asset inflation in the context of a flawed and incomplete liberalization process. Six elements are important to understanding how this process played out in Japan.

First, financial institutions had more portfolio flexibility than they had ever had in the past. This is especially true for small depositories; as with the savings and loan industry in the United States during the 1980s, credit cooperatives aggressively pursued lending in speculative real estate ventures during the bubble phase, and, like their U.S. counterparts, did so without much oversight. These credit cooperatives, especially those in the agriculture sector, contributed significantly to real estate price inflation. Second, the shift to a slower growth path after the first oil price shock in 1973 reduced the corporate sector's reliance on bank credit and services. As a result, banks sought out new markets outside traditional corporate finance and were willing to assume new and often higher risks for which they had little previous experience. Third, the main bank system began to unravel in response to financial liberalization, which, in the past, had provided the only system to evaluate and monitor risk. No widely available financial-disclosure framework was available to replace the main bank system. Fourth, the relationship among bank capital, equity prices, real estate prices, and bank lending ensured a strong feedback relationship between these variables so that once started, asset inflation could easily become self reinforcing. Fifth, the regulatory monitoring system lagged behind market developments, and "administrative guidance" could not keep pace with the fast changing financial environment. Sixth, complete deposit guarantees encouraged risk taking at the very time that the BOJ provided the liquidity and financial liberalization provided the asset-diversification powers. The risk-incentive nature of government deposit guarantees or the moral hazard problem of government deposit guarantees played an important role in accounting for the coincidence of asset inflation and financial liberalization in Japan.

Speculative Excess and Liquidation

The speculative excess phase occurs when asset price increases at rates that rational observers know are unsustainable, but "herd" behavior and a variety of psychological factors[2] continue to attract buyers, and, as a result, asset prices increase further than they did even in the irrational exuberance phase. At some point, asset prices collapse. The cause of the collapse might be the failure of a financial institution or large corporation or the revelation of fraud. But in Japan's case, the collapse was caused by BOJ policy.

By 1989, the BOJ became concerned about real estate and equity prices, and the rate of inflation was beginning to increase. The BOJ began to consider an increase in the discount rate despite opposition from the MOF. On May 1989, despite the MOF's objections, the BOJ commenced raising the discount rate from the postwar historical low of 2.5 percent to 3.25 and eventually to 6 percent in August 1990.

---

[2] See Minsky (1982), Kindleberger (1996), and Shiller (2005) for detailed discussion.

Asset prices continued to increase for a short period. The high point of equity prices occurred in January 1990 when the Nikkei index reached 38,922, after which equity prices commenced an unprecedented decline. As of May 2007, equity prices recovered to only about 45 percent of their high at the start of 1990. Real estate prices continued to increase until late 1991 but then commenced declining and only as of late 2006 have shown signs of increasing. As of late 2006, the real estate price index also stood at about 45 percent of its high value in 1991. The asset inflation and collapse in terms of magnitude and capitalization renders Japan's experience one of the most important examples of an asset bubble and burst in recorded history.

The collapse in asset prices became the shock that invoked the "accident waiting to happen" scenario discussed earlier. The decline in asset prices caused a severe recession as spending declined, weakened the balance sheets of financial institutions and corporations, and set into motion a regulatory and political response wedded to the old regime that ultimately became responsible for almost fifteen years of economic distress for Japan.

The Story up to 1990

Japan developed a set of economic and political institutions in the post-war period that provided impressive macroeconomic performance and growth, provided economic security to the population, and generated a distribution of income considered more equal than most Western economies, except for Nordic countries. This should not be taken to imply that the Japanese public was completely satisfied with the outcome or the social contract established by the LDP, bureaucracy, and corporations. There were many political scandals, resentment over the "old boy" system of the iron triangle, and resentment by workers not covered by lifetime employment or self-employed small subcontractors dependent on the large corporations. Nonetheless, Japan established a strong record of economic, financial, and political stability. The institutions responsible for the record were collectivist in nature and involved a large degree of government regulation and administrative control over the real and financial sectors of the economy. Although Japan had a full-fledged democracy, political institutions were more responsive to producers than consumers.

In the 1970s and 1980s, Japan found itself facing a new set of economic, political, and technological forces that were shifting much of the world away from collectivist-managed economies toward more open, competitive, and individualist structures. Japan was forced to begin a transition toward more open and competitive markets. However, the response was limited to only part of the financial system. Japan successfully resisted redesign of its other economic institutions and political institutions. Japan's financial transition in the late 1970s and 1980s appeared successful by any reasonable standard, especially in comparison to the financial disruptions being experienced by many other countries. Japan appeared to be a "model" of financial liberalization. However, the process was flawed and generated an accident-waiting-to-happen situation.

The flawed financial liberalization process permitted imprudent lending and investing on the part of financial institutions that made it relatively easy for asset prices to increase at rates that could not be justified by economic fundamentals. At the same time, the BOJ provided liquidity to support the asset inflation because its attention was directed elsewhere and it did not appreciate the flaws in the liberalization process. The decision to initiate tight monetary policy in May 1989 and the decision to impose a "cold turkey" tight monetary policy caused the burst of the bubble economy.

Even at this stage, however, it is not clear Japan would have experienced a decade and half of lost economic and financial development. It was the embedded attitudes and policies of the members of the iron triangle – bureaucrats, politicians, and corporations – that elevated the probability of policy errors. Japan's economy and public came to pay a high price for being wedded to the key elements of the old regime.

5

Economic and Financial Distress from 1990 to 2001 and the Turning Point

Introduction

The immediate effect of the collapse of asset prices in 1990 and 1991 was recession, disinflation, and weakened balance sheets for financial institutions and corporations; however, this economic and financial distress intensified over the decade. The decade has frequently been characterized as Japan's "lost decade" in terms of lost financial and economic development, but because the economic and financial distress continued until 2005, one could just as easily refer to the entire period as a decade and half of lost financial and economic development. The 1990s also witnessed political instability and uncertainty with the end of the "1955-System" of LDP rule and party realignment.

This chapter focuses on the economic and financial distress of the 1990s and ends with a summary of the most important policies of the Koizumi government starting in 2001. Although economic and financial distress continued for several more years, the economy would experience a significant turning point after Koizumi became prime minister.

The Cabinet Office's official business cycle turning points (see Table 5.1) indicate that Japan experienced a series of business cycles during the past decade and half. The three "expansions" after the collapse of asset prices with the most recent starting January 2002 and continuing through late 2007 mask a stagnant economy. Real GDP growth averaged 1.2 percent from 1991 to 2003, the year in which most observers conclude that the economy began a sustainable recovery. In 1998 and 1999, Japan experienced declines in real GDP. The last time that real GDP declined was in 1974. The unemployment rate in the 1990s almost doubled from the low rates of past decades.

**Table 5.1. Turning points and stage
of business cycle**

Peak – February 1991
Recession
Trough – October 1993
Expansion
Peak – May 1997
Recession
Trough – January 1999
Expansion
Peak – November 2000
Recession
Trough – January 2002
Expansion

Source: Japanese Government Cabinet Office,
Indexes of Business Conditions, http://www.esri.
cao.go.jp/en/stat/di/di-e.html.

The rate of price increases declined (disinflation) in the early 1990s
from an already low inflation rate, and then after 1994 the price level
declined (deflation). Despite official pronouncements by the BOJ that
deflation ended in 2006, measured inflation remained low. Japanese
price indexes possess well-known upward biases despite official statements that there are no or only small biases. That is, if the measured
price index indicates a 1 percent increase in the price index, the "real"
percentage change, taking measurement error into account, is likely
to be close to zero or negative, depending on the magnitude of the
measurement error.

The weakened balance sheets of banks and other financial institutions were manifested by a large nonperforming loan problem estimated at various times in the 1990s to be 6 to 12 percent of total
loans. The official nonperforming loan estimates published by the
MOF intentionally understated the problem for much of the period.
The nonperforming asset problem extended to the government banks
and many of the other FILP-agencies as well. Realistic estimates of
the nonperforming loan problem in Japan by the late 1990s in both
private and public financial institutions indicated that nonperforming
assets totaled about 25 percent[1] of GDP.

---

[1] Doi and Hoshi (2003) estimated that nonperforming assets in the FILP system represented
about 16 percent of GDP, whereas Cargill, Hutchison, and Ito (2000) estimate private bank
nonperforming loans at about 10 percent of GDP.

The Japanese banking system by the end of the 1990s was insolvent if assets were valued at market prices. Japan's DIC was insolvent by the end of 1994. Corporations and small business were in no better condition. Many failed. However, extraordinary efforts by the banks and government to prevent failures of large corporations were made during the 1990s. Many were kept from bankruptcy by bank loans that had little chance of ever being repaid and by the practice of "evergreening"; that is, replacing bad loans with new loans. It became common to refer to Japan's many trouble banks and corporations as "zombie"[2] banks and corporations. Banks and corporations that should have been buried (declared bankrupt) but had the appearance of being alive (zombies) only because of extraordinary efforts of the banks and the government to engage in forgiveness and forbearance based on the assumption that asset prices would recover and the banks and corporations would be able to work themselves out of the problem.

This hoped recovery of asset prices did not occur. Real estate prices continued to decline until 2006 and at that time still represented only about 45 percent of their peak in 1991. Equity prices declined and rose. But as of 2006, they recovered to only about 45 percent of their high in early 1990. The collapse of asset prices weakened the financial system, given the feedback relationships between asset prices and bank lending embedded in Japanese financial institutions.

The government's response to the collapse of asset prices and subsequent economic and financial distress was denial. When denial was no longer credible, the government justified inertia and slow policy response by understating the magnitude of the problem. When the financial and economic distress continued and policy makers could no longer postpone a meaningful response, the preferred policy response was mutual support or the convoy system, nontransparency in the form of creative accounting, and forgiveness and forbearance to conceal the magnitude of the financial distress. This response sequence was predictable from the existing set of economic and political institutions,

---

[2] The phrase "zombie" was used to characterize savings and loan associations in the United States during the 1980s that were insolvent, but kept operating because of forgiveness and forbearance policies of the regulatory agencies and politicians. The phrase drawn from horror stories had been used before, but became part of the common language of describing the outcome of forgiveness and forbearance policies in both Japan and the United States. This reference to "zombie" institutions came from a cult-horror film in the 1960s called *The Night of the Living Dead*.

which had largely remained in place despite an official policy of financial liberalization.

Policy errors by the BOJ, the MOF, and conflicts between these two institutions discussed in the next chapter intensified the economic and financial distress. The BOJ continued a "cold turkey" tight monetary policy after the collapse in asset prices, and then when it shifted monetary policy toward ease in 1992, it was not sufficiently expansionary and permitted the price level to fall after 1994. The MOF's fiscal policy was likewise counterproductive. The MOF implemented a series of stimulus packages in the 1990s that were notable for the amount of "pork" and loan guarantees that did not have large positive effect on the economy. These were designed partly to support the LDP government's client industries. The end result was large deficits and massive amounts of government debt.

The deficits likely reduced private spending because of well-known crowding out effects of government deficit spending in the absence of monetary accommodation[3]; however, the magnitude of the crowding out effects is debatable. The Japanese public must have understood that the deficits would be resolved by tax increases in the near future, given the conservative fiscal attitudes of the government and the increased social security and healthcare burdens that were expected from the aging of Japan's population. This view was vindicated by another policy error on the part of the MOF – the ill-timed fiscal austerity policy of 1997 – the termination of special income tax cuts, a consumption tax increase from 3 to 5 percent, various spending cuts, and an increase in health care copayments. Combined with lack of aggressive monetary policy, these fiscal actions pushed Japan in late 1997 and all of 1998 into an abyss of deflation, declining output, and further financial distress.

Overall, the economic and financial distress during the 1990s and the start of the new century is remarkable. Before 1990, it appeared that Japan did everything right in terms of managing the economy and adapting to the new economic, political, and technological forces with a policy of domestic and international financial liberalization. In

---

[3] Even under the most favorable view of the Keynesian model, government deficits generate some degree of crowding out. Macroeconomic theory and empirical evidence identifies several channels of crowding out and concludes that crowding out is a major problem of any fiscal policy. In Japan, the inherent "pork barrel" component of government spending suggests a large crowding out component to any fiscal stimulus package.

the 1990s, the economic and financial distress indicated that Japan was having difficulty doing anything right.

Government Response to the Economic and Financial Distress of the 1990s

How did the economic and financial crisis unfold in the 1990s? In this regard, it is appropriate to focus on the financial system, as it was the flawed approach to financial liberalization that generated the accident-waiting-to-happen situation. It was the effect of declining asset prices that deteriorated bank and corporate balance sheets, and it was flawed monetary policy that intensified the financial crisis. This perspective is not meant to imply that other factors were not important. But to understand Japan's economic and political problems after 1990, the financial system should be the first focus. The key events of the government response through 1999 are discussed by Cargill, Hutchison, and Ito (2000). The following summarizes and extends that discussion.

Denial, Understatement, and Forgiveness and Forbearance – 1990 to 1994

Despite the collapse of asset prices and recession, the government continued to express faith in Japan's economic and political institutions and regarded the decline as temporary. Once asset prices recovered, the Japanese economy would continue to expand as it had in the 1980s. The public likewise continued to have faith in Japan's institutions, and many basked in the light of the huge capital gains in real estate and equities enjoyed even in the face of price declines in the first few years of the 1990s.

By 1991, however, the MOF was forced to recognize official bankruptcies of financial institutions; however, the failures were confined to fewer than ten small banks and credit cooperatives over the 1991 to 1994 period. The failures were resolved by finding a stronger "white knight" institution to assume the assets and liabilities of the failed institutions with assistance from the DIC. Although this was a major departure from the past policy of no failures of financial institutions and indicated how serious the financial distress was even in the first few years of the 1990s, the approach to dealing with troubled institutions showed nothing had really changed. Shareholders were usually compensated for the book value of their shares, no depositors lost funds, few managers if any lost their jobs, and many of the nonperforming loans were "evergreened" by reissuing a new loan to replace the nonperforming loan.

The MOF insisted that the small number of failures of small-sized depository institutions did not represent any fundamental problem in Japan's financial system. The center of the financial system – consisting of the large banks – was officially declared solid. The MOF, however, took extraordinary steps to conceal and understate the growing nonperforming loan problem in the banking system. In 1992, when the MOF started publishing statistics on nonperforming loans for the then twenty-one major banks (city banks, long-term credit banks, and trust banks), the statistics were reported only for the twenty-one combined banks rather than individually. Nonperforming loans were not reported for regional banks until 1994. Outside observers regarded the official statistics as a gross understatement because of the narrow definition of nonperforming loans, "creative accounting" gimmicks, and the common practice of evergreening bad loans by banks.

The intentional understatement was especially acute in the case of the *jusen* industry.[4] The MOF was aware by 1992 and 1993 that the *jusen* industry was insolvent but did not disclose this fact, hoping that real estate prices would recover quickly and that the housing loan associations would work their way out of the problem. The delay was not merely because of a general preference for forgiveness and forbearance but also because many former MOF officials were in management positions in the seven housing loan companies (Toya, 2006, p. 117). This is a clear case of how *amakudari* and the iron triangle contributed to Japan's economic and financial distress in the 1990s.

The MOF engaged in other actions designed to cover up the distress. The MOF permitted banks to issue debt to build up their capital and then pressured life insurance companies to purchase the debt. The MOF pressured the PSS to use life insurance reserves to purchase equities to reverse the decline in prices. The MOF encouraged the establishment of a private-bank nonperforming loan warehouse called

---

[4] Cargill, Hutchison, and Ito (1997), chapter 6, provides a detailed discussion of the evolution and collapse of the *jusen* industry.

the Cooperative Credit Purchase Cooperation in 1992 to remove non-performing loans from the balance sheets of depository institutions; however, few of the housed loans were sold. This was merely an effort to improve the appearance of balance sheets of depository institutions.

The 1990 to 1994 period represents a growing financial crisis first denied and then understated by the MOF. The only policies adopted by the MOF were based on forgiveness and forbearance to give financial institutions time to work their way out of the problem. This, in turn, was based on the belief that asset prices would soon recover.

Institutional Change Wedded to the Old Regime – 1995 to October 1996

The economy started to improve after 1993, and equity prices ceased declining and registered a gain in 1994. Real estate prices, however, continued to decline. The MOF was unable to conceal the extent of nonperforming loans and the number of troubled financial institutions. By 1995, the MOF was pressured to adopt more aggressive policies and provide more transparent estimates of the magnitude of the nonperforming loan problem. In late 1994, two credit cooperatives failed and the resolution of these two institutions in 1995 along with a third failed credit cooperative in 1995 exhausted the reserves of the DIC. The DIC was insolvent and although it had never been an important part of the safety net for the financial system since it first was established in 1971, the failure of Japan's deposit insurance agency raised concern about the extent of the financial distress. In 1995, the MOF was forced to publicly admit that the *jusen* industry was insolvent and that the nonperforming loan problem was larger than previously reported.

Five policy actions are worth noting. First, in late 1995, the DIC was significantly redesigned to play a more important role in maintaining the public's confidence in the banking system. The staff was greatly expanded, the DIC was moved from the BOJ to a separate location, and the DIC reserve base was increased by increasing deposit insurance premiums. The DIC was given new rules and authority to assist troubled financial institutions. This was a significant change as the newly reorganized DIC was the start of a shift away from implicit complete deposit guarantees to explicit limited deposit guarantees. Second, to provide time for the new DIC to become operational, the MOF announced in late 1995 the decision to place the full faith and credit of the Japanese government behind deposits for a six-year period. The MOF announced that the complete deposit guarantee would be removed April 1, 2001, when bank deposits would be insured only up to ¥10 million. Third, the MOF adopted a new preemptive policy of dealing with depository institutions before they reached a point of no return referred to as Prompt Corrective Action (PCA) policy. PCA involved more transparent, objective, and timely measures of bank performance to monitor nonperforming loans and the use of bank capital asset ratios to trigger administrative action. Fourth, in 1995, the MOF established the Resolution and Collection Bank to liquidate loans of failed credit cooperatives and established the Housing Loan Administration to liquidate loans of failed *jusen* companies. Fifth, in 1995, the MOF closed the seven *jusen* companies.

On the surface, these five actions appeared to be meaningful reform. However, on close inspection, the implementation of these policies combined with other actions of the MOF suggested little change in the basic attitude that forgiveness and forbearance in the context of mutual support and nontransparency was the best policy. This policy in the view of the government, even though inefficient by some standards, would provide sufficient time for financial institutions and corporations to work their way out their weak balance sheets. The old regime remained in place, judged by the continued understatement of nonperforming loans in the private banking system, the silence regarding nonperforming loans held by government banks, and the silence about nonperforming assets held by other FILP entities.[5]

Resolution of the *jusen* problem was based on the convoy system. Even though credit cooperatives had provided a little less than half of the *jusen* funding, the banks were required to write off most of the bad assets. The MOF implemented this uneven burden sharing of the debt of the *jusen* as a result of intense political pressure from the agricultural sector and under the belief that the banks were in stronger financial condition than credit cooperatives. The adverse reaction by the international community was reflected by a major increase in the "Japan premium" – the additional basis points that Japanese banks were required to pay for loans on the London interbank market (Figure 5.1).

---

[5] In December 1995, the MOF reported ¥38 trillion in nonperforming loans for all depository institutions. Cargill, Hutchison, and Ito (1997, p. 119) show that nonperforming loans were actually ¥46 trillion, representing about 6 percent of total loans outstanding and 10 percent of GDP. Other estimates of nonperforming loans were even larger. Doi and Hoshi (2003) estimate nonperforming loans and assets in the FILP system at about 16 percent of GDP.

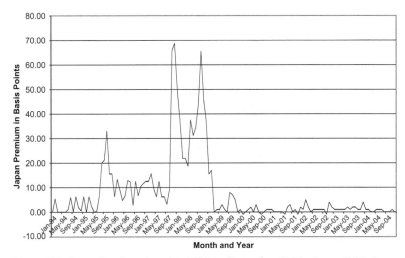

Figure 5.1. Japan Premium, January 1994 to December 2004. *Source:* BOJ, Long Term Time Series, Financial and Economic Statistics, http://www.boj.or.jp/en/type/stat/dlong/fin_stat/boj/cdab0130.csv.

In the summer of 1995, a bond dealer in the New York office of Daiwa Bank incurred significant losses. These were reported to the MOF but not the U.S. banking authorities as required by U.S. regulations. More significant, the MOF did not report the losses to the U.S. regulatory authorities for six weeks. This violated a long-standing understanding among regulatory authorities that they had an obligation to inform the host country of any serious financial problem with a financial institution in the home country operating in the host country. Daiwa was suspended from operating in the United States and forced to sell its U.S. operations to Sumitomo Bank.

Given the magnitude of the nonperforming loan problem, one would have anticipated a fairly large number of bank closings, forced mergers, and willingness to permit foreign banks to assume assets of domestic banks. These did not occur. The number of depository institutions receiving assistance from the DIC increased from two in 1994 to three and six in 1995 and 1996, respectively (Table 5.2, see page 117). The MOF had set up one bank-controlled nonperforming loan warehouse in 1992 (Credit Cooperative Purchasing Program) and two government-controlled nonperforming loan warehouses in 1995 (Collection and Resolution Bank and Housing Loan Administration); however, few of the loans assumed by these warehouses were sold. Rather than a warehouse, what Japan needed was a garage sale, but, again, based on a policy of forgiveness and forbearance, warehousing loans seemed to be a reasonable policy in anticipation of higher asset prices and economic recovery.

"Recovery," Big Bang, and the Asian Financial Crisis – November 1996 to October 1997

The LDP's Ryutaro Hashimoto became prime minister in 1996. There was a growing distance between the LDP and the MOF. The LDP was willing to adopt policies long opposed by the MOF, because the ministry had cooperated with the non-LDP coalition government in 1993–1994 and distanced itself from the LDP. This was pay back time.

There was much optimism in 1995 and 1996. Real GDP increased in 1995 and 1996 suggesting recovery, and although real estate prices continued to fall, stock prices began to recover in 1996. There was a sense that the most difficult structural issues had been settled and international confidence in Japanese banks was returning, manifested by a decline in the Japan premium. In this context, the Hashimoto administration decided to pursue an aggressive forward-looking strategy to render Japan's financial system one of the most important pillars of international finance.

This strategy was stated in the November 1996 announcement, referred to as the Big Bang,[6] because it envisaged a major redesign of Japan's financial system and was based on three principles: (1) to establish free, open, and competitive markets; (2) to ensure fair financial practices through transparent and enforced regulation and supervision; and (3) to initiate accounting, legal, and regulatory institutional reforms to make Japan's financial system internationally compatible. The Big Bang announcement did not itself spell out specific proposals as these would be developed through legislation and administrative decision making. The Hashimoto administration set 2001 as the date for achieving these policies.

The first result of the Big Bang announcement was a series of legislative changes in the spring and summer of 1997 and commitment to further institutional change. The most important include the

---

[6] The Big Bang terminology was first used to describe a series of financial liberalization policies in the United Kingdom in the mid-1980s. Toya (2006) provides a detailed discussion of the politics of the Big Bang in Japan.

following: (1) significant liberalization of foreign exchange transactions; (2) permitting financial holding companies which had been banned after World War II to prevent the resurrection of *zaibatsu*; (3) permitting more competitors in the securities business by expanding entry and eliminating the system of fixed brokerage commissions; (4) establishing the FSA as the primarily financial regulatory and supervisory authority in Japan; (5) revision of the 1942 BOJ Law; and (6) commitment to redesign the FILP and PSS.

The creation of the FSA was a major institutional change in Japan, as it reversed over one hundred years of the MOF's regulatory domination in the financial system. Revision of the BOJ Law provided the BOJ with enhanced formal independence and provided greater transparency for monetary policy. Revision of the BOJ Law was a long overdue reform. Consistent with the Big Bang strategy, although not an explicit part of the announcement, the Hashimoto administration also commenced in 1997 plans to redesign the FILP and PSS with the objective of reducing the role of government financial intermediation. These efforts led to the June 1998 legislation to separate the FILP and PSS discussed in the previous chapter.

In the first part of 1997, there was considerable optimism within Japan that the worst was over for both the economy and the non-performing loan problem. The increase in GDP in 1996 and continued increase in the first part of 1997 combined with the Big Bang announcement and subsequent legislative actions appeared to represent a turning point for Japan. This optimism was premature for several reasons.

Nonperforming loans remained large. Nonperforming loans in the private banking system represented 6 to 8 percent of total loans, and although the government was completely silent about nonperforming loans embedded in the FILP system, they were considered large. The Asian Financial Crisis started in the spring of 1997 in Indonesia and Thailand, spread to other Asian counties, and culminated with the near collapse of the South Korean economy in late 1997. Although Japan was not part of the capital flight and currency depreciation problems of those involved in the crisis, the financial problems seemed inconsistent with optimism in Japan. BOJ policy continued to provide little support for recovery, when judged by the decline in prices starting in 1995 and only small increases in bank credit. Deflation and expectations of continued price decline were inconsistent with any meaningful recovery. In addition, real estate prices continue to decline.

In hindsight, the optimism in Japan in early 1997 seems almost surrealistic, considering the events unfolding in Asia and domestic indicators of financial and economic health in Japan.

Financial Crisis, November 1997

The fragility of the Japanese financial system was dramatically revealed in late 1997. In November 1997, Sanyo Securities Company, Hokkaido Takushoku Bank, and Yamaichi Securities Company failed. Sanyo Securities was a medium-sized institution; however, Takushoku was a major city bank, and Yamaichi was one of the Big Four securities firms. The failure of Takushoku was especially serious because it showed that the government was unable to protect the largest banks, which it had promised in late 1995 when the MOF announced a complete deposit guarantee. The MOF had long claimed that the financial distress in the form of nonperforming loans and failures of depository institutions had not reached the center of Japan's financial system. The failures of these institutions within a month suggested otherwise.

Both external and internal events help explain why Japan's system began a downward spiral in late 1997 that continued into 1998. The Asian Financial Crisis exposed Japanese financial institutions to increased risk to the extent that they had loans directly or indirectly tied to the rest of Asia. The crisis heightened the sense of unease and rendered financial markets more susceptible to any shock. The effects of the Asian crisis appeared to spread in 1998 to areas outside of Asia, when the Russian government defaulted on its internal debt and devalued its currency, when Brazil experienced significant capital flight in late 1998 and devalued its currency in January 1999, and when the hedge fund, Long Term Capital Management failed in 1998.

Internally, Japan's financial system was weak, burdened with nonperforming loans and a regulatory structure that encouraged moral hazard and, hence, was susceptible to any shock. The shock came in the form of a policy error by the MOF and the Hashimoto government regarding fiscal austerity designed to reduce the government's deficit. The fiscal policy error was made worse because the BOJ had failed to achieve price stability after 1994 and permitted the price level to fall.

The BOJ's failure to prevent deflation after 1994 generated a weak economic environment. Falling prices not only reduced wealth by lowering the value of real estate, but also increased the cost of servicing existing debt.[7] Deflation is more serious than inflation, especially in an economy with large amounts of nominal debt. Deflation increases the real burden of servicing debt and, hence, increases bankruptcy. Increased bankruptcy reduces the willingness of banks to lend, which in turn reduces the ability of the central bank to stimulate the economy. Thus, the failure of monetary policy to prevent deflation played an important role in the financial and economic collapse of Japan in late 1997 and 1998. But monetary policy was not the shock that brought Japan close to collapse.

The Japanese government made concerted efforts to eliminate fiscal deficit throughout the 1980s and achieved a balanced budget by the end of the decade, thanks partly to large tax revenue gains from the economic growth experienced in the 1980s. The large deficits, however, reemerged after 1990, as the Japanese economy declined. The collapse of asset prices and recession in the early 1990s reduced revenue, and in an effort to stimulate the economy, the government carried out a series of economic stimulus packages and increased spending directly through the general budget and indirectly through an increase in the FILP budget. The deficit spending, however, did little to solve the fundamental problems of the Japanese economy. Large chunks of the spending were directed to the sectors electorally important to the governing LDP (local cities and governments in rural areas, construction, and loan guarantees) rather than sectors that would have benefited the entire economy. The result was a rapid growth of government gross debt without much to show.

In 1997, the Hashimoto government embarked on a fiscal austerity program to reduce the deficit and outstanding gross debt with a combination of spending cuts and increases in the tax and health care burdens of citizens, including an increase of the consumption tax rate from 3 to 5 percent. The administration believed that recovery was ongoing and the Japanese economy was strong enough to withstand the contractionary effects of fiscal austerity. This assumption proved to be incorrect. The economy was weak, and the austerity program caused the sharp decline in real GDP in the fourth quarter of 1997 and throughout 1998.

---

[7] The role of deflation in increasing the burden of servicing existing debt was emphasized by Fisher (1933) as the major factor behind the Great Depression in the United States.

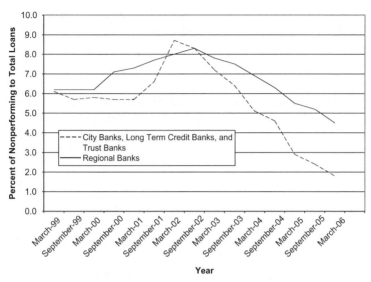

Figure 5.2. Large Banks and Regional Banks, Nonperforming Loans, March 1999 to March 2006. *Source:* FSA, Transition of Non-Performing Loans Based on the Financial Reconstruction Law, March 2006, http://www.fsa.go.jp/en/regulated/npl/20060808/table01.xls.

Financial Distress and Meaningful Policy Response, 1998 to August 2000

The financial and economic collapse shocked the Japanese regulatory establishment and raised concern worldwide that Japan's decline combined with the Asian financial crisis threatened the entire world financial system. In January 1998, the MOF acknowledged that the nonperforming loan problem was much larger than previously reported, based on new definitions and classifications of nonperforming loans for city banks, long-term credit banks, trust banks, and regional banks (Figure 5.2). The new estimates of nonperforming loans were more in line with outside estimates and showed that despite almost eight years of MOF policies to eliminate the nonperforming loan problem, the problem had largely been unchanged and, if anything, had grown worse. Even these statistics were considered conservative because of the widespread practice of evergreening bad loans. Lack of transparency still existed in other parts of the financial system. No effort was made to provide transparency regarding nonperforming assets embedded in the FILP system, which, according to Doi and Hoshi (2003), were significant.

In early 1998, the government committed ¥30 trillion of public funds to resolve the nonperforming loan problem. These funds would be used to assist closing of insolvent depository institutions and arranging asset purchases by other institutions. Of this amount, ¥13 trillion was to be used directly to inject capital into the banking system, and ¥17 trillion was allocated to the DIC to assist troubled financial institutions on request. The DIC was given new authority to raise public funds to purchase preferred stock and debt from troubled banks and was given expanded authority to arrange mergers. This commitment of public funds and willingness to assist troubled institutions was an indication that the government had finally recognized the seriousness of the financial distress; however, the execution of the public assistance was a failure because of unwillingness to depart form the old regime of mutual support.

In March 1998, the government injected ¥1.8 trillion to twenty-one banks (nine city banks, three long-term credit banks, six trust banks, and three regional banks). However, because of an unwillingness to make decisions as to relative degrees of risk among the twenty-one banks, the ¥1.8 was distributed almost evenly. The amount was far too small to have any significant effect, and more important, there was little effort to require due diligence and require the receiving banks to make a commitment to reduce nonperforming loans and restructure their portfolios. The March 1998 capital injections were widely criticized and further reduced the government's credibility to manage the crisis. The Japan premium increased as a result.

The LDP received a resounding vote of no confidence from the public in the July 1998 upper house elections. Prime Minister Hashimoto resigned shortly thereafter. His replacement, Prime Minister Obuchi, promised more aggressive action to end the economic and financial distress. In October 1998, a number of important changes in institutions and attitudes occurred. The Financial Reconstruction Commission was established December 1998 to coordinate policy as part of the prime minister's office and oversee the newly formed FSA. The commitment to resolve the financial crisis was increased from ¥30 to ¥60 trillion. The government combined the two previously established entities for disposing of nonperforming loans (Resolution and Collection Bank and the Housing Loan Administration Corporation) in the Resolution and Collection Corporation. The new entity could purchase nonperforming loans from solvent as well as assume loans from insolvent institutions at market prices. The Long Term Credit Bank and Nippon Credit Bank were nationalized, both of which had been recipients of the March 1998 capital injection. The government adopted a more liberal attitude about foreign purchase of Japanese financial institutions; for example, Merrill Lynch was permitted to purchase Yamaichi Securities Company, and foreign investors competed for Long Term Credit Bank.[8]

The government announced a more aggressive application of PCA to deal with a troubled institution before it reached the point of no return (failure) and imposed a high cost on the taxpayer. The number of institutions coming under supervision increased significantly in 1998 and 1999, and the number of bank failures likewise increased significantly (Table 5.2). The FSA commenced operations in June 1998 and by the end of 1999 had reviewed all of the large banks and most of the regional banks. The FSA closed several large banks in 1998, including the Long Term Credit Bank and the Nippon Credit Bank, and in 1999 closed several regional banks. In January 2001, the FSA was reorganized to absorb the functions of the Financial Reconstruction Commission, which was dissolved.

The March 1999 capital injection to fifteen banks (eight city banks, one long-term credit bank, five trust banks, and one regional bank) was large enough to make a difference (¥7.8 trillion versus the ¥1.8 trillion in March 1998) and the distribution was contingent on the bank's financial condition and required meaningful management plans to reduce nonperforming loans, increase loan loss reserves, and reduce size.

To reduce the inherent conflicts between the bureaucracy, the financial system, and the business sector, the National Public Services Ethics Act of 1999 for the first time imposed reporting requirements on heads of government agencies for gifts of even small amounts. This was only a dent in the long-established practice of favors but, at least for the first time, official action was taken to reduce the extent of the iron triangle and reduce the role of *amakudari*.

BOJ policy attempted to deal with declining prices by adopting in February 1999 a zero interest rate policy (ZIRP). The BOJ conducted

[8] Tett (2003) provides a detailed and fascinating discussion of the rise and fall of the Long Term Credit Bank and how foreign investors turned this Japanese "basket case" into a profitable banking institution now known as *Shinsei* Bank.

Table 5.2. Number of depository
institutions receiving assistance
from the deposit insurance
corporation, 1992 to 2006

Fiscal	Number of Cases of Financial Assistance
Year	–
1992	2
1993	2
1994	2
1995	3
1996	6
1997	7
1998	30
1999	20
2000	20
2001	37
2002	51
2003	0
2004	0
2005	0
2006	0
Total	180

Source: DIC of Japan, Financial Assistance by Year, http://www.dic.go.jp/english/
e_katsudou/e_katsudou1-2.html.

policy to target the call rate at 0.15 percent or virtually zero for all
practical purposes. This was unprecedented in postwar central banking
experience.

Continued Economic and Financial Distress and BOJ
Policy – August 2000 to March 2001

Despite more aggressive government action, the nonperforming loan
problem remained serious because of continued willingness to give
financial institutions time to work out their problems; that is, forgiveness and forbearance remained the preferred policy. Despite the more
aggressive and independent work of the FSA, the FSA was headed
by politicians whose electoral prospects often were more important
than resolving the nonperforming loan problem. The resolution plans
developed by the FSA looked good on paper, but the implementation
was not very aggressive as judged by the trend in nonperforming

loans. According to Figure 5.2, official estimates of nonperforming loans continued to increase after 1999. The unprecedented move by the BOJ to adopt ZIRP did not materially change the rate of deflation.

The economy and financial system remained vulnerable. Any shock or decline in economic activity was sure to intensify financial distress. A shock came in the form of the ill-timed shift toward tight monetary policy in August 2000 by the BOJ. In February 1999, the BOJ adopted ZIRP to reverse the deflation process partly because of intense internal and external pressure. The BOJ, however, was uncomfortable with this policy believing it to be too expansionary and continually worried that the economy would expand too rapidly. The BOJ was looking for any excuse to return to "normal" policy with positive short-term interest rates; however, the majority of central bank observers were critical of the BOJ's intentions to shift to a tighter policy. Observers outside the BOJ in fact questioned why the BOJ was not pursuing even more expansionary monetary policy rather than considering a shift toward tighter monetary policy.[9]

Despite much criticism, the BOJ increased the targeted call rate from 0.15 to 0.25 percent in August 2000. This shift toward tight policy in the context of a weak economic and financial system led to a recession starting in November 2000 (see Table 5.1). The BOJ returned to the ZIRP and by March 2001 targeted the call rate at essentially zero percent and adopted a policy referred to as Quantitative Easing Policy (QEP) designed to inject even more reserves into the banking system beyond what was called for to keep the call rate at zero. The new policy focused on the "current account balances" held by banks at the BOJ. The QEP was designed to increase current account balances far in excess of required reserves. This was accomplished by purchases of government securities by the BOJ or what is referred to as open market operations. The increased excess reserves in the banking system, in turn was expected to induce increased bank lending. The new QEP, however, was not pursued aggressively until the latter part of 2002 (Figure 5.3).

Japan again appeared to have reached another low point and began another recession in November 2000, resulting in declining real GDP for part of 2001. The number of depository institution bankruptcies

---

[9] Several papers and comment papers presented at the Bank of Japan's 2000 international conference held in Tokyo are indicative of the criticisms leveled at the Bank of Japan at that time (Bank of Japan, 2001). Also, see chapters 5 and 6 in Cargill, Hutchison, and Ito (2000).

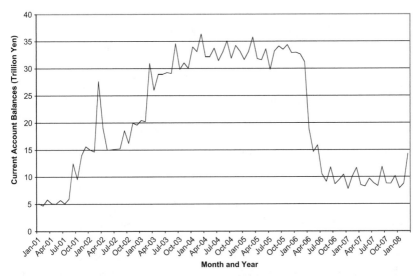

Figure 5.3. Current Account Balances Held by Banks at the Bank of Japan, January 2001 to March 2008. *Source:* BOJ, Long Term Time Series, Financial and Economic Statistics, http://www.boj.or.jp/en/type/stat/dlong/fin_stat/boj/cdab0130.csv.

increased, along with an increase in the nonperforming loan problem. Prices continued to fall. As the century came to an end and the new century started, there was increasing concern that Japan would enter into a second "lost decade" of economic, financial, and political distress.

The Turning Point: Koizumi

A major change takes place April 2001 when Koizumi won over the more conservative LDP backed Hashimoto to become prime minister. Koizumi promised to end the decade-long economic and financial distress by a series of institutional changes that would sharply differ from the past. Koizumi promised to end the nonperforming loan problem by achieving more aggressive restructuring of the banking and corporate sectors and ridding Japan of its zombie banks and corporations. Koizumi promised to reduce government spending, reduce the FILP budget, and redesign the entire system of government financial intermediation, including privatization of the postal service.

Subsequent chapters will discuss various aspects of Koizumi's influence in detail; however, it is fitting to end this discussion of economic and financial distress in the 1990s by mentioning various Koizumi policies or actions that generated a turning point in Japan's transition.

The nonperforming loan problem continued to worsen in 2002 as a result of recession. Despite the fact that official statistics indicated an increase in nonperforming loans in 2002, the head of the FSA, Hakuo Yanagisawa, announced that Japanese banks were solvent and reasonably capitalized. This was an astounding statement. Koizumi removed him as head of the FSA September 2002 and appointed Heizo Takenaka as FSA head.[10]

Takenaka was an academic economist with no political connections. Previously, all of the heads of the FSA were politicians. Takenaka was given the responsibility for reducing nonperforming loans by half in three years. To do this required putting far more pressure than previously on banks to cut off zombie corporations and allow bankruptcies, mergers, and acquisitions to take place including allowing foreign acquisition of Japanese banks. Nonperforming loans declined significantly after 2003 for the large banks, and although the nonperforming loan problem declined for regional banks, it remained higher than for the large banks as of 2006. There still remained a fairly large nonperforming loan problem for the large number of small credit cooperative type depository institutions, although, even for these, the nonperforming loan problem trended downward (Figure 5.4).

As a result of the decline in nonperforming loans and general improvement in bank and corporate balance sheets, the new deposit insurance system established in 1995 was made operational. The MOF in 1995 had announced a complete deposit guarantee to provide time for the financial system to adjust to a deposit insurance limit of ¥10 million per deposit. It was anticipated that the deposit insurance limit would be in place by April 1, 2001. This turned out to be impossible given the economic and financial distress that persisted to the first few years of the new century. On April 1, 2003, the new system was put into place over a two-year period. As of 2005, Japan, at least on paper, operated with the same type of explicit but limited deposit insurance system as in the United States and in many other countries. That is, the government sets a limit on the amount of deposits subject to a guarantee in place of the implicit guarantee under the old regime that all deposits would be guarantee by the government.

BOJ policy increasingly came under criticism by other central banks and observers of central bank policy for allowing prices to decline and

---

[10]   Hoshi and Ito (2004) provide a review of the FSA's performance from 1998 to 2004.

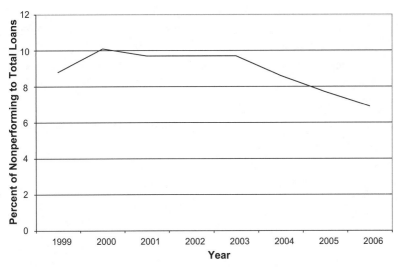

Figure 5.4. Credit Cooperatives, Nonperforming Loans, March 1999 to March 2006. *Source:* See Figure 5.2.

exiting the ZIRP in August 2000. The BOJ found almost no outside support for its policies. The BOJ in March 2001 adopted QEP but did not aggressively pursue this policy until late 2002. The change in BOJ operations was largely a result of increasing criticism by Koizumi and other politicians. They suggested that the BOJ should be a more aggressive "deflation fighter"; if the BOJ was unable to be a more aggressive deflation fighter, the BOJ Law might need to be revised to impose an explicit inflation target. The BOJ was opposed to any effort to impose an inflation target, as this was viewed as a step back from the newfound formal independence in the revision of the BOJ Law. As a result, the current account balance increased significantly in late 2002 and remained high through early 2006. Koizumi continued to pressure the BOJ in early 2003 when he was considering a new governor to replace the retiring governor in March 2003. In appointing the new governor, Koizumi made sure that the BOJ under his leadership would cooperate with the government on the effort to end deflation. Although central banks should not be susceptible to political pressure, this is one case in which the pressure was deserved and achieved a positive result.

PSS and FILP reform was initiated under the Hashimoto government, but it was Koizumi who carried out an aggressive program to reform and reduce the role of the PSS and the FILP in the economy. Many of these policies will be discussed in a later chapter focusing on

Koizumi and Japan's fiscal program. Koizumi was not able to redesign these institutions as thoroughly as planned; nonetheless, the ultimate postal privatization proposal that became law in late 2005 was a major achievement in many respects. Although PSS and FILP reform began under the Hashimoto government, Koizumi's contribution to the process was impressive.

6

Why Did the Economic and Financial Distress Last So Long?

Introduction

The Japanese economy by the end of Koizumi's tenure stabilized and reached a point of sustainable growth. Although Japan experienced several recovery periods since 1990 only to be followed by decline and instability, the recovery that started in 2003 has been more substantial. In the late 1990s and first year or two of the new century, there was considerable discussion about the potential for another decade of economic distress. As of September 2006, this type of discussion has all but disappeared. This does not imply an absence of economic and political challenges facing Japan in the near future. It does mean, however, that for the first time in a decade and half, the Japanese economy and political systems at the end of 2006 could realistically have a more positive attitude about the future. This view needs to be qualified to some degree because Japan's economic recovery has been based narrowly on the export sector, the political impasse and uncertainty that emerged with the LDP-CGP (Clean Government Party) government's loss of the majority in the July 2007 upper house election and the opposition parties' controlling the upper house, and continuing indications that the potential for deflation has not been completely rung out of the Japanese economy.

On the positive side, real GDP increased 2 percent in 2006, unemployment declined, although it still remained high by historical standards, equity prices increased, and, for the first time since 1991, real estate prices and rents in Tokyo begun to move upward. The nonperforming loan problem had been drastically reduced, although there remained concern about the amount of nonperforming loans held by credit cooperatives. Large numbers of depository institutions were closed. Their assets and liabilities were assumed by other institutions with support from the FSA and DIC. Japan began to seriously deal with its economic and financial problems under the Koizumi government. Koizumi brought new leadership to resolving the economic and financial distress that had accumulated by the end of the 1990s, initiated more aggressive structural changes than previous governments, and shifted decision making away from the LDP and the bureaucracy by enhancing the role of the prime minister in Japan's policy making. Koizumi left office with a historically high level of public confidence.

The previous chapters focused on the economic and financial stability of the 1980s, the clash between the new international economic and political environment and Japan's version of financial liberalization, and the resulting economic and financial distress in the 1990s and the first few years of the new century. References were made at various points in the discussion to the political distress in the 1990s, to the Koizumi government, and to political institutional redesign; however, the focal point was on the financial transition. Subsequent chapters will discuss the other broader aspects of Japan's economy in terms of political institutions, other economic institutions and policy, the changed social contract between the government and the Japanese people, and the economic and social problems facing a more open and competitive Japan.

This chapter ends the economic and financial perspective of Japan's transition since 1980 by posing the questions, "Why did the economic and financial distress persist for such a long period of time?" or "Why was Japan a reluctant reformer?" Japan's economic and financial distress from 1990 to 2005 has been the subject of much discussion as to how one of the world's largest economy could experience such a long period of distress especially in light of the spectacular success Japan achieved before 1990. The delay in recovery is the more remarkable when Japan is placed in the context of other Asian economies adversely impacted by the Asian Financial Crisis. Korea[1] and several other Asian economies recovered by 1999 and 2000 and, yet, as they recovered, Japan "celebrated" almost a decade of economic, financial,

---

[1]   South Korea is the most interesting counterexample to Japan because of its size and because its economic institutions resembled those of Japan more than any other Asian economy. In fact, Korea's economic institutions might have been even more rigid than Japan's in the postwar period. Cargill and Patrick (2006) discuss relative economic and financial performance in Korea and Japan and offer various factors that might account for the difference. Also, see Lee (2003).

and political distress and would experience several more years of difficulty. Table 6.1 presents a schematic of the major economic events in Japan from 1980 to 2006.

One can immediately dismiss some obvious answers to why Japan's distress lasted so long. It was not because Japan lacked material resources. Despite the distress, Japan remained one of the wealthiest economies with a high standard of living, possessed substantial amounts of international reserves so that currency flight was never a serious concern, and continued to generate favorable trade balances. It was not because Japan lacked intellectual resources or understanding. It was not because Japan was the first to experience the outcome of a flawed liberalization process. By the early 1990s, the world had provided many cases of what contributes to a flawed financial liberalization process and policies required to resolve the resulting economic and financial distress.

In some respects, the question has been partially answered in references to why Japan adopted a flawed financial liberalization (Chapter 4) and references to Japan's general approach to markets. What is intended in this chapter is to provide a broader perspective rather than merely focusing on those elements that generated a flawed financial liberalization process, expand on Japan's attitude toward markets, and focus on fiscal and monetary policy errors. In this regard, BOJ policy errors are the most critical to understanding the length of the distress.

It is useful to bifurcate the factors accounting for the long period of stagnation[2] into those specific to Japan and those of a more general character. The "Japan-specific" factors relate to the "uniqueness" of Japanese institutions that constrained institutional change in Japan. The "general" factors focus on fiscal and monetary policy errors that could have occurred in any institutional environment.

Japan-Specific Restraints on Institutional Redesign

There are many Japan-specific factors that can be identified; however, to focus on broad issues, they can be categorized into six groups: first, the belief among Japanese policy makers that Japan is special and

---

[2] Part of the discussion of the difficultly of institutional change is taken from Cargill (2006), with added detail about how to account for BOJ policy in the 1990s and the first few years of the new century.

Table 6.1. Major turning points in japan's economic and financial transition since 1980

Japan commences financial liberalization in late 1970s and early 1980s
↓
Flawed financial liberalization process in the 1980s
↓
The BOJ's easy monetary policy in the second half of the 1980s combined with flawed financial liberalization generates asset inflation
↓
Asset prices collapse in 1990 and 1991 in response to the BOJ's tight monetary policy starting May 1989
↓
Government response in 1990s to the effect of declining asset prices – denial, understatement, forgiveness, and forbearance
↓
The BOJ's easy monetary policy commences in 1992, but insufficient to prevent disinflation through 1994 and deflation after 1994
↓
Hashimoto government austerity program in 1997 – including increase in consumption tax from 3 to 5 percent
↓
Japan at the abyss of deflation, recession, and financial insolvency in late 1997 (three large financial institutions fail) and all of 1998 (increase in nonperforming loans, increase in corporate bankruptcies, nationalization of two large financial institutions)
↓
New financial and supervisory regime begins to emerge in 1998
↓
Despite weak economy and continued deflation, the BOJ shifts to tight monetary August 2000 – recession, increase in nonperforming loans, and continued deflation – the BOJ reverts to pre-August 2000 policy and adopts new approach focused on increased reserves (current account balance) to the banking system
↓
Koizumi becomes prime minister April 2001 with more aggressive approach to resolving economic and financial distress – pressure on FSA to resolve nonperforming loan problem and pressure on the BOJ to provide more liquidity to end deflation
↓
Nonperforming loans decline and economy begins tentative recovery in 2003 that by 2006 appears sustainable – deflation declines but still a potential problem
↓
Koizumi steps down September 2006

not subject to Western types of market failure; second, the matrix of cultural and social relationships institutionalized in the financial system delayed resolution of the financial distress: third, general distrust of markets and Schumpeterian "creative destruction"; fourth, the iron triangle maintained the status quo, limited policy actions to forbearance and forgiveness, and the lack of critical nongovernment organizations limited public challenges to these policies and limited any public forum for problem solving; fifth, complacency on the part of policy makers and the public until the late 1990s; and, sixth, political instability and uncertainty resulting from the electoral reform of 1994 and party realignment.

The Belief That Japan Is Special

Japan was very slow to recognize how the features of forgiveness, forbearance, and mutual support encouraged moral hazard. Moral hazard refers to the incentive to assume risk by the insured that is adverse to the insurer. Japan's entire financial system was geared toward reducing risk and limiting bankruptcy. However, financial liberalization provided greater ability to manage financial portfolios, and, hence, greater ability to assume and manage risk. Government guarantees of private risk taking provide incentives for the private sector to take on more risks – this is the basic essence of moral hazard. The extensive system of implied insurance represented by government policy encouraged imprudent lending and risk-taking.

Japanese authorities were aware of the problems experienced by the United States and other Western countries as they implemented financial liberalization policies in the 1970s and 1980s, but attributed these problems to characteristics of Western economic institutions. Japanese policy makers perceived their economic and financial institutions immune from the type of market behavior exhibited in these countries. They most likely based this view on the historical performance of the Japanese financial system, belief in the ability of administrative guidance to prevent imprudent behavior on the part of market participants, and, most important, on the belief that Western economic behavior was fundamentally different than Japanese economic behavior.

This belief in specialness was especially true of moral hazard. Japanese policy makers regarded moral hazard as relevant only for individual-based Western-type economic systems. Moral hazard had little relevance for a financial system based on social relationships in which mutual support and limiting risk were primary objectives. Likewise, Japanese policy makers regarded the type of regulatory–market dialectic common in the United States as appropriate only for a formal codified legal system that permitted "loop-hole mining." In a system dominated by administrative guidance, informality, and mutual support, market participants were more likely to refrain from actions that were not expressly permitted by the regulatory authorities, whereas in the United States, market participants would only refrain from actions that were expressly prohibited. Moral hazard was viewed as unique to individualistic rather than collectivist type economic institutions.

This belief system on the part of Japanese policy makers persisted well into the 1990s. Even at this point the role of moral hazard is less than universally accepted in Japan. Reluctance to accept the role of moral hazard in the financial liberalization process has been a major factor limiting institutional redesign of the financial system and, hence, a major factor in prolonging financial and economics distress.

Social and Cultural Characteristics Imbedded in Japanese Finance

Lee (1992 and 2002) and Lincoln (2001) argue that Japanese culture and belief systems make it difficult to adopt market-oriented financial institutions. Japanese culture and belief systems are rooted in Japan's collectivist orientation and aversion to risk.

Lee emphasizes the inherent social relationships between various Japanese groups institutionalized by the economic system in general. Reluctance by Japanese authorities to alter those social relationships constrains any institutional redesign of the economy. In contrast, social relationships play a significantly less important role in the economic institutions of the West.[3] Lee argues that although some degree of liberalization is in Japan's best interest, the transition has been resisted in Japan and other Asian economics to a much greater extent than in the United States.

Lincoln emphasizes the same point but directs more attention to the unwillingness to adopt a market orientation to the financial system. The matrix of social relationships, cultural characteristics, and

---

[3] Germany, however, has a system similar to that of Japan, characterized by banking-based finance and long-term relationships between banks and corporations.

economic institutions in Japan – especially the financial system – create binding constraints on reform toward transparency, open money and capital markets, and risk-taking. The essence of Lincoln's argument is as follows. Markets require formality, whereas informality is a chief characteristic of Japanese society. Markets require a focus on short-run (profit-maximization) and limited dimensional transactions (price and quantity), whereas Japanese financial institutions focus more on long-run (maintaining market share) and multidimensional transactions (complex customer relationships that go far beyond price and quantity to include management services, arranging connections with other firms, etc.). Markets require specialization and division of labor independent of social relationships, whereas Japanese economic and financial institutions directly incorporate social relationship characteristics such as long-term relationships, mutual support, and limiting risk. Markets require bankruptcy as a penalty function, whereas Japanese economic institutions are designed to limit market risk and, consequently, bankruptcy. Markets require transparency, whereas Japanese institutions emphasize nontransparency and façades or "face saving".

Cargill and Royama (1988) express a similar perspective in terms of the nature of the lender-borrower relationship in Japan and the United States and use Japan's flow of funds for the period from 1970 to 1975 to allocate the flow of funds into "customer" and "market" relationships for each country. The "customer" lender-borrower relationship is multidimensional, cooperative, and long-term – that is, it is a customer-based relationship designed to adapt to changes in the environment in a manner that is beneficial to both sides. This customer relationship is the essence of the *keiretsu* or main bank system that evolved from the prewar *zaibatsu*. Even the securities markets in Japan before 1980 involved strong customer relationships between lenders and borrowers. In contrast, the "market" lender-borrower relationship is limited to two dimensions (price and quantity): competitive, and short-term. Securities markets in the United States clearly meet this standard, and much of intermediation finance also satisfies the requirements of a market relationship between lenders and borrowers. Cargill and Royama (1988, p. 44) present statistics drawn for each country's flow of funds accounts that indicate dominance of customer relationships in Japan and the dominance of market relationships in the United States. These statistics present one effort to quantify the cultural issues raised by Lee and Lincoln.

A telling indication of the lack of interest in market-oriented financial transactions is the almost complete lack of courses in finance or MBA programs at Japanese universities until recently. This is beginning to change but, in the past, there was little interest in training Japanese students, even those destined for careers in either the public or private components of the financial system, in what would be standard empirical and theoretical finance concepts extensively taught in Western universities.

General Distrust of Markets and Schumpeterian "Creative Destruction"

Japan never embraced markets to the degree they were embraced in the United States (Johnson, 1982). Perhaps this attitude grew out of the concern over Japan's limited resources, limited usable land, and exposure to natural shocks. Japan viewed markets as too uncertain in the context of an economy with only small degrees of freedom to develop. The attitude may have also been due to Japan's negative perception of the West starting from Commodore Parry's forced entry to Japan in 1853 and the view market ideology was merely a political tool used by the West to expand its influence throughout Asia.

"Creative destruction" in the form of bankruptcy and change are important market foundations designed to ensure efficiency. Markets function best when participants are permitted to assume and manage risk to enhance profits. Mistakes result in a penalty function in the form of bankruptcy. Markets were never intended to support the status quo but, rather, to encourage change as competition led to new technology and innovation, lowered costs of existing products, or led to new products. Markets are in constant change with their reliance on "creative destruction." The decline of firms and loss of jobs in one sector is offset by more efficient sectors and the creation of new products and new jobs.

Japanese attitudes and institutions in the 1980s came into sharp conflict with these elements of the market system, especially the emphasis on creative destruction. Japanese economic and political institutions were designed to limit risk and change and, on balance, were biased toward the status quo. However, Japan was being pressured to permit more risk taking, permit more change, and disrupt the status quo. Japanese policy makers had difficulty understanding why they should redesign their economic institutions given the impressive record of economic growth and industrialization starting with the Meiji Restoration of 1868 and only seriously interrupted in the 1940s as a result of Japan's militarist ambitions. Japan was thus unwilling to alter the key elements of its economic and financial institutions and pursued financial liberalization only to the degree that it dealt with an immediate practical problem. As a result, Japan's financial liberalization process was unbalanced, incomplete, and flawed.

The Iron Triangle, Lack of Strong Political Leadership, and Lack of Critical Nongovernment Organizations

The mutual support among the LDP, bureaucracy, and their client industries, including financial institutions, known as the iron triangle, made it relatively easy to engage in denial and understatement, and, when action was required, to pursue policies based on forgiveness and forbearance. The iron triangle was solidified by *amakudari* and non-transparency. Forgiveness and forbearance policies designed to protect the status quo not only failed to resolve the financial and economic distress but created a more hazardous environment that elevated the ultimate economic and political cost of resolution. The interdependence of one element on the other made it difficult to initiate change in any direction. Likewise, the pork barrel politics of the FILP ensured that the extensive set of government financial institutions would not be meaningfully reformed, the nonperforming assets embedded in the FILP system would be concealed, and, when concealment was no longer possible, the government would find a way to forgive and forebear any meaningful resolution.

A strong prime minister might have been able to overcome the iron triangle's resistance to change, if Japan's political system had allowed for such strong leadership. A strong prime minister could have initiated policy action, appealed to the public, and balanced conflicting interests. In times of crisis, strong leadership at the highest levels of government is required to resolve the distress. However, as we reviewed in Chapter 2, the power of the Japanese prime minister was constrained by several features of Japan's political institutions until Koizumi assumed power in 2001. This lack of political leadership contributed to Japan's economic and financial distress by increasing the probability of inaction.

The relative lack of effective nongovernment organizations, such as research institutions, "think tanks," and the news media contributed to the long period of distress in Japan because ineffective policies could more easily be pursued without challenge. The importance of nongovernment organizations is based on the common response of government to any type of economic, financial or political distress. Government regulatory authorities have an incentive to deny the existence of a problem. Once denial is no longer a credible policy, government then has an incentive to understate the magnitude of the problem using accounting gimmicks, withholding information, and on occasion outright lying. Once government recognizes that actual policy is required to deal with a problem, such as the savings and loan mess in the United States or the collapse of the housing loan industry (*jusen* industry) in Japan, the preferred policy is forgiveness and forbearance. The policy of forgiveness and forbearance is a delaying action designed to give financial institutions and the market time to work themselves out of the problem and often is based on an implicit understanding of mutual support between regulators and the regulated entity. Theory and experience show forgiveness and forbearance only leads to higher economic and political costs in the future to resolve the problem. All governments have an incentive to engage in forgiveness and forbearance; however, the ability to pursue this type of policy is critically dependent on the role of nongovernment organizations.

Nongovernment organizations have a difficult time in Japan because of the closed system of information and pervasive "old boy" system of mutual support. They also have a difficult time in the United States for many of the same reasons, but, on balance, outside groups have been more effective in the United States than in Japan. The differences are not a result of the makeup of these groups but, more important, a result of the set of institutions that defined their operating environment. This point can be illustrated by the experience of an interesting and influential nongovernment entity in the United States known as the "Shadow Financial Regulatory Committee" and efforts to establish a similar group in Japan.

In the late 1970s, a group of well-known economists formed the Shadow Financial Regulatory Committee in the United States. They already had established reputations. They commenced focusing their papers, presentations, and publishing official statements of the Shadow Committee on the policy errors being made for regulatory authorities and politicians. Like a "shadow behind the government," this group studied and commented on the various financial and monetary policies of the U.S. government. During the turbulent period in the late 1980s and early 1990s, some members of the group occasionally appeared on television and radio. They were able to shed light on the various financial disruptions, especially the savings and loan and banking problems. They were not appreciated by government regulatory authorities. Yet this group was very effective and, in fact, they had a significant influence on the content of the 1991 Federal Deposit Insurance Improvement Act. This was a major change in regulatory framework and philosophy that has become a model for much of the world, including Japan. The U.S. shadow group is sponsored by the American Enterprise Institute, and there are now European, Latin American, and Asian shadow groups all acting independently of each other, although they do have a joint conference every two years[4].

In 1998, a Japan Shadow Financial Regulatory Committee was established and modeled on the U.S. committee. This was a major achievement in a culture that prides itself on nontransparency, mutual support and consensus. Unfortunately, the Japan group did not have the same impact on public policy as its counterpart in the United States and has not released a large number of statements. The Japan group as of 2008 has released five statements in English (3 in 1998 and 2 in 2005) and participated in two joint statements with committees in Europe and the United States (1 in 1999 and 1 in 2000) according to its Website. The Japan group membership includes well-known academics and represents a broad spectrum of areas. The Japan group continues and hopefully will come to play a more important role over time.

Complacency – Japan Did Not Perceive Itself in Crisis until the Late 1990s

There is an interesting comparison between South Korea and Japan that suggests another Japan-specific restraint on reform. Before the Asian Financial Crisis, South Korea had long been criticized for its inefficient financial institutions, irrational allocation of credit, and large nonperforming loan problem that had emerged in the 1970s. Korea devoted some attention to these concerns and officially adopted numerous financial liberalization measures in the 1980s. Despite some progress, the general assessment up to 1997 was that financial liberalization was even more rhetoric than substance compared to Japan.

---

[4] Information on the shadow groups can be found at the American Enterprise Institute Website (http://www.aei.org/research/shadow/projectID.15/default.asp).

Korea's efforts were designed to be just sufficient to secure acceptance into the OECD, which Korea achieved in 1995, but not meaningful enough to change the basic structure of the financial system. Korea, like Japan, found it difficult to accept the necessity to make fundamental changes when their economy had achieved so much success in such a short period of time. Korea's financial institutions more than any other Asian country were closest to the prewar Japanese financial institutions, Korea's *chaebol* (company groups) were more similar to Japan's prewar *zaibatsu* than Japan's postwar *keiretsu*.

In late 1997, when Korea's economy and financial system collapsed, policy makers correctly perceived a crisis situation that required decisive action. As such, Korea in 1998 and 1999 moved swiftly to bail out private banks, permit foreign investment in banks, and reform corporate governance. Central bank policy was constrained to prevent both inflation and deflation by adopting a formal inflation-target framework. The economy recovered rapidly, and by 2000, Korea had appeared to return to sustained economic growth. Thus, the crisis environment provided an incentive to initiate fundamental institutional redesign.[5]

Japan did not perceive itself in a crisis situation, with the exception of the turbulent period from the fourth quarter of 1997 to early 1999. Japan's lost decade is more one of lost potential, than of actual decline. Real GDP per capita did not decline over the decade of the 1990s, though it did increase slower than previously (Figure 1.5). This overall measure of the standard of living however, masks a deterioration in the standard of living for the average Japanese household as explained in Chapter 10. Japanese homeownership is broad-based and although real estate prices have declined as much as 60 percent, the turnover rate of homeownership is low. Despite the decline in real estate prices and stock prices, household financial wealth is large. The large corporations have shielded themselves from Japan's inefficient financial institutions by shifting much of their production and financial operations outside of Japan; that is, they have "opted out" (Schoppa, 2001) of providing political pressure to reform the system. The LDP continued to benefit politically from the support by banks that did not wish to see a more aggressive resolution of the nonperforming loan problem, from the support of corporations and business firms that did not wish to see a more aggressive resolution of the

---

[5] Cargill and Patrick (2006) and Lee (2006) present a comparative perspective on Korea and Japan.

nonperforming borrower problem, and from the PSS and FILP that did not wish to see a reduction of government financial intermediation. At the same time, the deadweight loss had not yet been perceived by the public to be serious enough to demand change. Japan was not in danger of a currency crisis because it had virtually no external debt, international reserve assets were large, and the world continued to purchase Japanese goods. Thus, in many respects, the household, business, and political sectors did not perceive a crisis until late 1997 through 1998.

Decision Making in the Context of Electoral Reform

Complacency was one reason for the lack of more decisive action on the part of the government through the mid-1990s. However, this was also a period of significant change in Japan's political institutions because of electoral reform in 1994 and ensuing party realignment. Until the late 1980s, Japan was noted for a stable political environment because of the dominance of the LDP, the permanent role of the bureaucracy, and their relatively stable relationship to client industries and firms. The public tolerated money politics, corruption, and the distributive politics of the iron triangle because the LDP had delivered strong economic performance and fulfilled a social contract that produced social stability.

In the late 1980s, a series of scandals involving payments to politicians and bureaucrats by private firms caused considerable public outrage for a public that in the past had tolerated the widespread practice of money politics in Japan. Political reform emerged as an important issue, and political parties enacted electoral reform. These events are fully discussed in Chapter 7; however, we should briefly note them here because they were another reason for policy malaise and the lack of policy innovations in the 1990s.

The 1994 electoral reform changed the incentive structure for politicians and parties and set in motion large-scale party realignment. Politicians changed party affiliation and political parties repeatedly broke up and merged, as politicians tried to ensure their reelection and to be in the party that they expected would gain control of government. As a result, politicians consumed much of their energy and resources in their electoral and power concerns and were unable to pay sufficient attention to the pressing economic and financial problems during the 1990s. Combined with their failure to recognize the depth of the economic problems, politicians were unable to consider policy innovations to deal with the economic and financial distress. In this environment, they were more likely to fall back on the familiar conventional approach rooted in their mutual support system of the past. It is not clear whether in the absence of political uncertainty and confusion, politicians would have been willing to consider anything but the traditional approach. Nonetheless, their preoccupation with political and electoral survival as a result of political instability and uncertainty made it more difficult for them to not only focus on the economic and financial distress, but, more important, made it difficult to consider new approaches to resolving the distress. This lack of attention thus contributed to Japan's lost decade.

General Restraints: Bank of Japan Policy

Not only did BOJ policy in the second half of the 1980s contributed to asset inflation, BOJ policy in the 1990s and into the first part of the new century represented a major constraint on recovery. As of late 2007, there still continues to be the potential for BOJ policy to interfere with recovery. The BOJ plays an important role in the economy and, as such, we should review its history briefly.

The BOJ from the mid-1970s to the first half of the 1980s achieved a remarkable record of price stability while defying the conventional wisdom that legally dependent central banks generated higher inflation rates than legally independent ones. These years represent the high point of BOJ policy in the postwar period and drew widespread academic and policy interest to BOJ policy outcomes and central bank institutional design. In the late 1980s and 1990s, however, the BOJ was criticized for accommodating asset inflation and then for a "cold turkey" response to the asset bubble in 1989 followed by anemic expansionary policy after 1992 almost universally regarded as insufficient to prevent prices from falling (Hetzel, 2003, and McCallum, 2003). In the first half of the 1990s, Japan experienced disinflation, followed after 1994 by a gradual but persistent fall in the price level that only by 2006 showed signs of increasing. The disinflation and deflation adversely affected the financial and real sectors and limited Japan's ability to recover from the collapse of asset prices.

The deflation period appeared to be ending in late 2007. Combined with an expanding economy, the BOJ on March 9, 2006, announced a gradual end to its ZIRP, first established in February 1999, and to the QEP initiated as of March 2001. At the same time, the BOJ announced that it was adopting a price stability objective of ultimately keeping the inflation rate between 0 and 2 percent, with a focus on the midpoint. Although not a formal inflation target, the announcement was designed to express the BOJ's definition of the price stability objective in 1997 BOJ Law. In July 2006, the BOJ raised the targeted call rate from 0.10 to 0.25 percent and in March 2007 raised the targeted call rate to 0.50 percent.

The failure of the BOJ to prevent deflation has generated much debate between the BOJ and the academic profession as well as debate among the BOJ and the MOF, Koizumi, and the Diet. The public nature of this debate was manifested by a seminar given May 2003 in Tokyo by Ben Bernanke, then a member of the Federal Reserve Board of Governors and currently chair of the Board (Bernanke, 2003). The criticism focused broadly on the entire period of monetary policy in the 1990s and on concern that the BOJ was exiting too rapidly from the QEP in light of the premature shift to tighter policy in August 2000. Even though the Bank's QEP significantly increased in late 2002 and 2003 and the rate of deflation declined, the BOJ was still subject to criticism for past policies, resisting calls for more expansionary policy and resisting an inflation-target framework. This generated interest in modifying the newly enhanced independence achieved in 1998. Heizo Takenaka, minister of Internal Affairs stated in December 2005 that monetary policy is not the sole responsibility of the BOJ (*Economist,* December 17, 2005). The BOJ's March 2006 announcement to focus on an inflation rate between 0 and 2 percent might be interpreted as a move to fend off any institutional redesign by the government unfavorable to the BOJ, especially in the form of an explicit inflation target.

The consequences of the ten-year deflation have been significant both in economic and political terms. In the next section, we discuss the adverse effects of deflation in general and especially in the context of preexisting conditions in Japan during the second half of the 1990s and the first few years of the new century. Then we turn to a discussion of why the BOJ might have followed a deflationary policy for so long despite overwhelming evidence deflation adversely affected the Japanese economy.

Deflation Is a Serious Problem

Deflation recently has come to be recognized as a serious macroeconomic problem beyond the experiences of Japan (Burdekin and Siklos,

2003). The Federal Reserve and European Central Bank in May 2003 expressed concern about the potential for deflation. Krugman (1999) reintroduced the concept of the 1930s liquidity trap to account for what was happening in Japan and what was likely to become a more general problem of "depression economics" elsewhere (Krugman, 2002). Cargill and Parker (2003, 2004a, and 2004b) discuss the sources of deflation, the effects of deflation, and the relationship between deflation and monetary policy from an institutional, theoretical, and econometric perspective. Their discussion can be summarized as follows.

First, because deflation has been a rare event in the postwar period, contracts are likely to be adjusted much more slowly in response to a deflation of x percent than an inflation of x percent. Second, the nominal rate of interest is bounded from below by zero; hence, deflation increases the real rate of interest and reduces investment spending when deflation occurs in the context of low nominal interest rates. Third, deflation increases the cost of servicing debt and increases bankruptcy further reducing spending and weakening balance sheets of financial institutions. This is a variation of Fisher's (1933) "debt-deflation" process described seventy years ago in the context of the decline in economic and financial activity in the United States from 1929 to 1933. The increased bankruptcy rate reduces the money multiplier as banks become less willing to lend. Fourth, even perfectly expected deflation may reduce current consumption as a result of the asymmetric effect on future prices and the real interest rate, as consumers wait for cheaper prices in the future. Specifically, because the nominal interest is bounded from below by zero, deflation increases the real interest rate and provides incentives to save. Fifth, deflation changes the relative prices between money and commodities and tends to increase the demand for money (hoarding), making it more difficult to restore expectations of price increases by monetary policy.

Deflation generates a discontinuity for monetary policy or liquidity trap in the sense that deflation shifts the demand for money upward (velocity declines), reduces consumption, reduces investment, and reduces the money multiplier, thereby reducing the ability of the central bank to reverse course. This is a different type of liquidity trap than the standard textbook Keynesian case used to rationalize the ineffectiveness of monetary policy in the 1930s. In this case, the central bank is responsible for the upward shift in money demand and, in turn, the central bank has the ability to reverse the liquidity trap by aggressive monetary ease. Hence, the phrase "discontinuity in monetary policy" might be more appropriate than liquidity trap. Estimates of the demand function for money in Japan using quarterly data find a significant (at conventional levels of confidence) upward shift in money demand and downward shift in the consumption function (annual data) in the 1990s that can be statistically related to the decline in prices. The statistical evidence also shows that the money multiplier declined along with the price level.

Although much of this literature is technical, the bottom line is straightforward. Central banks should never allow the price level to fall for any long period of time. Declining prices increase the cost of servicing outstanding debt, increase bankruptcy, reduce consumption, and reduce the ability of monetary policy to affect the economy. These effects of deflation are well documented in the theoretical and empirical literature on central banking.

Why Did the BOJ Permit Deflation?

It is difficult to account for the BOJ's behavior, especially given the lessons learned from the history of central bank policy during the 1930s. The major lesson from that period is that central banks had the ability to reverse the decline in prices in many cases but did not do so for a variety of reasons. The decline in prices greatly intensified the economic and financial distress of the 1930s for many countries. The following summarizes the various explanations that have appeared in the literature on BOJ policy.

It's Not My Fault Trap

The BOJ has stated on a number of occasions that structural problems, aftermath of the collapse of asset prices, or Chinese cheap imports were responsible for the deflation process, and that these events were outside the influence of monetary policy (Noland and Posen, 2002). Did the BOJ have the power to reverse disinflation and deflation that characterized the 1990s? The BOJ has found little support for its position that deflation was out of its control or that the BOJ pursued a policy of ease during the 1990s. To paraphrase Milton Friedman's famous statement about the relationship between money and prices over the long run – that at all times, inflation or deflation is a monetary phenomenon.

Conservative Central Banker

The BOJ's history suggests it has an aversion toward inflation and that it regards measured inflation rates close to zero as price stability. In a sense, the BOJ meets the requirements of the conservative central banker solution to the time inconsistency problem in which central banks have an inflation bias. Time inconsistency refers to a bias that central banks have toward inflation independent of any political influence. Masaru Hayami (2000), Governor of the BOJ from 1998 to March 2006, left few doubts about the inflation aversion of top BOJ officials when he criticized some who argued "tolerating a little bit of inflation" would be beneficial to the Japanese economy (Hayami, 2000, p. 2). The March 2006 decision to end QEP and adoption of "soft" inflation target further emphasizes the bias against inflation. The BOJ's view that a 1 percent inflation rate is consistent with price stability places it among the most conservative of central banks in industrial economies. One percent is a low inflation rate given the well-known measurement errors in the price index.

Independence Trap

Formal independence in 1998 came to the BOJ quickly and was as much the outcome of a political effort to reduce the role of the MOF in the financial system as it was to modernize the BOJ's legal charter and to achieve an institutional design similar to central banks in other industrial countries. As such, Cargill, Hutchison, and Ito (2000) argued that the BOJ became overly cautious and inward in its decision making. In a sense, the BOJ became a "prisoner of its own independence." Not only did BOJ policy become more risk averse in adopting nontraditional policy as the deflation process became more apparent in 1998 and 1999, but also the BOJ became politically more insular and unwilling to interact with the MOF or others for fear that this would represent a loss of independence.

Policy Error Trap

It is possible that the BOJ simply made a series of policy errors – not unheard of even in recent central banking history. The turbulent environment of 1998 when the governor and deputy governor resigned over a scandal in the banking section combined with the appointment of Hayami as governor may have generated an environment for error.

Some of the policy statements of former Governor Hayami in particular suggest a lack of understanding about monetary policy. Ito (2004) provides an excellent discussion on this point.

War of Attrition with the MOF

The BOJ has expressed concern over the MOF's policies of expanding the debt both to finance spending and to support a policy of forgiveness and forbearance in dealing with troubled financial institutions. The BOJ regards the level of private and public debt as socially excessive and resists accommodating the expansion in debt (Hayami, 2000). One BOJ economist (Okina, 1999, p. 193) defended monetary policy in the late 1990s because easier monetary policy would be used by the government to accommodate increasing levels of debt. Monetary expansion could easily become a "drug" that would be difficult to give up if the BOJ adopted a more aggressive policy.

Balance Sheet Trap

The BOJ at times expressed concern that easy monetary policy, especially the QEP, exposed the Bank's balance sheet to solvency and interest-rate risk problems. This is because the BOJ increasingly relied on open market operations (purchasing government bonds) to increase current account balances held by banks at the BOJ (see Figure 5.3). In the view of the BOJ, the large government bond portfolio exposed it to solvency and credibility problems when interest rates rose as the economy recovered. Higher interest rates reduced the value of the bond portfolio and the BOJ's balance sheet would deteriorate as bonds would have to be sold to reduce liquidity when the economy recovered. Also, the larger the bond portfolio, the more reluctant the BOJ would be in exiting from the ZIRP and QEP, according to Fujiki, Okina, and Shiratsuka (2001). Thus, concern about the effect of a large government bond portfolio may have limited the degree of monetary ease the BOJ was willing to pursue.[6]

The Debt Trap

This is a more theoretical version of the war of attrition between the BOJ and the MOF. The Japanese economy accumulated a significant

---

[6] This issue is discussed in Cargill (2005).

amount of debt in the 1990s with a meaningful percentage of private debt considered nonperforming. The large government deficits increased the amount of government debt so that the gross government debt to GDP ratio in 2007 is 160 percent, among the highest in the world. Cargill and Guerrero (2007) developed a game model to suggest that deflation might have been a rational policy on the part of the BOJ to limit the amount of government debt. Specifically, the model shows that a central bank is temped to use "deflation surprises" as a disciplining device to keep the levels of real debt under control. Deflation increases the stock of real debt, thus making it more difficult for the market to absorb more debt, and deflation increases the real interest rate, thus making debt service more burdensome.

Which Explanation is Correct?

Each explanation with the exception that the BOJ had no control over the price level contains an element of truth, although no one explanation provides the entire answer as to why the BOJ failed in the fundamental responsibility of any central bank to prevent deflation as well as inflation. This issue will continue to be debated for a long time. The last time that central banks failed in their responsibility to prevent declining prices was in the 1930s. This is not to imply that the two situations are the same from a quantitative perspective; however, there are important qualitative similarities between BOJ policy in the 1990s and the experiences of a number of central banks in the 1930s, especially that of the Federal Reserve (Cargill, 2001).

Koizumi and the BOJ

In the later part of 2002, the BOJ shifted to a more aggressive monetary policy by significantly increasing the size of the current account balance based on the QEP initiated March 2001. The call rate was already essentially zero. The impact on bank reserves was immediate and although it did not increase the growth rate of money, it provided much needed liquidity to the banking system and began to change expectations that the BOJ was serious about reversing the deflation process. This shift in policy was a direct result of increasing criticism from the LDP and Prime Minister Koizumi, and the realization by the BOJ that it would be forced to accept an explicit inflation target and, hence, lose some of its newly found legal independence unless it showed more willingness to increase liquidity.

In order to maintain its legal independence, the BOJ may have been willing to give up some of its substantive independence in other areas. Koizumi made it very clear in the newsmedia in early 2003 before making the final decision on the BOJ's new governor that he would only appoint someone to replace Hayami if that person would be willing to be a "deflation fighter." Koizumi appointed Toshihiko Fukui March 2003 to replace Hayami. The BOJ maintained a more expansionary policy than previously judged by the behavior of the current account balances held by banks at the BOJ. There is little doubt Fukui's appointment was contingent on Fukui's promise to make the solution of deflation the top priority. Thus, the BOJ for the time being avoided having an explicit inflation target imposed on its operations.

This is another instance of the importance of political leadership to revolve financial and economic distress in Japan. The willingness of Koizumi to question BOJ policy, make the appointment of the governorship contingent on more expansionary monetary policy despite the newly-established formal independence of the BOJ, and implicitly threaten to modify some of the Bank's formal independence achieved in 1998 encouraged the BOJ to adopt a policy more conducive to recovery.

General Restraints: Japan's Fiscal Program

Japan's fiscal program consisted of the general budget for the central and local governments based on the familiar revenue-spending framework and the FILP based on a flow-of-funds framework. The general budget stipulates government revenues from various taxes, fees, and bonds and how the revenues are allocated to various components of government spending. Japan's general budget is similar in concept to any country; however, the FILP budget is a special feature of the Japanese fiscal program that constitutes a major part of the financial system. The FILP budget was referred to as Japan's second budget, drafted by the government and approved by the Diet along with the general budget. The FILP funds came primarily from postal savings deposits, postal life insurance, and national pension contributions. The FILP budget consisted of allocations of these funds to a system of government banks, enterprises, corporations, and local governments, which collectively were referred to as FILP agencies.

The two components of the fiscal program – the general budget and the FILP – will be discussed in detail in Chapters 8 and 9; however, at this point, we need to explain how Japan's fiscal program in the 1990s made reform more difficult and prolonged the economic and financial distress.

The general budget began to run large deficits in the early 1970s in response to the oil price shock of 1973 and a slower growing economy. Government spending increased to offset the adverse effects of higher oil prices and appreciation of the yen, while tax revenue grew at a slower rate because of the slower growth of the Japanese economy. In the late 1970s, the MOF initiated efforts to reduce the deficit. By the late 1980s, it had almost achieved the goal of a balanced central government deficit.[7] The collapse of the Japanese economy and nonperforming loan problems quickly returned the general budget to deficit status. The deficit and outstanding government debt increased significantly over the decade and into the first few years of the new century. The government conducted a series of fiscal stimulus packages during this period that had little positive impact on the economy and wasted valuable resources in the process. The spending programs were influenced by political considerations as the 1994 electoral reform and party realignment generated much uncertainty about how politicians would win reelection under the new electoral system and how political parties would win control of government. The shift to fiscal austerity in 1997 by the Hashimoto administration was a major policy mistake that led to a sharp fall in economic activity.

The net result of the large deficits was, at best, neutral and more likely negative in the 1990s. Deficit spending is subject to crowding out effects on private spending even in the most activist formulation of the Keynesian model. It is likely crowding out effects occurred in the 1990s as the Japanese public understood that taxes would be raised. Aside from any crowding out effects the deficits supported unproductive sectors and delayed meaningful structural change. Deficit spending was not likely to contribute to the overall economy because much of it was implemented to support nonproductive sectors of the economy

---

[7] Cargill and Hutchison (1997) discuss the process of deficit reduction in the 1970s and 1980s.

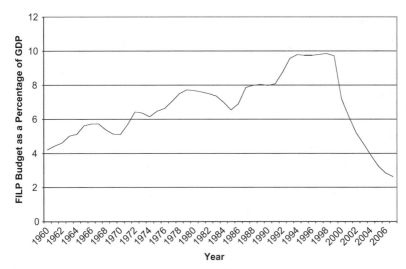

Figure 6.1. FILP Budget as a Percentage of GDP, 1960 to 2007. *Source:* GDP data from Figure 1.2 and FILP budget data from Figure 9.2.

by extensive loan guarantees and "pork barrel" infrastructure projects at the local level.

The FILP budget increased as a percentage of nominal GDP throughout the 1990s as government banks increased loans to the business and household sectors (Figure 6.1). Corporations and other businesses increased their dependence on funds from public financial institutions as private banks reduced their lending. Much of these funds were being allocated to weak sectors of the economy as part of the mutual support system. Ultimately, this delayed resolution of firms that had little chance of becoming profitable. As a reflection of the expanding FILP budget, postal deposits increased and were becoming an increasingly important financial asset for the household sector (Figure 6.2).

The relative increase in the importance of postal deposits in the 1990s reflected growing concern by the public about the safety of private banks, especially smaller banks. In fact, the Ministry of Posts and Telecommunications, then regulatory authority for the PSS, actually used the post offices to inform individuals that postal deposits were much safer than private bank deposits during this period of uncertainty. As a result, private depository institutions lost funds to the PSS, which in turn exacerbated the problem. Post offices were informed

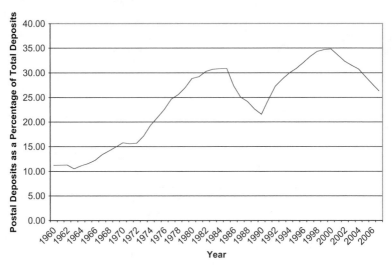

Figure 6.2. Postal Savings as Percentage of Total Deposits, 1960 to 2007. *Source:* Postal deposits, 1960 to 1999 (Cargill and Yoshino, 2003); postal deposits, 2000 to 2007, Bank of Japan Website, Money Stock, http://www.boj.or.jp/en/theme/research/ stat/money/ms/index.htm; bank deposits, 1960 to 1974 (Cargill and Yoshino, 2003); bank deposits, 1975 to 2003, Ministry of Internal Affairs and Communications, Historical Statistics of Japan, Finance and Insurance, http://www.stat.go.jp/english/data/ chouki/14.htm; and, bank deposits, 2004 to 2007, Bank of Japan Website, Assets and Liabilities of Domestically Licensed Banks, http://www.boj.or.jp/en/theme/ research/stat/asli_fi/index.htm.

in 1993 by the government to cease using the banking problems to encourage postal deposit growth, but the practice continued in a more subtle manner.[8]

Not only did the disintermediation of funds from bank deposits to postal deposits weaken the financial condition of the private banks, but the increased flow of funds into the PSS permitted the government to allocate a large amount of resources to client industries, many of which were unproductive.

This was part of a more general problem presented by the PSS. The implicit guarantee of private bank deposits by the government in the first half of the 1990s appeared less firm than it had in the past. The DIC had never been an important part of the deposit guarantee system in Japan and, in any event, the DIC was insolvent by late

---

.[8]   The disintermediation of bank deposits to postal deposits in Japan is discussed in Kuwayama (2000), Okina (2000), and Cargill and Yoshino (2003). See O'Hara Easley (1979) for a similar episode in the United States during the 1930s.

1994. Thus, the public came to view postal deposits as safer because they represented direct government debt rather than claims offered by private institutions. Even after the MOF issued the complete deposit guarantee in late 1995, postal deposits were increasingly viewed as safer than private bank deposits. In addition, postal deposits paid a higher effective interest rate. The existence of postal deposits thus complicated the problems of the private banks, as they increasingly had to compete with public institutions.

7

The Transition of Political Institutions in the 1990s and the New Century

Introduction

Society is in a constant state of change even though change may be too subtle or gradual to notice. Japanese politics under the LDP's one-party dominance was changing in a similar manner – change was present but subtle. The political regime during the postwar period looked stable, for the most part: The same party ruled the government for almost four decades. The interest-based competitive and cooperative relationships among politicians, bureaucrats, and socioeconomic interests dominated the policy-making process on issues vital to their interests. Politicians engaged in the same old distributive politics. Despite repeated calls for the reduction of corruption and money politics, ruling LDP politicians went about their usual business, and little changed in the way of money politics and pork barrel politics. Most of the time, the interests of citizens and consumers were given secondary attention by policy makers, unless they threatened the LDP's electoral prospects. And many politicians implicated in corruption scandals kept getting reelected to the Diet, and the LDP continued to be the party in power.

Yet, under this apparent tranquility, there were also changes. The LDP's electoral strength lay more in rural than urban areas. But the party's electoral support experienced long-term decline, partly as a result of the movement of Japanese people from rural to urban areas during the high growth period and because of the decline of the agricultural population that had supported the LDP. The LDP's other electoral bases – such as the distribution, construction, and transportation sectors – also became relatively stagnant industries and the sources of economic inefficiencies.[1] The economic costs of the LDP's policy support for those client industries became large. The electoral rationale for protecting those industries with stagnant or declining labor populations – as opposed to supporting new industries with growing labor populations – also became thin. The LDP was not the only party facing long-term decline in electoral support. The opposition parties experienced similar decline. The LDP (and the opposition parties) needed to cultivate and mobilize votes among so far unexplored socioeconomic groups and/or broaden their range of electoral bases. In the 1990s, particularly, the percentage of voters who did not support any existing party increased dramatically. Those non-party-identifiers now represent about 50 percent of the voting population.

The stable political regime began experiencing large-scale changes at the start of the 1990s. The end of the 1980s also showed some signs of change, with the revelation of the Recruit scandal, Prime Minister Noboru Takeshita's resignation as a result of his involvement in the corruption scandal, the LDP's loss of the majority in the upper house in 1989 for the first time in its history, and electoral reform becoming a policy issue.[2] At that moment, however, the political situation could have gone in any direction – back to normalcy and stability or to change – depending on a variety of factors. As it turned out, electoral reform became one of the catalysts of the political change that Japan was to undergo in the 1990s.

This chapter first reviews the political changes of the 1990s. It then explains further changes induced by both electoral reform and associated changes and induced by idiosyncratic Prime Minister Koizumi (2001–2006). These changes in Japan's political regime are important, because they help explain the large swing in Japan's budget policy between the 1990s and 2000s from an expansionary fiscal policy to fiscal austerity. They also help explain various liberalization and deregulation market reforms introduced in the 2000s. Reforms

---

[1] Political changes in Japan were, thus, caused partly by changes in the domestic and international economy, in the sense that economic changes altered the economic and political power of the traditional industries, which, in turn, induced changes in politics (Gourevitch, 1986).

[2] Recruit was a bribery scandal involving insider trading and many prominent politicians. The chairman of Recruit, a publishing and telecommunications firm, offered shares in a Recruit subsidiary shortly before going public to favored individuals including politicians. Even though the scandal crossed party lines, the LDP was especially hurt.

shifted the Japanese economy toward a more U.S.-style market economy, although this was in the Japanese context and was not nearly as extensive as that of the U.S. economy.

Political Corruption and Call for Political Reform

The origin of the political change goes back to the late 1980s. A series of political corruption scandals emerged, starting in 1988 (Recruit, Kyowa, and Sagawa scandals). Japanese politics under LDP rule had been replete with money politics and corruption scandals. But it was different this time, as the Recruit scandal involved many LDP leaders – including former and current prime ministers, finance minister, and chief cabinet secretary – as well as the highest-ranking bureaucrats and even the chairpersons of the opposition Democratic Socialist Party (DSP) and the Clean Government Party (CGP). The magnitude of the corruption case overwhelmed the Japanese public's traditional tolerance of money politics and corruption involving the exchange of political favors and money. It ignited public anger against politicians and exacerbated public distrust in the accountability, efficacy, and legitimacy of the government. The public and media demanded "political reform" to reduce or eliminate money politics and corruption. The LDP and opposition parties felt that they had to carry out "some reform" to soothe public demands and avoid electoral retribution.

Some LDP politicians (as well as academics) attributed money politics and corruption to Japan's electoral system – the MMD system. The public did not particularly demand electoral reform (Sakamoto, 1999b). But pro-reform LDP politicians from this point on tried to replace the MMD with an SMD system. Electoral reform was eventually enacted in 1994 and became a trigger to political changes that were soon to follow, including large-scale party realignment and the control of government by coalition governments. In the past, the LDP was almost always able to form single-party majority governments without coalition partners.

Pro-reform politicians and observers attributed money politics and corruption to Japan's MMD system with the single nontransferable vote (SNTV), claiming that it entailed candidate-centered elections, large campaign spending, and particularistic pork barrel politics. Under this system, two to six representatives were elected from a district, and candidates of the same party (mostly the ruling LDP) competed with each other in the same districts. Their need to run successful campaigns against party colleagues (as well as candidates of opposition parties) encouraged constituency services and large campaign spending to manage their personal vote-mobilization machines (Hirose, 1989; Ishikawa and Hirose, 1989). Competition based on policy issues was an ineffective strategy for those who stood on the same party platforms where party discipline was strong.

The LDP lost the majority in the 1989 upper house election for the first time in its history. The loss was a result of the Recruit scandal as well as liberalization of beef and oranges imports, which alienated the party's traditional electoral base (farmers), and the new consumption tax legislated by the LDP. It is important to note this, because the LDP has not regained a majority in the upper house since 1989, which in turn has required the LDP to form coalition governments with another party or two to date.[3]

The LDP's Split and Fall from Power, Electoral Reform, and Party Realignment

In 1993, power struggle within the LDP and policy conflict over electoral reform led to the passage of a nonconfidence motion against Prime Minister Kiichi Miyazawa, when pro-reform LDP politicians voted for the motion submitted by opposition parties. The prime minister dissolved the lower house, and 54 pro-reform LDP politicians left the party and formed two new conservative parties (Renewal Party and New Party Harbinger). In the lower house election, the LDP could not obtain a majority and lost the control of government for the first time in its history, when eight non-LDP parties agreed to form a coalition majority government. The coalition parties and LDP passed electoral reform in 1994 replacing the current MMD with a mixed SMD-PR (Proportional Representative) system.[4]

---

[3] The LDP is currently in a coalition government with the CGP, because it does not control the majority in the upper house, although it has a large majority in the lower house. The LDP's coalition government lost the majority in the July 2007 upper house election. As a result, the LDP lost the status as the largest party in the house, while the Democratic Party of Japan (DPJ) became the largest party in the upper house.

[4] Sakamoto (1999a) provides a detailed description of the political process during the period.

The electoral system exerts significant influence on the behavior of politicians and political parties. An SMD system tends to create a two-party system, which in turn results in single-party majority governments because an SMD system marginalizes small parties. Small parties have difficulty winning a percentage of votes large enough to win plurality and either are eliminated over time or merge with other parties to achieve size. A PR system tends to produce a multiparty system and consequently multiparty coalition governments or minority governments, as it makes it possible for small parties to survive electoral competition. Politicians and parties have different incentives under different electoral systems. Change in the electoral system induces change in politicians' incentive structure and, hence, behavior.

Japan's new mixed system is SMD-dominant and is advantageous for large major parties for two reasons. First, there are more SMD seats (300) than PR seats (180). Second, although the PR portion of the system makes it possible for small parties to gain representation, small parties tend to get marginalized because they are not large enough to win SMD seats and have to rely on PR candidates to mobilize votes, whereas, for large parties, vote mobilization by SMD candidates mobilizes votes for their parties in PR elections also.[5]

The change in the incentive structure as a result of electoral reform induced large-scale party realignment in Japan. After 1993, politicians changed party affiliation, and political parties repeatedly broke up and merged, as politicians tried to ensure their reelection and to be in the party that they expected or hoped would gain control of government. The alignment process is not over as of late 2007. Figure 7.1 illustrates the movements of political parties. The LDP came back to power in 1994 in a coalition with the Social Democratic Party (SDP) and Harbinger. Since 1993, Japan has been ruled by coalition governments by the LDP and other parties most of the time. As a result, politicians consumed much of their energy and resources in their electoral and power concerns, and Japanese political parties paid less than full attention to the pressing economic and financial problems during the 1990s. This lack of attention contributed to Japan's economic and financial distress in the 1990s.

---

[5] Small parties running candidates only in PR districts suffer from a collective action problem, whereas large parties running candidates in both SMD and PR districts do so only to a lesser extent.

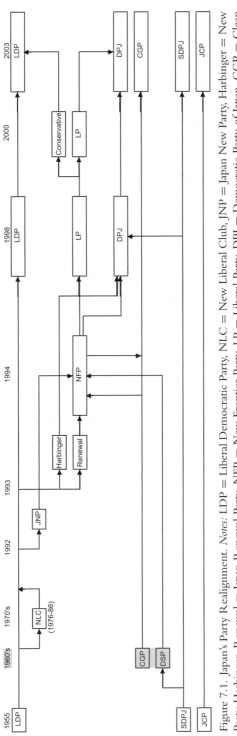

Figure 7.1. Japan's Party Realignment. *Notes:* LDP = Liberal Democratic Party, NLC = New Liberal Club, JNP = Japan New Party, Harbinger = New Party Harbinger, Renewal = Japan Renewal Party, NFP = New Frontier Party, LP = Liberal Party, DPJ = Democratic Party of Japan, CGP = Clean Government Party (*Komeito*), SDPJ = Social Democratic Party of Japan (formerly, Japan Socialist Party [JSP]), DSP = Democratic Socialist Party, JCP = Japanese Communist Party.

The small parties that currently exist (SDP, CGP, and JCP [Japanese Communist Party]) will continue to exist on a small scale, assuming that they do not merge with other parties because the presence of PR seats in the electoral system enables them to survive elections. Japan's party system is thus likely to have two major parties (the LDP and DP[6]) and a few smaller parties under the current electoral system. Japan is also likely to be governed by coalition governments more often than not, because it is not easy for the governing party or parties to win majority control in both the lower and upper houses at the same time.[7] It has been over a decade since electoral reform and, as of 2007, Japan's party system is moving toward a relatively stable state.[8]

Economic and Financial Distress and Government Inaction

Japan's policy-making system had difficulty dealing with the pressing economic and financial problems of the 1990s. The first half of the 1990s witnessed significant economic and financial distress and a growing nonperforming loan problem in the banking system that was attracting international concern. Bureaucrats and politicians continued their traditional approach of responding to economic problems with denial and understatement, and when actual policy action could no longer be avoided, policies were based on forgiveness and forbearance.

The tendency toward inaction was magnified by the political parties' need to adjust to the new political environment. Frequent coalition governments have been a necessity, because the LDP or any other party did not have majority control in the Diet most of the time during this period, and never in the upper house. Coalition governments were possible also partly because after the end of the Cold War and the collapse of communist regimes and the rise of neoliberal thinking in economic policy, leftist and centrist parties' economic policy positions moved rightward in Japan, as in many other industrial democracies.

[6] DP member politicians came from the LDP, DSP, and SDP.
[7] Bills need to be passed by both houses of parliament.
[8] The SDP and JCP have difficulty merging with the DP (or the LDP) because of their policy distance. The CGP also has difficulty joining any party, because it is a party supported by a denomination of Buddhism called *Soka Gakkai* and other parties have reservations about being associated with a strongly religious party. This is why Japan's system may not move to a pure two-party system.

As a result, the policy distances between leftist and rightist political parties became smaller. This new political environment, for example, led to the prime ministership by the SDP leader, Tomiichi Murayama, as head of the LDP-SDP-Harbinger coalition government from 1994 to 1996.

Party realignment of this magnitude meant that there was a large degree of uncertainty and instability that could potentially affect the policy-making capabilities of government. Such was the case, to a certain extent, in Japan. Japan faced intense economic and financial distress in the 1990s and into the first years of the new century. The uncertainty and instability of the new electoral system negatively affected the ability of the successive governments led by the LDP and others to effectively respond to the economic shocks. As a result, less attention was devoted to policy innovations needed for economic recovery and, thus, it was easier to rely on conventional and familiar policies rooted in the old Japan. The LDP also suffered intraparty power conflict, as it always had, and it further reduced the ability of the government to conduct effective and coherent economic policy. Karube and Nishino (1999), for example, show that during the height of the 1997 economic crisis, the Hashimoto administration's policy making was significantly hampered by his own LDP's intraparty conflict and the lack of cooperation from the party. The worsening economic and financial distress intensified the intraparty power conflicts, which in turn reduced further the ability of the government to conduct effective and coherent economic policy.

Policy malaise also was caused by the highly institutionalized distributive politics of the LDP, its reliance on traditional Keynesian spending, and the strong incentive to ensure continuity and the status quo established under the LDP's one-party rule since 1955. These factors made it difficult for the Japanese government to conceive policy innovations to respond to the economic crises effectively. Change came after Koizumi became prime minister in 2001, but even he was unable to execute large-scale policy changes until his last year of tenure, because of the strong influence of antireformers in the LDP and their alliance with interest groups and the bureaucracy. It was really only in his last year, after he received an overwhelmingly clear popular mandate in the 2005 lower house election, that he was able to carry out significant economic reforms.

There were signs in 1996 that the economy was improving. A number of reforms had been enacted to close the *jusen* industry, establish a deposit insurance system, and provide for more meaningful intervention to resolve troubled financial institutions. Nonetheless, serious structural problems remained. Some argue that the Big Bang announcement of November 1996 was a coherent policy to deal with these problems. However, closer analysis of the announcement suggests that the program did little, if anything, to correct the flaws in the Japanese economy, especially in the financial system (Cargill, Hutchison, and Ito, 1998).

Prime Minister Hashimoto resigned in 1998, following his LDP's defeat in the upper house election. This loss was partly a result of growing public dissatisfaction with the government's economic mismanagement in light of the economic and financial collapse starting in the last quarter of 1997 and continuing in 1998. The public had already expressed its dissatisfaction with the government's handling of the *jusen* industry in 1995, when politicians were surprised at the negative public reaction when only about 5 percent of the ¥14 trillion bailout was to be financed with public funds. In March 1998, the government made the first distribution of public funds to twenty-one troubled banks without any due diligence and without any effort to determine the probability of success. The ¥1.8 trillion capital injection was essentially divided into twenty-one equal parts and distributed as such – this was the old Japanese approach to dealing with a problem. This distribution of funds was an economic disaster. In fact, two recipients of funding – the Long Term Credit Bank and the Nippon Credit Bank – were nationalized in late 1998. The March 1998 distribution of public money to troubled banks, combined with the general dissatisfaction of the public with the government's handing of the growing economic and financial distress, cost the LDP in the upper house elections and forced the resignation of Hashimoto.

During the 1990s, Japanese politics was in flux, because of all the changes and uncertainties introduced to the policy-making world that had been governed by a stable set of highly institutionalized procedures and norms under LDP rule. In addition, the severity of the economic problems and confusion added to the political uncertainties. Politicians and political parties almost blindly tried to solve the economic problems with the familiar policy tools and approaches that they had always used, while trying to ensure their electoral survival and control of government.

Despite this less than positive assessment of the Japanese government's inability to deal with the growing economic and financial distress and to depart from the policy responses embedded in the old regime in the 1990s, it would be an error to conclude an absence of any meaningful progress. Some significant changes were made in the organization of government and political institutions in the 1990s and set the stage for a new political regime and economic policy making in the first decade of the new century. Koizumi, who would lead the government for five years starting in 2001, was able to take advantage of the benefits of the institutional changes to enhance prime ministerial policy-making capabilities and confront the elements of the old regime. Before turning attention to Koizumi's reforms, however, it is useful to review the important changes in Japan's political institutions that took place in the 1990s. These are electoral reform, administrative reform, and central bank redesign.

Electoral Reform and Implications for Prime Minister Leadership

Electoral reform not only induced party realignment and governance by coalition governments as discussed earlier, but also helped create a policy-making environment in which a prime minister could take strong policy initiatives if conditions warranted. Compared to counterparts in other Western parliamentary democracies, the Japanese prime minister traditionally had weak policy-making power, because his power was constrained by his party and LDP factions, the bureaucracy, client industries and businesses, and the opposition parties. Japan's norm of consensual decision making made it possible for these other actors to have the power to block the prime minister's policy attempts. Power diffusion among these political actors and the consensual norm created multiple veto players in the policy-making system (Tsebelis, 2002).

The 1994 electoral reform introduced a system of government subsides to political parties, which served to reduce LDP factions' power and concentrated power more in the party leadership. Before the reform, the LDP's faction leaders had solid financial sources that they used to control their factions and their members. Finance was one of the sources of the power of the LDP factions, which had the informal power to select the prime minister or override an existing prime minister. The new system restricted campaign fund donations to individual legislators like faction leaders and, instead, created government subsidies to be distributed to political parties. This gradually shifted the financial source of power from faction leaders to party leadership, which, in the LDP's case, is headed by the party president – the prime minister. Thus, the reform served to reduce the power of LDP factions. This potential for power shift was not immediately recognized or utilized by the successive prime ministers in the 1990s, but Koizumi skillfully used it for the first time after he came to power in 2001. And it was one of the contributing factors for his successful postal privatization and other reforms.

By the start of the new century, policy positions and the attributes of party leaders became more important elements in Japanese politics. This resulted from both electoral reform and the conscious effort by politicians and political parties to increase the importance of policy issues in electoral and policy competition. Previously, policy issues played a marginal role in policy competition and elections among political parties for much of the postwar period. The selection of the LDP president, and thus the prime minister, for example, was determined largely by factional competition within the party that did not have much policy component. Policy competition among political parties was characterized more by negotiations, deal-making, concessions, compromise, and collusion, rather than by policy debate. In election campaigns, politicians and parties depended on networks of supporters' associations (*koenkai*) in which support for politicians was based more on personal relationships, exchange of favors, and distributive politics for vote mobilization. Policy debate was a relatively minor concern among politicians.

The importance of policy debate increased, however, at the start of the new century, as politicians and political parties began to consciously compete with each other based on policy platforms. Policy competition now plays an important role in electoral competition among political parties. It is also an important component even in the selection of the LDP president, which used to be governed by power and money competition among LDP factions; although the selection of party leaders for now is still largely determined by the consideration of which leader will win more votes in elections, rather than being based on policy platforms *per se*.

The importance of policy issues increased somewhat when Koizumi competed for the 2001 LDP presidential election with the proposal of postal privatization and a more aggressive policy to resolve Japan's economic problems. Policy issues increased importance more when the DP started election campaigns based on policy platforms and the LDP led by Koizumi followed suit. By the 2006 LDP presidential race, policy debate became routine, although the outcome was still largely determined by the public popularity of the candidates.

Governance on the basis of policy issues is one of the goals pro-reform politicians tried to achieve by electoral reform. They claimed that they could turn Japan's candidate-centered election campaigns into policy- and party-centered ones by introducing an SMD electoral system. An SMD system does not always induce party-centered campaigns, which can be seen by looking at U.S. campaigns with an SMD system and candidate-centered elections. Nonetheless, this was an important goal of the pro-reform politicians. Combined with their conscious effort to guide Japanese politics toward that goal, policy now plays a much more important role in Japan than previously. Of course, this is also, importantly, because Japan faced major policy issues at the turn of the century as compared to the past. Policy positions of party leaders and their attributes have begun to matter in electoral competition among political parties and the selection of the LDP president. This in turn has shifted more power into the hands of party leaders (to the extent that party leaders are still popular among the public and party legislators). The popularity of party leaders among the public is likely to be an important determinant of electoral results in national elections. This will give party leaders more power over party politicians, all other things being equal. But if they are unpopular or lose elections, parties will be quick to replace their party leaders.

The increased importance of policy discussion and public support for party leaders or the prime minister has made it possible for the prime minister to carry out loss-imposing policies in various sectors of the economy, as long as he enjoys public popularity. This in turn has weakened the iron triangle. Previously, the prime minister had great difficulty pursuing policies that imposed costs on the LDP's client industries and firms, because he would meet with opposition by those industries and the LDP politicians who drew money and votes from them and even by the bureaucratic ministries that wanted to protect industries under their jurisdiction. Because of power diffusion in the political system, the prime minister had difficulty overriding these veto players, each of whom had a certain level of power to block the prime minister's policy initiatives. This made it difficult for the prime minister to pursue policies supported by the general public but not by the LDP's client industries.

Increased importance of policy debate and of public support for the prime minister made it possible for him to pursue loss-imposing policies to a greater degree than previously, if he enjoyed great public support. Public support gave the prime minister a mandate to carry out policies opposed by the iron triangle. In this context, individual LDP politicians could not easily override the prime minister's policies as in the past, because a popular prime minister enhanced the party's electoral prospects and because recalcitrant politicians could damage their electoral prospects by obstructing policy initiatives by the popular prime minister.

Administrative Reform and Implications for Prime Minister Leadership

In the late 1990s, the LDP government carried out administrative reform, and this would have impact later on the power of the Japanese prime minister and the power relations among the executive branch, the governing party, and the bureaucracy. The reform was formulated during the Hashimoto administration and came into effect in 2001, just before Koizumi's election as prime minister. Thus, Koizumi had the benefit of the new policy making environment and, with public support, took as much advantage of the new institutional framework as possible to pursue his agenda.[9]

In short, administrative reform provided an institutional environment in which the prime minister could take strong policy initiatives and leadership vis-à-vis other actors such as the governing party and bureaucracy, if the prime minister would be willing to do so and was popular enough among the public to have a clear popular mandate. The reform strengthened the power of the prime minister vis-à-vis bureaucratic ministries and cabinet ministers in setting the policy agenda, taking strong policy initiatives, and leading the cabinet. It was

---

[9] There were also other reforms: establishment of the FSA; separation of the PSS from the MOF and establishment of a public corporation to manage the PSS; and reform of the BOJ. The redesign of the PSS is considered in the next chapter because it needs to be placed in the context of Japan's fiscal program. But it is important to emphasize that separating the PSS from the MOF (effective April 1, 2001) dramatically reduced the ability of the ministry to influence the allocation of postal deposits in the FILP budget. BOJ reform is considered in the next section of this chapter.

also intended to move budget-making power from the MOF to the prime minister's office.

Surprisingly, the prime minister did not have these powers in the previous Cabinet Law. Although many may wonder why, the prime minister's power over his cabinet members was not clearly specified in the earlier law, which became one of the factors constraining his power. In combination with Koizumi's conscious efforts to concentrate power in his executive branch to carry out his policy initiatives in the midst of policy opposition, the revision of the Cabinet Law helped change the power balance among the executive branch, the governing party, and the bureaucracy. As a result, the prime minister can now take strong policy initiatives, if he is willing to and has a clear popular mandate. Intention and public mandate are important qualifications because the new formal rules would not prevent the ruling party and bureaucracy from trying to override the prime minister if those actors saw that the prime minister did not have public support. When the prime minister is not buttressed by public support, he will still be vulnerable to pressures from the other political actors who had often served as veto players under the LDP's one-party rule. The reform also reduced the number of government ministries from twenty-two to twelve plus the Cabinet Office.

The Council on Economic and Fiscal Policy (CEFP) was established to lead and guide the Japanese government's economic policy and placed under the prime minister's office. These functions had previously been performed by government ministries, such as the MOF, Ministry of International Trade and Industry (MITI),[10] and the Economic Planning Agency. This reform was designed to move policy making power from government ministries to the prime minister. But the power of the CEFP is not automatic. Its power depends on the willingness and ability of the prime minister and other policy makers to utilize the CEFP as the main economic policy formulation and decision making body and on the political conditions that may or may not allow it to perform such a role.

Prime Minister Yoshiro Mori (April 2000 to April 2001) did not utilize the CEFP; as a result, it did not play any significant role. However, Koizumi tactically used the CEFP to push his economic policy

---

[10] In 2001, the MITI changed its name to the Ministry of Economy, Trade, and Industry (METI).

agenda. The CEFP consequently played a major role in overriding the policy opposition by the bureaucracy, LDP, and *zoku* politicians. The CEFP was one of the most important factors accounting for the successful implementation of many reforms during the Koizumi administration. The CEFP's role, however, declined toward the end of the Koizumi administration, as Koizumi's interest in using it to advance his policy agendas declined and some LDP politicians successfully shifted some power from the CEFP back to the LDP. The CEFP played a much more limited role under the Abe administration (2006–2007) and succeeding Fukuda administration (2007–). Thus, the CEFP still has the potential to play an important role in the economic policy-making process of the Japanese government, but its role is highly dependent on whether the prime minister is willing to utilize the CEFP and on other political conditions.

Prime Minister Koizumi took full advantage of the institutional changes and concentrated power in his executive branch to carry out his policy initiatives in the midst of opposition from the LDP, bureaucracy, and the various client industries and firms. In hindsight, this development was a result of Koizumi's political determination, skills, audacity, and his strong popular confidence levels. It is uncertain whether future prime ministers will be able or willing to exercise the same level of leadership against the LDP and the bureaucracy.

In 2006, Abe replaced Koizumi as the LDP president and Japanese prime minister. But Abe was unable to take strong leadership. At first, Abe enjoyed high public approval and, in fact, this was why the LDP elected him prime minister. He was in a good position to take strong leadership and pursue his policy initiatives. He had some success in his nationalistic agendas. Abe legislated the national referendum required for constitutional revision, revised the education basic law requiring the teaching of morals and patriotism in school, and promoted Japan's Defense Agency to a higher level of importance as the Ministry of Defense. This nationalistic agenda, however, failed to appeal to citizens who remained concerned about economic conditions, their economic insecurity and disparity, and Japan's malfunctioning social security system.

The LDP under Abe's leadership suffered a major loss in the July 2007 upper house election as a result of Abe's lack of political skills and leadership and because of multiple scandals surrounding his cabinet, which severely diminished public support for him. The public was especially outraged with the revelation that Japan's Social Security

Agency had amassed fifty million cases of unidentified social security contributions made by participants of the national pension system over the years as a result of its negligence. Abe resigned in September 2007, after one year in office without achieving much more than his nationalistic agendas, which was possible mostly because of his LDP's overwhelming two-thirds majority in the lower house achieved by the previous Koizumi administration in the 2005 lower house election. Thus, Abe's case is one in which the lack of political skills and experience limited his policy-making leadership.

Prime Minister Yasuo Fukuda assumed power October 2007. Fukuda has so far been much more conciliatory and accommodative to LDP politicians and bureaucrats than Koizumi. Fukuda is a consensus-seeking politician typical of old LDP leaders. As a result, he is very unlikely to push policies that would be opposed by the LDP and bureaucracy. Thus, despite the political institutional changes in Japan in the past decade, the kind of strong leadership exercised by Koizumi is contingent on the prime minister's individual attributes and political skills.

Central Bank Reform and Political Implications

The BOJ became more independent from party government influence in 1998. The pre-1998 BOJ was under the control of the MOF, and monetary policy was subject to influence by the MOF and the LDP government for macroeconomic or fiscal policy needs or for political needs. Despite the dependence of the BOJ on the government, the BOJ generally had a good price stability record through much of the postwar period, especially after 1973 when it was no longer required to use monetary policy to maintain the fixed exchange rate standard. Cargill, Hutchison, and Ito (1997) argue that, despite the lack of formal independence, the BOJ was more politically independent than indicated by the formal relationship between the BOJ and the government as specified in the BOJ Law.

Nonetheless, the BOJ conducted expansionary policy from time to time to accommodate the needs of the domestic economy, international policy coordination, and even domestic politics. The Japanese government used monetary policy to reduce current account deficits by suppressing aggregate demand and imports in the 1950s and 1960s (Ishi, 2000). During the late 1960s and early 1970s, the BOJ conducted a highly expansionary monetary policy to sustain double-digit GDP growth and to maintain the undervalued exchange rate fixed at ¥360 and later at ¥308 to the dollar. While the BOJ supported the objective of limiting yen appreciation because of the negative impact of the appreciation of the undervalued yen,[11] the BOJ became increasingly concerned about inflation. The BOJ was forced by Prime Minister Kakuei Tanaka to lower the discount rate despite clear signs of inflation and the BOJ's desire to tighten monetary policy. This monetary expansion first supported by the BOJ and then resisted by the BOJ led to "wild inflation" in the early 1970s (Cargill, Hutchison, and Ito, 1997).

Although the BOJ emerged from the "wild inflation" period of the 1970s with enhanced informal independence, monetary policy could still be influenced by the government according to the BOJ Law. In the second half of the 1980s, the BOJ pursued an expansionary policy at the government's direction as a result of policy coordination agreements by the G5 (Plaza Accord) and G7 (Louvre Accord) to support the dollar and limit yen appreciation. This expansionary policy accommodated asset price inflation and resulted in the bubble economy. Monetary policy during the 1980s became the default stabilization instrument of the government, because the LDP government and the MOF consistently pursued deficit reduction throughout the decade and did not want to use fiscal policy for countercyclical economic stimulus (Ishi, 2000).

These accommodations by the BOJ of party governments' needs were possible, because the BOJ was not formally independent from the government. At the same time, it would be a mistake to conclude that the BOJ was at the edge of inflationary monetary policy for two reasons. First, the Japanese government was in general averse to inflation since the 1970s and generally did not interfere with BOJ policy if it appeared that doing so would generate inflation. Second, the BOJ had emerged from the "wild inflation" period in the early 1970s with enhanced informal independence and made price stability its primary goal in 1975.

The BOJ in 1998 became more independent from politicians in general and the MOF in particular. Although politicians and the MOF were able to influence BOJ monetary policy in the past, they

---

[11] The undervalued yen was an important component of Japan's effort to support the export sector.

have had less success since 1998. There have been instances in which politicians and party governments (including cabinet ministers and LDP leaders) have attempted to influence BOJ policy to be more stimulative; however, the BOJ has been able to resist those efforts to a greater extent than previously because of its newly gained independence (Fujii, 2004).

The BOJ's new independence, however, may not be as solid as it appears for two reasons. First, the BOJ in late 2002 showed that it was susceptible to political pressure when it shifted to a more aggressive monetary policy partly as a result of political criticism that its past policy was insufficient to reverse the deflation process. In fact, it was made known by policy makers that if the BOJ did not adopt a more aggressive policy against deflation, the newfound independence might be modified by imposing an explicit inflation target on the BOJ. Second, even after the BOJ shifted to a tighter monetary policy – what the BOJ calls the "normalization" monetary policy – by ending the QEP and ZIRP in 2006, the BOJ was reluctant to raise interest rates because of actual and potential political backlash. This does not imply the BOJ is not concerned that higher interests might bring back deflation, but only to indicate the decision making process of the BOJ appears to incorporate a political component despite its new found formal independence. The BOJ has been careful not to confront politicians with a definite contractionary monetary policy, as politicians have criticized BOJ policy in the past for not being sufficiently expansionary to end deflation.

The long-term impact of central bank reform on the Japanese economy is not clear at the time of this writing. The BOJ will likely come under greater political pressure in the future, particularly because of recent changes in the political system – more policy-based party competition and increased possibility for alternation of parties in power. Political parties now fiercely compete with each other with different economic policies. Potentially, they can demand different monetary policies of the BOJ. In fact, even the LDP alone has an internal division on fiscal and monetary policy, jockeying for their preferred policies, respectively. Multiple rejections in early 2008 of nominees for the position of BOJ governor and deputy governors by the Diet demonstrated the possibility that the BOJ's monetary policy may be subjected to political influence even after the central bank reform of 1998. The LDP government nominated candidates for the governor and deputy governor, but the nominees were rejected multiple times by the opposition parties that controlled the upper house (appointment requires approval by both houses of the Diet).[12]

Thus, the BOJ's future monetary policy may be influenced by which political parties and politicians gain the upper hand in economic policy making, those supporting the BOJ's policy position or those opposing it. This factor may make monetary policy difficult for the BOJ. Formal independence and transparency provide the BOJ with better ability to resist these pressures than previously and politicians may found themselves frustrated more than previously in attempting to influence monetary policy; however, the BOJ has yet to demonstrate an ability to pursue price stability and maintain public confidence, judged by the over-a-decade-long deflation.

The Policy-Making Process during the Koizumi Administration

Most of the political changes discussed to this point are those induced by changes in formal institutions or rules, and were already in place by the time Koizumi came to power in 2001. During his administration, however, Koizumi also significantly changed Japan's policy-making process by changing the way informal rules of policy making were exercised. Most of the changes in informal rules were possible because of idiosyncratic attributes of Koizumi and, thus, there is no guarantee that his successors will be able to manage policy making in the same manner. But some of the changes made by Koizumi will remain in place because they set a precedent for the potential leadership role that the prime minister can achieve.

It is useful to specify Koizumi's idiosyncratic attributes because they played a role in his administration. Koizumi was not afraid of alienating the LDP and the iron triangle of the LDP, bureaucracy, and client industry. Nor was he afraid of leaving the LDP or being expelled by the LDP. If anything, the more he confronted the LDP, the higher his public approval became. Usually, political actors can enforce informal rules and practices and obtain compliance among themselves, because

---

[12] The opposition parties' rejections of the nominees were not over monetary policy or the nominees' policy positions. The rejections resulted from a political conflict between the LDP and the opposition DP and from the DP's preference not to appoint former MOF officials to the governorship.

they calculate that the negative consequences of norm violation are costly.

Koizumi was not much influenced by these potential negative consequences and felt much freer to break the rules in the LDP, because he did not have a great stake in the LDP. He had never belonged to a mainstream faction in the LDP before his Mori faction became large after his prime ministership. He was not even a leader of a faction, although he was a nominal leader of the Mori faction before he was elected LDP president. If anything, he was very hostile to all mainstream factions (such as the former Takeshita faction) that had always put the minority factions at a disadvantage. A cost of rule violation for a prime minister would have been a loss of support from his LDP and a loss of power and influence. Koizumi would not have minded leaving or destroying the old LDP. In fact, he planned to leave the LDP and pursue postal privatization as a non-LDP prime minister, if he lost power in the LDP (Shimizu, 2005). Thus, Koizumi had little to lose by breaking LDP rules and norms and antagonizing the LDP. Not many LDP politicians would be willing to alienate the party. As a result, they could not have broken LDP norms to the same degree as Koizumi.

The changes reviewed here are those Koizumi made in the way informal norms, rules, and practices of the LDP government were exercised in the LDP or between the LDP and executive branch led by the prime minister. These are not changes in formal institutions. Because of the long period of LDP dominance for much of the postwar period, changes in the norms and practices within the LDP significantly affected the way government policy was formulated. Koizumi was able to achieve the changes in informal practices because his goals for change were buttressed by the changes in the formal institutions discussed earlier, which were made to enhance the power of the prime minister. Unconventional, reform-minded Koizumi came to power at an opportune time. Put differently, Koizumi's resolute reform intentions and forceful political style alone might not have enabled him to successfully enact economic reforms, if it had not been for the change in formal institutions. Nor would the changes in formal institutions alone have made possible the economic reforms in the absence of the unconventional political leader.

Previously, the obstacles to the Japanese prime minister's policy initiatives were the LDP's powerful intraparty factions that controlled the selection of the prime minister (LDP president) to varying degrees, the LDP's *zoku* politicians who formed alliances with client industries and bureaucratic ministries and exercised policy influence in various policy areas, and the bureaucracy that had oligopolistic power in policy formulation and protected the industries under their jurisdiction. The Japanese prime minister needed to gain the support of these powerful veto players in order to advance policies that impinged on their vested interests. When the prime minister's policy was opposed by any of these actors, he had to either abandon the policy or engage in consensus building with the policy opposition. When persuading the opposition, he was usually forced to make serious concessions and compromises to the opposition, which often watered down the parts of the policy that originally invoked opposition.

Koizumi gradually shifted power from these veto players to the executive branch by emasculating them. He accomplished this by breaking some informal practices and customs that had been institutionalized and practiced inside the LDP and that had given power to the veto players.

First, Koizumi weakened the power of the LDP's factions by violating the practice of the factions' control over the selection of cabinet ministers and by making the post assignments himself. In the past, LDP factions (faction leaders) nominated cabinet minister candidates, and prime ministers unconditionally accepted the lists submitted by the factions. Their power over post assignments had long been a source of their power, because LDP politicians (and the prime minister) had to belong to and support factions in order to obtain a cabinet seat. The factions had some control over the prime minister, not only because they had influence on prime minister selection to begin with, but also because cabinet decision had to be made by unanimity and the factions controlled the cabinet ministers – that is, theoretically and legally, cabinet ministers controlled by LDP factions potentially could veto the prime minister's policy. The exercise of a veto by cabinet ministers did not happen for the most part, because the prime minister avoided such a situation by heeding the policy preferences of LDP factions. This inevitably constrained the Japanese prime minister's policy-making power.

Koizumi weakened the power of the LDP's factions by making the ministerial assignments himself. In order to eliminate policy interference by LDP factions, Koizumi conducted cabinet minister selection on his own and completely disregarded the LDP factions' power over those assignments. Koizumi appointed only those politicians who supported his policies and were not likely to oppose him. In fact, when he tried to dissolve the lower house in 2005 over his postal privatization, one cabinet minister did not agree to the lower house dissolution. House dissolution requires a unanimous decision of the cabinet. Koizumi secured unanimous cabinet support by firing that minister. Thus, Koizumi successfully reduced the LDP factions' influence and increased his own power in his administration's policy making. Put differently, Koizumi increased his policy-making power by creating a situation in which supporting LDP factions would not get LDP politicians cabinet seats but supporting the prime minister's policy would.

Second, toward the end of his tenure, Koizumi took control over candidate nominations in the 2005 lower house election from the LDP factions. Koizumi selected candidates himself along with the LDP leadership that remained loyal to him. Party nomination in elections is important to LDP candidates, because of the value that the LDP had for vote mobilization, fund-raising, and name recognition. Before Koizumi, the LDP factions controlled candidate nomination. But when he dissolved the lower house to hold an election, Koizumi refused to give any party nomination to the LDP politicians who had voted against his postal privatization bill. Those LDP politicians were still free to run in their districts as independents but not as LDP politicians. In addition, in those districts, Koizumi nominated opposing LDP candidates to penalize and defeat those unnominated LDP members. In most of those cases, he handpicked a candidate who had name recognition or appeal. Many of Koizumi's choices won seats and defeated the LDP incumbents who had opposed Koizumi. This strategy was much more confrontational than those used previously in the LDP. By adopting this strategy, Koizumi showed LDP members that the prime minister could damage the careers of dissenting politicians, made it difficult for them to oppose him, and, as a result, concentrated power in the prime minister's office.

Third, Koizumi undermined the power sources of *zoku* politicians and the LDP as a whole by bypassing them in making the policy they opposed. Previously, there existed a firmly institutionalized informal rule for the government to send policy proposals and bills to the LDP for review and approval before submitting them to the cabinet and the Diet. Proposals would be subjected to review and approval in the LDP's Policy Affairs Research Council (PARC) and Executive Council. This procedural norm gave the LDP and its *zoku* politicians (who had policy influence and expertise) the power to reject any proposal they opposed or proposals opposed by their client industries and firms. Once rejected by the LDP, proposals would be either abandoned or revised. In the case of revision, the prime minister would be expected to engage in extensive consensus building efforts and make concessions, resulting in a much different proposal than the one originally submitted. This gatekeeping power gave the LDP and *zoku* politicians considerable power and weakened the power of the prime minister.

Prior to the landslide victory in the 2005 lower house election, Koizumi was subject to these constraints by the existing and accepted policy-making norms of party review and of consensus building. Many of his policy initiatives, as a result, were watered down and emasculated by the LDP and *zoku* politicians (e.g., the privatization of the PSS and Highway Public Corporation). Koizumi was willing to confront opposition by the LDP and *zoku* politicians before the 2005 election; however, the vote of confidence given to Koizumi by the public in the election dramatically increased his ability to bypass the informal rules. Knowing his willingness to bypass or override LDP opposition and the public support Koizumi enjoyed, the party and *zoku* politicians needed to consider the possibility that he might actually do so, and that it might be better for them to accept the general direction of his policies and win particular policy concessions, instead of trying to block the policies as a whole. This made it possible for Koizumi to achieve the policy changes that would have previously been almost impossible, no matter how many concessions to the opposition offered by Koizumi.

Koizumi was extremely hostile to *zoku* politicians and bureaucratic ministries that had strong ties with special interests. In essence, Koizumi was hostile to all three actors that formed the iron triangle in Japanese policy making. He was determined to override their opposition to his reforms. In order to bypass the attempts by the LDP and *zoku* politicians to block his policies, Koizumi made extensive use of the CEFP and set the CEFP at the center of policy making and executed policy changes without the interference of the LDP and *zoku* politicians. He appointed economists and business leaders to the CEFP who were not part of the iron triangle. He made the proceedings of the CEFP meetings public so as to make it difficult for *zoku* politicians, special interests, and bureaucrats to openly push for the protection of special interests and block legitimate reform in the public eyes. Koizumi thus skillfully controlled the power of *zoku* politicians, client industries, and bureaucrats. Toward the end of his administration, he further weakened the power of *zoku* politicians by imposing a term limit for the chairs of the PARC committees to reduce their influence.

The most important legacy made by his administration is that Koizumi set a precedent. Koizumi showed that a Japanese prime minister could resolutely purse his policies and override opposition by conventionally invincible *zoku* politicians and bureaucrats.

8

Political Economy of Japan's Fiscal Program

Introduction

Japan's fiscal program has undergone significant change in the late 1990s and the first years of the new century. The fiscal program consists of the general budget for the central and local governments based on the familiar revenue-spending framework and the FILP based on a flow-of-funds framework. The general budget stipulates government revenues from various taxes, fees, and bonds and how the revenues are allocated to various components of government spending. The FILP is referred to as Japan's "second" budget, because of its size and importance. Both the general budget and the FILP budget are drafted by the government and approved by the Diet. The FILP funds came primarily from postal savings deposits, postal life insurance, and national pension contributions. The FILP budget allocated funds to a system of government banks, enterprises, corporations, and local governments, which were referred to collectively as FILP agencies. Starting in 2001, FILP funding sources changed and a major redesign of FILP and the PSS occurred.

There were many catalysts for the change in Japan's fiscal program, but one of the more important was the growing recognition that Japan's conventional fiscal program was the source of economic inefficiencies and prevented Japan from adjusting to the new reality of the globalized international economy, which put competitive and efficiency pressures on most industrial nations. The general budget often was used as an instrument of stabilization policy in the context of Keynesian demand management. The governing LDP used various expenditure components of the budget to maintain and advance their electoral power via distributive spending on legitimate public works as well as on low-productivity or declining sectors of the economy, which were the party's electoral bases. The FILP budget likewise was used in the same manner by the government – as an instrument of stabilization and vote mobilization. The LDP government's proclivity for the use of fiscal policy as an electoral tool, however, was partly checked by the fiscally conservative MOF.

Japan's fiscal program accumulated economic inefficiencies over decades and contributed to Japan's stagnation in the 1990s and the first few years of the new century. The failures of the fiscal program and its growing incompatibility with the new economic environment generated a series of reforms starting in the late 1990s that have resulted in significant redesign. This chapter reviews Japan's fiscal program through the 1990s, including the institutional redesign of the fiscal program starting in the late 1990s, whereas the next chapter focuses on Koizumi's fiscal consolidation and market reforms during the period from 2001 to 2006. The first section of this chapter discusses the budget in the 1990s in general terms; the second section provides a more detailed development of the budget and budget policy objectives bifurcated into two periods: before the 1990s and during the 1990s; and the third section discusses the FILP budget over the same two periods.

Fiscal Conservatism out the Window in the 1990s, Except in 1997

Japan accumulated a massive level of government gross debt in the 1990s for two reasons. First, the growing debt was partly a result of the multiple recessions lasting for almost a decade and a half. During economic downturns, fiscal deficits increase as social security spending (e.g., unemployment benefits) increase and tax revenues from individual and corporate income taxes decline. This is the part of deficit that would increase even in the absence of any policy action.

Second, Japan's debt accumulation was also a result of the existing political-economic regime. The particular nature of the regime contributed to government debt by giving the government a propensity to continuously rely on Keynesian deficit spending that turned out to be marginally effective in resolving the economic distress and promoting

growth in the 1990s. The ineffective economic policy helped prolong the recessions, amplifying the automatic stabilizers and further
increasing deficits and debt, as a result.

Japanese policy makers viewed the general budget as a countercyclical stabilization instrument and thus fiscal stimulus as an obvious
response to the economic distress. Keynesian spending increases made
sense in the context of the LDP's propensity to use the fiscal program for distributive economic policy. The fiscally conservative MOF
would have normally opposed deficit spending for economic stimulus.
But such fiscal conservatism in normal times was overshadowed by the
magnitude of the economic recessions, the concern by the LDP to
reverse the economic decline, and the distributive predisposition of
the LDP government's fiscal policy. As a result, Japan witnessed large
deficits and debt as well as an increasing role of the FILP budget in
flow of funds in the 1990s.

There was little willingness to depart from Keynesian fiscal stimulus.[1] The propensity for Keynesian spending closed off a shift toward
fiscal consolidation and neoliberal market reform, which would reduce
government spending and impose painful short- to medium-term
costs on the LDP's constituents as well as on the general public. Businesses and citizens were hurt by the recessions. Such reform would
worsen the recessions at least in the short run and make the situation worse for businesses and citizens. Nonetheless, deficit reduction
remained in the background and resurfaced in 1997. In the midst of
a weak economy and financial system, the LDP government and the
MOF implemented a ¥9 trillion increase in tax and health care burdens
on citizens to reduce the deficit. This policy shift to fiscal austerity
almost immediately turned out to be a mistake and contributed to
the decline in real GDP in the last quarter of 1997 and throughout
1998. Thus, there were two policy objectives at work in Japan – one
to expand the budget and incur large deficits and the other to reduce
deficits. Both had adverse effects.

Why did the LDP and LDP-led coalition governments in the 1990s
resort to Keynesian expansionary policy? It is because that was what the
LDP government had almost always done in the past, and the Japanese

---

[1]   This is despite widely accepted views that government spending generated crowding-out
    effects on private spending. In the 1970s and 1980s, the Keynesian-monetarist debate focused
    much attention on the crowding-out effects of government deficit spending. Even Keynesian-
    oriented participants to the debate recognized that there were significant crowding-out
    effects, although not as high as 100 percent, as claimed by some.

economy had always bounced back from recessions, setting aside the issue of whether the economic recoveries were a result of Keynesian spending. Spending increases were also an attractive economic policy tool for LDP politicians who faced multiple elections, in the midst of protracted economic recessions in the 1990s and the LDP's declining electoral strength during the decade. Politicians felt that fiscal austerity and market reform were not electorally popular and were detrimental to their electoral goals. Of course, the LDP government might have instead opted for reform, if it had known the nature and severity of the Japanese economy. But until the economic crisis of 1997, the government – the LDP and bureaucracy – did not, or did not want to, recognize the real magnitude of Japan's economic problems.

The expansionary fiscal policy conducted throughout the 1990s may have prevented the economy from falling into deeper recession. On balance, however, numerous stimulus packages were ineffective in placing the economy on the recovery track, particularly in the face of the economic and financial distress and the negative consequences of policy mistakes by the LDP government and the BOJ in 1997 and 2001. The most serious outcome of the ineffective stimulus packages, however, was that they delayed the necessary structural reform of the Japanese economy.

Setting aside the general issue of whether fiscal demand management is effective, the ineffectiveness of Japan's fiscal expansion in the 1990s was partly a result of the particular way it was carried out by the LDP government; that is, much of the spending increase was directed to areas in which the spending failed to bring large long-lasting economic benefits or improvements in factors of production or in the productivity of the economy.

Why did the LDP government in 1997 shift to tight fiscal policy by significantly reducing government spending and increasing taxes and health care burdens? There was a need to cut deficits because growing government debt was unsustainable, but, until 1997, deficit reduction took a back seat to stimulating the economy. It was also overshadowed by the LDP government's propensity to expand spending during recessions. In 1996 and the first part of 1997, however, there were indications that the economy was recovering, Japan had made a number of institutional changes, and many believed that Japan had turned the corner. Japan had closed a number of insolvent financial institutions; closed the *jusen* industry; redesigned the DIC; imposed a blanket government deposit-guarantee through April 1, 2001; adopted a more aggressive approach to dealing with troubled financial institutions before they became insolvent; and announced the Big Bang policies in 1996 followed by legislative action in the spring and summer of 1997. In this environment, policy makers, the LDP government, and the MOF believed that the economy was sufficiently on a recovery track and was now able to absorb the negative shock of fiscal austerity. This was a misjudgment. The ill-timed tax increases in 1997 – in combination with an acute financial contraction and subsequent economic crisis resulting from the failure of three major financial institutions – brought Japan to the abyss of depression and deflation in 1998. Sanyo Securities, Hokkaido Takushoku Bank, and Yamaichi Securities all failed in late 1997 and their failure shocked the private and public sector and showed that economic and financial distress had not been resolved despite the appearance of some recovery in 1995 and 1996.

Japan's fiscal policy in the 1990s was a failure because of almost blind reliance on traditional Keynesian deficit spending and a premature shift to fiscal austerity without fully appreciating the depth of economic and financial distress in the economy. The government immediately reverted to expansionary fiscal policy after the crisis in late 1997 and 1998.

Koizumi came to power in 2001 after ten years of failed fiscal policy. He was an unconventional LDP politician as described in the previous chapter and held different views than the traditional LDP about policies to revitalize the Japanese economy. He reversed the LDP government's previous Keynesian spending and initiated efforts at liberal economic reform. Not all of his reform attempts were entirely successful, and some of his reforms such as fiscal consolidation built on policies unsuccessfully initiated by the Hashimoto administration. Nonetheless, Koizumi reversed a decade of fiscal expansion and carried out wide-ranging economic and government reforms. The next chapter focuses on Koizumi's reforms including fiscal retrenchment. As a prerequisite, this chapter reviews the general budget and FILP budget developments up through 2001.

The General Budget: Pre-1990s

Until the early 1970s, the Japanese government's fiscal policy was conservative in that government spending levels were low by international standards and the government maintained balanced budgets, although government spending and tax revenue increased over time as a result of rapid economic growth. The government did not use fiscal policy as a countercyclical tool in the postwar period until the 1965 recession, when it conducted an expansionary fiscal policy and issued budget deficit bonds for the first time since the Dodge Line was established (Okazaki, 1998). During the 1970s, government spending saw a rapid rise both in total spending and in individual spending categories. The use of deficit spending with deficit bonds became common after 1975 through 1990. The LDP government's use of public works in rural areas as an instrument of economic stimulus and vote mobilization had started during the rapid growth era.

The Japanese government's fiscal policy became sharply expansionary starting in the early 1970s in terms of both absolute amounts and as a percentage of GDP. The early 1970s were a period when the LDP government started systematically using fiscal spending on a larger scale to court its client sectors and constituencies to buttress its electoral strength. Prime Minister Kakuei Tanaka (1972–1974), above all, contributed greatly to the LDP government's electoral use of fiscal manipulations by initiating an extensive use of clientelistic distributive politics. The LDP government intensified the allocation of government resources to rural areas, farmers, and small businesses, all of which were part of its electoral bases.

The Tanaka administration's expansionary monetary and fiscal policy resulted in rampant or "wild" inflation in 1973. After the Nixon Shock in 1971 and the collapse of the fixed exchange rate system, the Japanese government implemented an expansionary monetary policy in an effort to restrict yen appreciation and stimulate the economy in recession resulting from yen appreciation.[2] The administration conducted an expansionary fiscal policy to stimulate the economy and promote the development of Japan's rural areas. The end result of this monetary-fiscal policy mix combined with the oil price shock was inflation of 11.7 percent in 1973 and 23.2 percent in 1974 (OECD, various years).

What was established and institutionalized during this period was a system of distributive politics and the one-party dominance by the LDP, which was made possible by the allocation of government resources and the close relationships between the LDP and its client

---

[2] The depreciated yen benefited Japan's exports by keeping export prices low.

sectors, industries, and regions.[3] The LDP provided its client sectors and regions with government resources. The client constituents, in turn, provided the LDP with votes and money. The LDP government provided abundant public works for the construction industry, rural regions, and farmers.[4] The LDP supplied direct income subsidies to farmers, as well as various protective measures that shielded Japanese farmers from foreign competition, including import bans and quotas, tariffs, and price controls. The LDP government assisted small businesses in distribution and manufacturing with preferential government loans, government-guaranteed loans, and tax deductions and exemptions. The government also protected small businesses from domestic and international competitors by severely restricting the opening of large discount stores.

Under this economic policy regime, large-scale redistribution of wealth from urban to rural areas and from efficient export industries (e.g., automobile, electronics) to less efficient industries (agriculture, distribution, construction, and transportation) took place in postwar Japan. This is because the LDP enjoyed strong electoral support in rural districts, and also many client sectors and industries were more concentrated in rural areas. It became the LDP government's conventional countercyclical economic measure during economic downturns to increase spending in public works and provide government or government-guaranteed loans to small businesses on preferential terms. In fact, Japan's relative income equality in the postwar period was partly caused by this large-scale redistribution of wealth from urban to rural areas and from Japan's efficient industries to the inefficient domestic sectors.

The government conducted contractionary fiscal and monetary policies between 1973 and 1975 to control inflation (Okazaki, 1998). A recession set in, and in 1974 the Japanese economy registered negative economic growth (−1.2 percent) for the first time in the postwar period (OECD, various years). The government maintained tight fiscal and monetary policies until 1975, as price stability had become one of the top priorities of the government. But government spending continued to rise throughout the 1970s after Tanaka's resignation and the first oil crisis.

---

[3] Hirose (1981), Ishikawa and Hirose (1989), and Calder (1988) provide detailed discussion on this issue.

[4] Farmers often worked as seasonal construction workers during off-farming seasons.

In response to the growing deficits, the Japanese government initiated in 1980 a concerted effort to reduce the fiscal deficit and gross debt frequently referred to in Japan as "fiscal reconstruction without tax increases."[5] As a result, in the 1980s, government spending leveled off in absolute terms. As a percentage of GDP, spending even decreased throughout the decade. The government imposed a cap or "ceiling" on the growth of the budget every year in order to balance the budget by reducing spending but not increasing taxes. In 1982, the ceiling was set at 0 percent growth from the previous year's level, and from 1983 on, it was set at 0 to −10 percent, depending on the spending items.

The exception to Japan's fiscal austerity in the 1980s was during 1986–1987 when the government conducted an expansionary fiscal policy in response to the slowdown in growth caused by yen appreciation, which, in turn, was the outcome of the 1985 Plaza Accord to first depreciate the dollar and then to support the dollar. This fiscal stimulus was also a response to foreign pressure to stimulate domestic demand (Okazaki, 1998) and to reduce Japan's huge trade surplus. Other than this one exception, the government's priority during the 1980s was fiscal consolidation, and the government was unwilling to use fiscal policy as a countercyclical tool. One outcome of this fiscal conservatism was to place the main responsibility of economic stimulus on BOJ policy that led to expansionary monetary policy in the second half of the 1980s and the bubble economy (Ishi, 2000).

Figure 8.1 illustrates major government expenditures in absolute terms from 1958 to 2006. Social security, public works, grants to local governments, and education and science all experienced rapid rises during the 1970s. This shows the Japanese government's expansionary fiscal policy regime during the decade. These spending rises were also partly due to the negative economic shock caused by the first oil crisis. Figure 8.2 illustrates the major expenditures as a percentage of GDP and shows that the spending increases in these expenditures outpaced economic growth during the decade. These trends, however, were reversed starting in the early 1980s. Fiscal consolidation continued until the very beginning of the 1990s, when the budget was finally balanced.

The effort to reduce the deficit was also accompanied by administrative reform to reduce the size of government and liberalize the

[5] Cargill and Hutchison (1997) provide an account of this policy attitude.

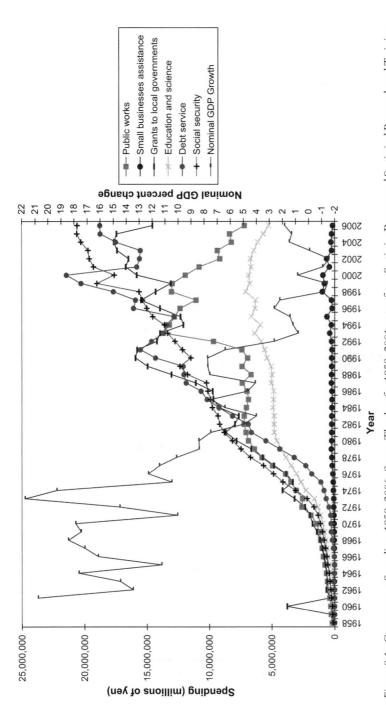

Figure 8.1. Government Spending, 1958–2006. *Source:* The data for 1958–2001 come from Statistics Bureau and Statistical Research and Training Institute, the Ministry of Internal Affairs and Communications, Nihon no Choki Tokei Keiretsu, [http://www.stat.go.jp/data/chouki/]. The data for 2001–2006 come from the Budget Bureau, the Ministry of Finance, Yosan/Kessan [http://www.mof.go.jp/jouhou/syukei/syukei.htm]. *Note:* The figures are actual expenditures at the end of each fiscal year, except for the year 2006 where the figures are those in the initial annual budget.

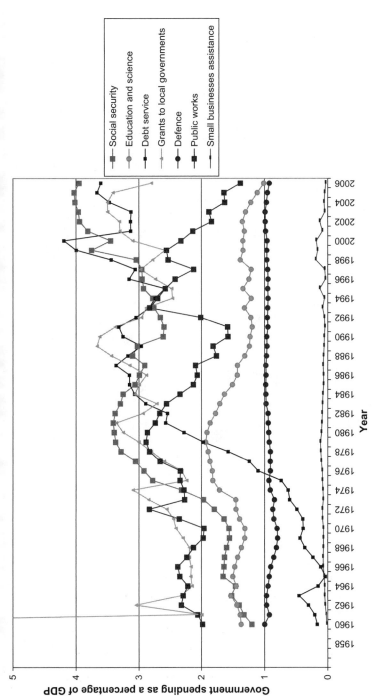

Figure 8.2. Government Spending as a Percentage of GDP, 1960 to 2006. *Source:* The data for 1960–2001 come from Statistics Bureau and Statistical Research and Training Institute, the Ministry of Internal Affairs and Communications, Nihon no Choki Tokei Keiretsu, [http://www.stat.go.jp/data/chouki/]. The data for 2001–2006 come from the Budget Bureau, the Ministry of Finance, Yosan/Kessan [http://www.mof.go.jp/jouhou/syukei/syukei.htm]. *Note:* The figures are actual expenditures at the end of each fiscal year, except for the year 2006 where the figures are those in the initial annual budget.

181

economy. The LDP government under Prime Minister Yasuhiro Nakasone (1982–1987) privatized the Nippon Telegraph and Telephone (1985), the Japan Tobacco and Salt (1985), and the Japan National Railways (1987). Nakasone wanted to pursue neoliberal market reform along the lines of the United Kingdom under Thatcher and the United States under Reagan in the 1980s. Japan's administrative reform and deregulation were pursued partly to satisfy international pressure to liberalize the economy. These deregulation policies, however, were more limited than those of Reagan and Thatcher. The Nakasone administration also implemented tax reform similar to Reagan and Thatcher with lowered and simplified tax rates, making individual income tax less progressive, and eliminating the tax exclusion for interest on small savings. In both figures, we can see that as the LDP government came to frequently rely on deficit bonds in the second half of the 1970s, spending on debt services sharply climbed.

Most of the expenditures leveled off in the 1980s as a result of fiscal consolidation. Figure 8.1 shows that spending on social security and debt services slowed down much less than other expenditures. The trend in social security expenditures was a result of the LDP government's drastic welfare expansion in the 1960s and the early 1970s before the oil crisis and the difficulty of reducing spending for entitlement programs quickly. The trend in debt services expenditures was due to the fact that even when the government reduced the annual deficit, it still had to finance the debt services for previous debt and to rely on deficit bonds until it eliminated the annual deficit in 1990. Nonetheless, Figure 8.2 shows that the Japanese government significantly curbed social security spending and debt services as percentages of GDP.

Grants to local governments show a different pattern, continuing their increases during the 1980s as well. This is a result of two factors. First, they are designed to increase during economic booms, because they are calculated as percentages of national tax revenues – when the economy is growing, tax revenues increase, and the grants increase accordingly. So this factor gives the grants a pro-cyclical component. But, at the same time, the LDP government uses the grants to local governments as a countercyclical tool during recessions, which increases the grants, while national tax revenue declines. Thus, this factor gives the grants a countercyclical component. The growth of this spending slowed down in the early 1980s as a result of the government's efforts at fiscal consolidation. But it shows a rapid increase in the late 1980s because of the increase in tax revenues brought about by the economic boom supported by the bubble economy during the period.

The bubble economy in the second half of the 1980s generated large tax revenue increases and combined with the slowdown in government spending (see Figures 8.1 and 8.2), the government balanced the budget by 1990. The government did not need to issue deficit bonds in 1991, 1992, and 1993. Spending on debt services decreased both in absolute terms and as a percentage of GDP in the early 1990s. This success at reducing the budget deficit was short lived. The collapse of asset prices and subsequent recession led to expansionary fiscal policy. After 1993, deficit spending and deficit bond issues skyrocketed because of the protracted, multiple recessions, resulting in the highest gross debt to GDP ratio among OECD countries by the end of the decade (Figure 8.3).

Thus, the general budget reflected three distinct phases over the four-decade period from the start of reindustrialization in the early postwar period to the early 1990s. First, during the reindustrialization and high-growth period from 1950 to the early 1970s, the budget was fiscally conservative both in attitude and outcome. Second, in the 1970s, the budget reflected fiscal expansionism and generated large deficits. Third, the 1980s was a period of fiscal conservatism as the government attempted to reduce the deficits generated in the 1970s. By 1990, the budget was balanced. In the early 1990s, however, the fiscal restraint of the 1980s was reversed, as the bubble in asset prices burst and ushered in fifteen years of economic distress.

The General Budget in the 1990s

The LDP government successfully contained fiscal spending in the 1980s and eliminated deficit spending in 1990. The successful deficit reduction was in part the result of the conservative bias of the MOF. By the early 1980s, the MOF skillfully persuaded LDP leaders of the crucial importance of deficit reduction, particularly in light of the projected aging of the Japanese population and enormous increases in social security and health care spending that a "grayer" Japan would require.

Fiscal restraint was put on temporary hold as the economy declined in the early 1990s. No one in the Japanese government expected at

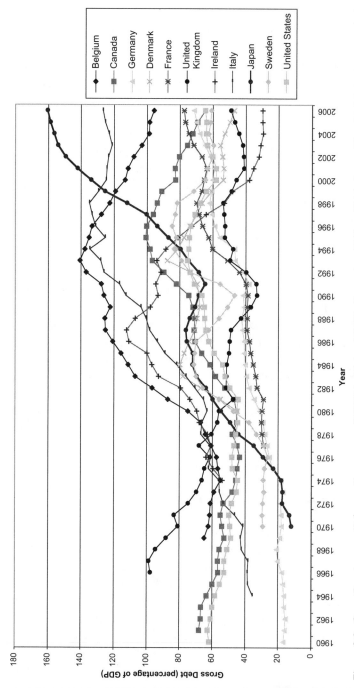

Figure 8.3. Gross Government Debt as a Percentage of GDP in Major OECD Countries, 1960 to 2006. *Source:* The OECD *Economic Outlook* (various years). *Note:* The values for 2006–07 are projections.

184

that time that fiscal expansion would continue for the next decade. Yet, as the recession and other economic problems continued, fiscal restraint became of secondary importance to the goal of ending economic stagnation. The Japanese government adopted an aggressive expansionary fiscal policy for most of the 1990s with the exception of brief but unsuccessful fiscal austerity policy in 1997.

Most components of government expenditures began to increase after 1990 (see Figure 8.1 and 8.2), especially after 1997, when Japan faced serious economic and financial distress manifested by the failure of a large bank and two securities companies, deflation, negative economic growth, and increasing unemployment. At the same time, tax revenues fell and the government accumulated gross debt. The debt service component of government spending (see Figures 8.1 and 8.2) increased sharply. The pattern of the LDP government's traditional fiscal spending behavior during recession was illustrated by increased spending for public works, grants to local governments, and small business protection. Public works were given particularly strong emphasis.

The Japanese government's Keynesian spending increases took place, partly because that was what the government had always used and apparently worked before the 1990s crisis. During the early postwar period of rapid growth, public works and other public investments worked as relatively effective tools of productivity gains and economic stimulus. The country was rebuilding its economy from the devastation of war, there was much room for the economy to grow, and, as a result, these public investments contributed to productivity gains and economic growth. But their positive effects on the macroeconomy had declined by the 1990s (Ihori, 2001; Ihori et al., 2002).

Table 8.1 lists the economic stimulus packages the government carried out between the collapse of the bubble and the Koizumi administration. The economic packages of September 1993 and February 1994 were implemented by the non–LDP eight-party coalition government led by Prime Minister Hosokawa (1993–1994). The government implemented thirteen economic stimulus packages between 1992 and 2001, and large chunks of the emergency expenditures were allocated to the LDP's traditional client sectors and areas, especially in the rural areas of Japan. The total amount of the policy packages was ¥141.3 trillion (approximately $1.2 trillion). Fifty-three percent of the total amount was spent on public investment, most of which was in public works. Nineteen percent was spent on small businesses.

Table 8.1. Economic stimulus packages implemented by the Japanese government, 1992–2001

August 1992	Total	¥10.7 trillion
	Public Investment	¥8.6 trillion
	Small Businesses	¥1.2 trillion
April 1993	Total	¥13.2 trillion
	Public Investment	¥10.6 trillion
	Small Businesses	¥1.9 trillion
	Tax Cuts	¥0.15 trillion
September 1993	Total	¥6 trillion
	Public Investment	¥5.15 trillion
	Small Businesses	¥0.77 trillion
February 1994	Total	¥15.3 trillion
	Public Investment	¥7.2 trillion
	Small Businesses	¥1.4 trillion
	Tax Cuts	¥5.8 trillion
April 1995	Total	¥7 trillion
	Public Investment	¥5.4 trillion
	Small Businesses	¥1.4 trillion
September 1995	Total	¥14.2 trillion
	Public Investment	¥12.8 trillion
	Small Businesses	¥1.3 trillion
April 1998	Total	¥16 trillion
	Public Investment	¥6.2 trillion
	Small Businesses	¥2 trillion
	Tax Cuts	¥4.6 trillion
November 1998	Total	¥20 trillion
	Public Investment	¥8.1 trillion
	Small Businesses	na
	Tax Cuts	¥6 trillion
June 1999	Total	na
	Public Investment	na
	Small Businesses	na
November 1999	Total	¥18 trillion
	Public Investment	¥6.8 trillion
	Small Businesses	¥7.4 trillion
October 2000	Total	¥11 trillion
	Public Investment	¥4.7 trillion
	Small Businesses	¥4.5 trillion
October 2001	Total	¥5.8 trillion
	Public Investment	na
	Small Businesses	¥4.5 trillion
December 2001	Total	¥4.1 trillion
	Public Investment	¥4.1 trillion
	Small Businesses	na

Sources: Nakao (2002), Ishi (2000), and *Asahi Shimbun* (various dates)

Together, seventy-one percent of total spending was allocated to the LDP's traditional client sectors – construction, distribution, small businesses, farmers, and rural regions.

The large number of emergency stimulus packages was a result of the protracted recessions and the effort by the LDP to protect its traditional electoral bases. Other than the two years of 1996 and 2000, Japan's economy was either stagnant or declining and, after 1994, deflation was a serious problem. The government's countercyclical spending increases through these stimulus packages were not effective in ending the economic stagnation. There continues to be debate about the specific causes of Japan's stagnation and the effectiveness of public investment in stimulating demand and promoting growth.[6] Despite the debate among economists with different views, it is safe to say that the LDP government's public investment in the 1990s was not as effective in stimulating growth as before that decade (Ihori, 2001; Ihori et al., 2002). This is not to deny the effectiveness of public investment across the board in promoting growth. If investment is made in such a way as to facilitate the productivity and efficiency of the economy, public investment can be an effective policy tool, as endogenous growth theory suggests. But the particularly way the LDP government implemented public investment was not the kind that would promote productivity and growth in the long run.

The LDP government expended massive public resources to sustain inefficient and redundant sectors, businesses, and workers, which needed restructuring instead. Its economic packages temporarily boosted these sectors and companies, but their stimulative effect was only short-lived and dissipated after their initial boost. These resources had a high opportunity cost because a more innovative policy could have used them to stimulate more productive sectors and resolve the nonperforming loan problems in the financial system. These fiscal expansions may have kept Japan's economy from falling into an even deeper recession; however, there were costs to fiscal expansion; crowding-out effects on private spending and the public's anticipations that higher taxes would be required in the future to resolve the large amount of outstanding debt. The continuation of government support for the unproductive sectors also delayed necessary structural reform and adversely impacted Japan's growth potential. The accumulation of unproductive capital acts as a drag on economic growth much like

---

[6] See Hamada and Horiuchi (2004) for a summary of this debate.

the albatross around the neck of the ancient mariner in Coleridge's *Rhyme of the Ancient Mariner.*

All things considered, it is difficult to make a positive case for the large number of stimulus packages and their size over the period from 1992 to 2001. They represented the LDP's traditional response to an economic downturn. The LDP adopted this policy because it appeared to have worked in the past; it was part of the political-economic regime that maintained the LDP's political power; and, the electoral reform of 1994 created uncertainty for politicians, and, in response, they attempted to court their traditional electoral bases. The LDP also experienced the decline of its electoral strength during the period, and the party leadership and individual politicians felt the strong urge to spend increased government money on their client sectors and constituencies. Japan's public investment would have been more productive if the LDP government had allocated resources to sectors and industries with future growth potential and in ways to facilitate technological advances and productivity gains. Eventually, the government realized this and began to increase spending in science, technology, education, and R&D toward the end of the 1990s.

The result of the massive fiscal expansions in the midst of stagnation and decline that led to falling tax revenues was an accumulation of government debt in the 1990s. In the early 1970s, Japan's government gross debt level was the lowest among the major industrial economies (Figure 8.3). As Japan's fiscal spending expanded in the 1970s, its gross debt grew rapidly. Japan's successful fiscal austerity policy in the 1980s slowed debt accumulation and eventually generated a decline in gross debt in 1988. Yet, gross debt began a steep rise in 1992, as the government responded to economic stagnation with drastic fiscal expansions. It continued to rise and, by the end of the 1990s, Japan had the highest level of outstanding government debt among the industrial economies. In contrast, most of the industrial countries in the 1990s engaged in debt reduction, and their debt levels declined over the decade. Debt reduction by countries such as Belgium, Ireland, and Italy that previously had the highest levels of gross debt was particularly impressive.

The high debt level in the 1990s rendered Japan's economy vulnerable to economic shocks and especially deflation. Deflation increased the real cost of servicing the outstanding debt; combined with the huge amount of private debt fixed in nominal amount, deflation generated a drag on the Japanese economy. The large debt constrained Japan's fiscal policy options in the event of any economic or political shock and placed stabilization responsibility on the BOJ. The BOJ, however, was unwilling to adopt nontraditional approaches to monetary policy, arguing that it had done all it could to stimulate the economy, especially after February 1999 when the BOJ adopted the ZIRP.

Fiscal Consolidation Debacle of 1997 in Detail

Faced with rapidly accumulating government debt, the Hashimoto administration (1996–1998) launched an aggressive campaign to reduce the deficit at the end of 1996. Various economic indicators showed signs that the economy was recovering. The administration and MOF concluded that Japan's economy could absorb the shock of fiscal austerity – both spending cuts and tax increases (Karube and Nishino, 1999). However, this conclusion was premature. Fiscal consolidation was supported by not only the LDP but also all opposition parties.

The administration passed the Fiscal Structure Reform Law in November 1997 (the same month Hokkaido Takushoku Bank, Sanyo Securities and Yamaichi Securities failed). The law stipulated that the annual fiscal deficit be contained under 3 percent of GDP by 2003 and that deficit bond issuance be terminated. It specified the amounts of specific spending reductions for the following three years – a reduction of total government spending in 1998 from the previous 1997 level; a 7 percent reduction in public investment in 1998 and further reductions in 1999 and 2000; zero or negative spending growth in defense and agriculture for the three years; containment of spending in social security and education for the three years; a 10 percent reduction in foreign aid in 1998 and further cuts in 1999 and 2000; and a reduction of grants to local governments in 1998 from the previous year's level. Thus, the LDP government's fiscal policy turned contractionary.

To pursue fiscal consolidation, the Hashimoto administration implemented a ¥9 trillion increase in citizens' tax and health care burdens in 1997 – a consumption tax rate increase from 3 to 5 percent (¥5 trillion), the termination of a temporary individual income tax cut (¥2 trillion) that had been in place for three years, and a 10 percent increase in company employees' healthcare copayments (¥2 trillion).[7]

---

[7] Karube and Nishino (1999) show (based on the results of their interviews with the core policy makers) that when assessing the contractionary effects of tax increases on the macroeconomy,

This shift to fiscal contraction could not have been timed better to do more damage. The law was enacted the very month that the financial and economic crisis emerged. Deflation continued; real GDP declined in the fourth quarter of 1997 and in each quarter of 1998; nonperforming loans among corporations and banks increased; and Sanyo Securities, Hokkaido Takushoku Bank, and Yamaichi Securities – Japan's major financial companies – failed. The MOF and the LDP government were not aware of the severity of the nonperforming debt problem until the bankruptcies of the three financial institutions were imminent (Cargill, Hutchison, and Ito, 2000; Karube and Nishino, 1999; Shimizu, 2005). Before this, the MOF had not thought that the problem of nonperforming loans was serious enough to destabilize the financial system. The very fact the LDP, the opposition parties, and the MOF supported the deficit reduction package in 1997 attests to their lack of understanding of the depth of the economic and financial distress.

The failure of the three financial institutions sent a shockwave through the financial sector, the entire economy, and the world. Their bankruptcies led to an acute financial contraction and severely depressed investment and consumption. The economy took a deep plunge. Up to this time, the MOF had been able to protect major financial firms. It had been a common understanding that the MOF would not let any major financial institution fail, either through "white knight" mergers in which strong firms merged with weaker firms or through encouraging BOJ lending to troubled institutions. The MOF tried to salvage the three institutions by orchestrating bailout plans involving other healthy financial institutions. But everything failed. The financial conditions of those companies were beyond the ministry's problem-solving capacity. The old Japanese financial system and convoy system were ended.

Why did Japan's economy take such a sharp decline in the latter part of 1997? A combination of factors was responsible. First, the Hashimoto administration's fiscal austerity had a contractionary effect. The economy was weak and susceptible to any shock.

---

various government ministries (the MOF, Economic Planning Agency, Ministry of Health and Welfare), and the Hashimoto administration failed to take into account an increase in health care copayments (¥2 trillion yen). This oversight resulted from Japan's policy-making system at that time, which was not well designed to oversee different parts of economic policy in their entirety.

Second, the failure of three major financial institutions interfered with the normal functioning of the financial system and fundamentally changed attitudes about the seriousness of the economic and financial distress, setting off a downward economic spiral. Their failures reflected the fundamentally weak financial system and the failure of seven years of government efforts to resolve the financial distress. They also made Japanese corporations, consumers, and other economic actors realize how serious the problem was and, as a result, depressed investment and consumption.

Third, partly as a result of the government's active campaign of fiscal consolidation, Japanese consumers were aware of the government's "fiscal crisis," and consequently only saw reasons why they should not spend and should save instead. They could only see reasons why they should anticipate future increases in their tax, health care, and social security burdens, and decreases in the benefits they would receive from those programs in the future. The population was rapidly aging, and the costs of social security and health care would increase. The massive government debt would have to be paid back by tax increases or spending cuts or both in the future. The public realized in 1997 that fiscal austerity was inevitable, when the government started reducing expenditures and increasing taxes and health care copayments. Combined with a weak economy, the public became increasingly concerned that even major corporations could go bankrupt, and concerned about the possibility of layoffs,[8] Japanese workers had not experienced such a sense of economic insecurity since the early 1950s. Given all of these factors, the private sector had little incentive to consume and invest, especially in an environment of falling prices.

Fourth, the BOJ had permitted the price level to fall from 1995. Deflation weakened balance sheets by increasing the cost of servicing debt; reduced the willingness of banks to lend because of increased bankruptcy risk from higher debt service cost; and increased real interest rates as nominal rates were very low, which in turn reduced investment and consumption, and increased the demand to hold money in anticipation of lower prices on goods and services.

As a result of the economy's sharp decline, the Hashimoto administration had no choice but to reverse fiscal austerity and resume an

---

[8] There had been layoffs in the past such as during the early 1970s but, compared to the late 1990s and early 2000s, layoffs were the exception.

expansionary fiscal policy in late 1997. It implemented a ¥16 trillion stimulus package in April 1998, including a ¥4 trillion individual
income tax cut (Table 8.1). But it was not effective enough to reverse
the economy's downward spiral. Real GDP declined in 1998 by 1 percent – the largest decline since 1974 – and the unemployment rate rose
to 4.1 percent. In the July 1998 upper house election, Hashimoto's
LDP suffered a major defeat. He resigned immediately following the
electoral outcomes.

The succeeding Obuchi administration (1998–2000) continued the
large-scale fiscal expansions and implemented two large stimulus packages totaling ¥38 trillion in 1998 and 1999. The administration also
passed a law in November 1998 to suspend the 1997 Fiscal Structure
Reform Law until the economy recovered. As indicated in Table 8.1,
the LDP government carried out a total of seven more large-scale
economic stimulus packages after Prime Minister Hashimoto's fiscal reform attempt. Japan's fiscal policy became sharply expansionary
again. Fiscal consolidation took a back seat to economic recovery and
did not return to the policy agenda until the inauguration of Prime
Minister Koizumi in 2001.

Prime Minister Obuchi suffered a stroke and fell into a coma in
April 2000. Yoshiro Mori was selected by the governing LDP as
successor as a result of the party's backdoor negotiations (back then,
still a common method of LDP leader selection) and became the prime
minister. He continued fiscal expansion in an effort to resurrect the
Japanese economy also without significant success.

The LDP government started an initially half-hearted attempt to
open economic policy making to analysis and advice by nonpoliti-
cians such as economists, major corporate leaders, and other specialists
during the Obuchi and Mori administrations. The much publicized
CEFP that Koizumi heavily utilized after 2001 was established under
the Mori administration. The effort under both the Obuchi and Mori
administrations, however, was largely symbolic and did not change
Japan's economic policy making. The CEFP did not play any significant role. Obuchi and Mori had intended to use the CEFP staffed with
nonelected specialists as a central policy-making body; however, the
LDP and its *zoku* politicians still retained significant political power
vis-à-vis the prime minister, and were not willing to confer to out-
siders any fraction of their control over government policy (Shimizu,
2005, chapter 4). Thus, the policy-making regime was largely the

same as before, and change in policy making would have to await the arrival of Koizumi.

Prime Minister Mori's approval ratings were low, and the LDP lost seats in the 2000 lower house election. Mori resigned in April 2001, as the LDP feared poor electoral performance in the 2001 upper house election under his leadership. Koizumi won the LDP presidential election over Hashimoto and became the prime minister. This was a rare event in the history of Japanese politics. In the past, those who aspired to be prime ministers were leaders of LDP factions who could rely on their faction members' support and votes. Koizumi, however, was not a faction leader. He made a career of challenging the traditional LDP and advocated privatization of Japan's postal services, which was the foundation of the FILP budget. The cause of the election of Koizumi was a desperate wish among the public and LDP supporters and members for change and a leader who could engineer economic recovery.

The Redesign of Japan's Fiscal Policy: Hashimoto and Koizumi

The Hashimoto administration's failure at reform of the general budget contrasts Koizumi's more successful fiscal austerity policy after 2001. Thus, in terms of the first component of Japan's fiscal program, Koizumi was more successful than Hashimoto in reducing government spending. But Hashimoto was successful in initiating reforms in the PSS and FILP budget – the second component of Japan's fiscal program. In fact, the Hashimoto administration's initiatives with the PSS and FILP provided an important foundation for reforms achieved by Koizumi.

What distinguishes the policy outcomes of the two prime ministers with respect to the general budget component of Japan's fiscal program? The difference does not lie in their policy goals. Hashimoto's motivations and goals for fiscal consolidation were the same as Koizumi's. As with Koizumi, Hashimoto aimed at structural reform without sanctuary and intended to cut into the LDP's vested interests, including public works, health care, and social security (Shimizu, 2005, chapter 2). There are several reasons to account for the difference in policy outcomes.

First, the Japanese government and public retained their faith in fiscal stimulus during the Hashimoto administration. Even after Hashimoto's resignation, it took three more years of failed fiscal stimulus packages to convince the majority of policy makers that traditional government spending would not end the economic distress. Koizumi was fortunate in that Japan had a record of almost ten years of failed fiscal stimulus packages; hence, it was easier for him to override proponents of spending increases and reverse fiscal policy. The public was more receptive to new remedies and a new leader who would provide new approaches after a decade of failed policy.

The second factor is the difference in the political and economic environment the two prime ministers faced. When Hashimoto attempted fiscal consolidation and failed because of the economic crisis, he faced a policy making environment characterized by divisions among the core policy makers (Hashimoto Cabinet and LDP leadership), lack of concentration of policy-making power, and the resulting lack of effective economic policy making. The LDP factions and *zoku* politicians had not been weakened sufficiently for a prime minister to override their opposition to reform. Hashimoto found himself in a power conflict with LDP party leaders in the midst of the confusion over the economic crisis in late 1997 and 1998 (Karube and Nishino, 1999; Shimizu, 2005). The rift between Hashimoto and the LDP leadership made it difficult for Hashimoto to take strong initiatives to effectively respond to the crisis, as LDP leaders blamed each other for the economic failure. The conflict between Hashimoto and the LDP also made it difficult for the MOF to actively pursue meaningful policy.

Koizumi faced a different environment. During his administration, the influence of the LDP factions and *zoku* politicians had declined. This was the result of Koizumi's intentional effort to weaken them and the cumulative effects of the electoral and campaign fund reforms of 1994 aimed to concentrate power in the party leadership rather than faction leaders and individual politicians. The net result was that Koizumi successfully concentrated policy-making power in the executive branch.

Third, the idiosyncrasies of Japanese legislative politics hindered the Hashimoto administration's swift response to the financial crisis in late 1997 and ensuing economic stagnation. The Fiscal Structure Reform Law that stipulated fiscal austerity was enacted only a short time after the failures of Sanyo Securities, Hokkaido Takushoku Bank, and Yamaichi Securities. The administration had to respond to the crisis with fiscal expansion in a way that would not contradict the law (Shimizu, 2005). This delayed policy implementation, and the remedial fiscal expansion was not wholehearted in the beginning. The institutional features of legislative politics also left the administration with no choice but to wait to announce an economic stimulus package until after it passed the contractionary 1998 budget in April. As a result, the administration was unable to respond swiftly with fiscal policy.

Fourth, Koizumi enjoyed much greater public support than Hashimoto and thus a greater ability to shield his policy proposals from opposition by the LDP, bureaucrats, and client sectors and constituency groups. Public support permitted Koizumi to claim a public mandate. Public support can increase a prime minister's policy-making capabilities, not only because of the normative power a stronger public mandate gives him but also because electoral and political incentives make it difficult for his party to oppose him; that is, the party needs a publicly popular party leader to win elections.

In sum, Hashimoto launched a meaningful fiscal reform effort in 1997, but the economy and financial system were too weak to absorb an austerity program, and events turned against him. The financial crisis hit Japan, and the economic condition was worse than his administration expected. In the face of the financial crisis, the administration's fiscal consolidation served only to further depress consumption and investment and deepen the economic crisis. The government was unable to detect the severity of the economic problems and take appropriate policy response to them, as its system of policy coordination across the ministries was weak (Shimizu, 2005). When economic conditions worsened and the incompatibility between Hashimoto's fiscal austerity and the need for fiscal expansion became evident, the LDP leadership was not willing to support Hashimoto. The schism between the LDP leadership and the Hashimoto administration deepened.

There is no doubt that Koizumi was far more successful in reducing the size of the general budget than Hashimoto for a variety of reasons. There is also no doubt that Koizumi carried FILP and PSS reform further than Hashimoto. However, Hashimoto achieved a major institutional change in the role of government financial intermediation in regard to Japan's second part of its fiscal program. Hashimoto initiated the redesign of the FILP system in 1998 and set into motion reforms that would change one of the most important elements of the old set of economic and financial institutions that dominated much of Japan's recent history.

The FILP Budget: Pre-1990s

The FILP budget was managed by the MOF and formulated along with the government budget. The FILP funds were used to promote policy goals in housing, social infrastructure and environment, welfare and education, small and medium businesses, agriculture and fisheries, roads, transportation, communication, industrialization, and international cooperation. The FILP budget was largely dependent on postal savings deposits and life insurance premiums collected by some twenty-four thousand post offices throughout Japan. The PSS was created in 1875, whereas the FILP system itself was a postwar development. The post offices transferred the majority of deposits and life insurance premiums to the MOF's Trust Fund Bureau, which combined these funds with funds from other sources (national pension premiums and government bonds) and distributed them to government banks and other FILP-financed entities or FILP agencies. The FILP agencies provided subsidized funds to targeted sectors of the economy. These agencies consisted of government banks that made loans to targeted sectors and numerous government corporations and enterprises.

The PSS and FILP were an important part of the old financial regime, the iron triangle, and were deeply entrenched in the Japanese economy. Despite two decades of financial liberalization policies and rhetoric in Japan from 1976 to 1998, these institutions not only continued to function but also became more prominent in Japan's financial system.

The PSS and FILP avoided reform for four reasons. First, they provided significant advantages to the participants. Post offices relied almost exclusively on *teigaku* time deposits, which provided a no-penalty option to withdraw funds after six months to take advantage of interest rate movements. As a result, *teigaku* deposits offered a higher effective interest rate than any time deposit offered by private banks.[9] Post offices were also more convenient, as their numbers exceeded

---

[9] The relative attractiveness of *teigaku* deposits compared to standard bank deposits is discussed in Cargill and Yoshino (2003, p. 65). Kamada (1993) demonstrates the comparative advantages of these deposits over any savings deposit offered by private banks.

those of private bank branches in every prefecture for much of the postwar period. Furthermore, funds obtained through the FILP were subsidized, and many borrowers would have been unable to obtain the same level of funding from the private banking system. Second, the ruling LDP used the FILP as an instrument to maintain and enhance its electoral strength, because local governments and many sectors of the economy were dependent to varying degrees on funds it provided. Allocation of FILP funds was very sensitive to the discretion of politicians and bureaucrats. Third, the PSS and FILP were so large and pervasive that reform was a daunting task at a minimum and, thus, policymakers were willing to put their reform on the back burner. Fourth, the PSS and FILP were immensely popular in Japan, criticized only by academics, private banks, and, on occasion, the BOJ. The size of the FILP expanded in the 1990s, as funds allocated to business and housing grew more rapidly than other FILP uses of funds, which mitigated the credit crunch at private banks caused by the nonperforming debt problem.

Redesign of the FILP Budget

The FILP budget continued to increase in the 1990s as the government funded public works and various other government programs with the FILP to spend its way out of the recessions. Not only did the FILP budget increase but also the PSS expanded in the 1990s. Postal deposits expanded for two reasons. First, they inherently offered more benefits and paid a higher effective interest rate than private bank deposits. Second, as the public became increasingly concerned about the health of the banking system, postal deposits appeared to be an attractive alternative because they were regarded by the public as directly guaranteed by the government; whereas, bank deposits at least until late 1995 were not directly guaranteed by the government. Instead, banks deposits were insured by the DIC which was unfamiliar to the public and in 1994 became insolvent.

The network of post offices was more important than merely providing the major source of funding to the FILP budget. It was the LDP's important electoral base. The national association of postmasters was one of the LDP's strongest and most crucial electoral support bases. The association had a high level of cohesion and organization as a vote mobilization machine and commanded large numbers of organized votes. Many LDP politicians relied on their votes and opposed change in the postal system.

Despite this widespread opposition to reform in the LDP, however, institutional redesign did take place in the 1990s, and major change was accomplished in 1998. This is one of the few high points of the Hashimoto administration. Two factors motivated reform of postal savings and the FILP.

First was the financial distress of the 1990s. The PSS complicated Japan's government deposit guarantee system and provided incentives to transfer private bank deposits to the PSS whenever the public became concerned about the condition of the banking system. The PSS itself encouraged this disintermediation in the early 1990s by emphasizing the safety of postal deposits over bank deposits, given the troubled banking system. The MOF in 1993 was required to pressure the Ministry of Posts and Telecommunications[10] to cease such activities. Although encouraging disintermediation was no longer official policy, the practice continued. Cargill and Yoshino (2003, pp. 130–139) discuss this issue in detail and provide statistical evidence of disintermediation[11] in the 1990s. Okina (2000) also draws attention to the disintermediation issue.

Second, there was growing concern over projected demographic trends in Japanese population, which placed a premium on increasing the rate of return on Japan's high savings rate. Increasing labor productivity through higher yield investment would be a major factor to stem a decline in the standard of living (income per capita) if current conditions prevailed. Many would argue that much of Japan's high saving has been wasted because of an inefficient financial system and, more specifically, because of the large amount of funds collected by the PSS and allocated by government financial intermediation.

The first two reforms in the 1990s were meaningful, but did not make an attempt to redesign the PSS. As discussed above, in 1993 post offices officially were informed to cease appealing to the fears of the public to attract deposits. In 1994, an agreement was reached between the regulatory authorities that the PSS would set deposit rates "close

---

[10] The ministry was reorganized in 2001 into today's Ministry of Internal Affairs and Communications along with the then Management and Coordination Agency and Ministry of Home Affairs.

[11] It is interesting to note that the U.S. postal savings system had a similar, but much larger, negative effect on the private banks in the 1930s (O'Hara and Easley, 1979). The U.S. postal savings system ceased functioning in 1967.

to" private bank deposit rates in an effort to reduce disintermediation. But these two reforms paled in comparison to the reforms that commenced in June 1998.

As part of the Fundamental Reform of the Central Government Industries and Agencies Law (June 1998), the formal relationship between the PSS and the FILP changed. Starting April 1, 2001, postal deposits, postal life insurance premiums, and national pension premiums were no longer provided to special accounts or government banks through the Trust Fund Bureau. The FILP agencies previously dependent on the Trust Fund Bureau were required to raise their own funds in the form of (a) FILP-agency bonds without a government guarantee, (b) FILP-agency bonds with a government guarantee, or (c) FILP bonds issued by the MOF, which essentially represented general government debt. In fiscal year 2001, twenty agencies previously financed by FILP commenced selling bonds without a government guarantee. Although these bonds provided only a small part of their funding and the remainder came from MOF bonds, this set the stage for a major change in how these entities obtained funding. The other agencies financed by the FILP continued to be supported by the government through the MOF. The new process was officially referred to in the budget as the Public Funding Mechanism, but the term FILP continues to be used to describe the process of allocating funds.

As a result, the new PSS was no longer required to transfer funds to the MOF and for all practical purposes became a stand-alone government bank. In June 2000, the Ministry of Public Management, Home Affairs, Posts, and Telecommunications (the new regulatory authority for the PSS) announced a strategy to manage postal deposits.[12] The portfolio "in principle" should consist of 80 percent in "safe" assets (government bonds, etc.), 5 percent in foreign bonds, 5 percent in foreign equities, and 5 percent in domestic equities, and the remaining 5 percent in money market instruments. The plan to hold 80 percent of postal deposits in government bonds and other safe assets essentially turned a major part of the PSS into a "narrow" bank.

The 1998 changes were of major significance and an achievement of the Hashimoto administration. However, they left many issues unresolved. The reform of the FILP and PSS would be accerated by Prime Minister Koizumi. Koizumi would build on the changes introduced in

---

[12] The ministry's English name was later changed to the Ministry of Internal Affairs and Communications. See footnote 10.

the 1998 reform and make the reform of government financial inter-mediation a major focal point of his structural reform. Thus, in terms of the FILP and PSS, both Hashimoto and Koizumi made contribu-tions. Although the Hashimoto administration failed to achieve fiscal consolidation, it did set into motion changes in the second component of the fiscal program that would change Japan's financial institutions with far-reaching effects.

9

Koizumi Administration's Reform in Broad Perspective: Fiscal Consolidation and Market Reform

Introduction

Prime Minister Koizumi came into office April 2001, when the economy was in serious, protracted stagnation and deflation, despite nine years of repeated government stimulus packages and the unprecedented ZIRP of the BOJ starting February 1999. In 2001, the economy was in renewed decline, and real GDP growth was only 0.21 percent in 2001, after a brief modest recovery in 2000 (2.4 percent real growth). The unemployment rate of 5.0 percent in 2001 was the highest in postwar history and was still climbing. Deflation continued with a 0.77 percent decline in the CPI in 2001 (OECD, various years). Observers in and outside Japan were wondering whether a "second lost decade" was in the making. The Japanese public and businesses felt helpless in the face of the seemingly insurmountable economic stagnation and ineffective government policy. They were desperate for any change or any political leader who could offer any alternative solution to the economic and financial distress that had passed the decade mark.

The Japanese placed their hope in Koizumi – very unconventional, energetic, and atypical of LDP leaders – when he emerged in 2001 with the promise of changing Japan and engineering economic growth and, if necessary, destroying his own LDP in the process.[1] Koizumi attempted reform in many areas of the economy and government intervention, some successfully and some not so successfully. They included the following: (a) fiscal consolidation including retrenchment

---

[1] Mulgan (2002) provides a detailed discussion of Koizumi's policy in the initial period.

of public works and the national government's financial grants to local governments; (b) deregulation; (c) the privatization of the postal services and highway and other public corporations; (d) the privatization or closure of government financial institutions; (e) the restructuring of the FILP system; (f) administrative reform to restructure government agencies and personnel; (g) reform of the government special account budget; (h) devolution – delegation of policy-making power from the national to local governments; (i) the restructuring of health care and social security systems to contain their cost expansion; and (j) stabilization of the financial system and ending the nonperforming loan problem embedded in the banking and credit cooperative system.

The central themes of Koizumi's reform programs were small government, deregulation, liberalization, privatization, and devolution. These reforms would transform the Japanese economy into a more open and flexible market economy with less government intervention and regulation, in which free-acting economic actors drive innovation, investment, and economic growth through market competition. Typical of conservative or neoliberal policy makers in other industrial democracies (not necessarily Japanese conservatives), Koizumi wanted to reduce government intervention and the amount of resources the government took from the private economy. He believed that the government's allocation of resources was inefficient and would severely limit Japan's ability to compete with the rest of the world. Thus, his reform efforts were concentrated on reducing the size of government and releasing the funds the Japanese government absorbed from the market in the form of taxes and postal savings and insurance back into the private economy. His policy platform was similar to the market reform and deregulation carried out by Margret Thatcher in the United Kingdom and Ronald Reagan in the United States in the 1980s.

It should be noted that Koizumi was not the first prime minister to take this approach. During the 1980s, Prime Minister Nakasone wished to carry out reform along the lines of the Thatcher and Reagan administrations. He succeeded in privatizing the national telephone, railway, and tobacco companies and in implementing tax reform similar to Thatcher's and Reagan's. But his reform did not go much further than these successes. Likewise, Hashimoto made efforts to reform Japan's economy but fell short because of misjudgment about the weakness of the economy and events beyond his control.

This chapter focuses on the reform efforts of the Koizumi administration (2001–2006).[2,3] The administration represents a turning point in Japan's transition. Economic, financial, and political institutions became more open, flexible, and responsive to the public in the first few years of the new century partly as a result of the reforms enacted during the Koizumi administration.

Reducing Government Spending

One of the Koizumi administration's most important policy priorities was the reduction of the fiscal deficit and eventually gross government debt. Fiscal consolidation during recessions is usually difficult in any country, because constituencies and political-economic actors demand government spending increases to stimulate the economy, and electoral incentives make politicians prone to increase spending, reduce taxes, or both. Automatic stabilizers built into fiscal policy – such as unemployment benefits and individual and corporate income taxes – increase spending and reduce tax revenues, even if policy makers do nothing to change fiscal policy. However, the Keynesian bias of the LDP government's fiscal policy particularly made spending increases during recessions likely and spending cuts difficult. After a decade of Keynesian expansions and continuing economic stagnation in the 1990s, however, Koizumi embarked on fiscal consolidation when he came in office in 2001. His fiscal reform stipulated that the government would achieve primary balance surpluses by the beginning of the 2010s. He further declared that his administration would carry out the structural reform of the Japanese economy, arguing, "No structural reform, no economic recovery."

The Koizumi administration reduced spending with relative success over a five-year period in areas where government spending had been notoriously inefficient and had not contributed to economic recovery – particularly, in public works and small business assistance.

---

[2] Koizumi stepped down from power per LDP party rules in 2006, and Prime Minister Shinzo Abe assumed power.

[3] We used Japanese newspapers (*Asahi, Mainichi, Nikkei, and Yomiuri Shimbuns*) and the government documents published by various government ministries on their Web sites for many of the factual descriptions in this chapter. When information is identical and widely found across multiple sources, we do not cite its sources. This comment also applies to Chapters 10 and 11.

Table 9.1. Annual growth of government budget, 2001–2006

Year	Social security	Education and science	Science	Grants to local governments	Defense	Public works	Economic cooperation	Small businesses assistance
2001	4.70	1.80	8.60	12.70	0.40	0.00	−3.00	0.20
2002	3.80		5.80	−3.30	0.00	−10.70	−10.30	
2003	3.90	−3.50	3.90	2.30	−0.10	−3.90	−4.70	−7.10
2004	4.20	−5.20	4.40	−1.00	−3.50	−4.80	0.50	
2005	2.90	−6.70	2.60	−1.00	−3.60	−3.80	−0.50	
2006	0.90	−8.00	1.10	−0.90	−4.40	−3.40	−6.60	

Note: The figures are all initial budgets at the beginning of the fiscal year.
Source: The Budget Bureau, the MOF, Yosan/Kessan (http://www.mof.go.jp/jouhou/syukei/syukei. htm).

Table 9.1 shows the annual growth of government budgets (initial budgets at the beginning of the fiscal year) in major spending categories during his administration (2001–2006). Table 9.1 illustrates that the administration cut spending in education, defense, public works, ODA[4] (Official Development Assistance), and small businesses almost every year. In the context of the overall budget, the rates of decline are small and represent minor changes in those expenditures. But the declines are notable nonetheless for at least three reasons.

First, each of these expenditures was guarded by LDP politicians, bureaucrats, and special interests, and Koizumi had to override their opposition. The power of Japanese prime ministers usually had been seriously constrained by other political actors and informal rules and, as a result, they did not have a great ability to override other actors' opposition in the postwar period. Bureaucratic ministries would do everything to protect their budgets, and no ministry would be willing to accept spending cuts. LDP politicians were in the position to protect their client ministries, industries, and constituencies and resist spending cuts. In this structural context, previous Japanese prime ministers were not successful in budget reduction, except during the 1980s where there was wide consensus among political parties, business, and the public on fiscal consolidation.[5]

Second, the LDP government's normal fiscal predisposition during a recession had always been to increase spending, particularly in

---

[4] ODA, to be precise, is economic cooperation, but most of it is allocated to foreign countries.

[5] Fiscal consolidation, however, is consistent with the policy preferences of the MOF which supports a balanced budget. Thus, prime ministers' past efforts at fiscal consolidation were almost always supported by the MOF.

public works and small business assistance to help its electoral bases in the construction, distribution, and agricultural sectors and local (rural) governments. But Koizumi managed to overcome the pressure to expand spending during a period of economic distress. Moreover, he achieved this in those policy areas where the alliances of LDP politicians, bureaucrats, and special interests were particularly powerful and exerted strong influence in the LDP – construction (public works), small businesses, and grants for local governments. In the context of the economic distress and the LDP's usual support for public works and small business spending, the Koizumi administration was exceedingly successful in achieving even minor reductions in these spending categories. The declines were not large, but their symbolic and practical meaning was significant in that Koizumi accomplished something his predecessors were unable to do.

Third, the prime minister had to implement budget cuts during a serious recession and deflation. They are difficult to implement during a recession because government spending cuts directly reduce aggregate demand and, hence, decrease GDP holding other things constant. The last thing any administration would want to do is to slow down the economy further. From this perspective, the Koizumi administration needed to reduce spending without suppressing growth, and the minor reduction rates were probably all that could reasonably be accomplished.

Education, defense, and ODA were also areas that received constant spending cuts under the administration. Spending cuts in these areas were still not easy, because each area faced an alliance of LDP politicians and bureaucrats that would oppose spending cuts. LDP politicians in these areas, however, were less powerful than those in construction, agriculture, commerce, and postal service. Moreover, defense and ODA do not have strong domestic special interests, which makes spending cuts politically easier than in areas that have strong domestic interests (foreign countries may oppose them, but people from foreign countries do not vote in Japanese elections and cannot hurt the LDP's votes directly).

During the Koizumi administration, the Japanese government shifted government resources from previous allocation to inefficient areas such as public works in rural areas, to the sectors and areas where public investment was expected to enhance the productivity and growth of the national economy. It shifted resources from the traditional sectors such as construction, distribution, and agriculture to dynamic sectors with great growth potential such as IT (information technology), nanotechnology, life science, and the environment. Although spending in education as a whole was cut during the administration, government spending in science and technology was increased every year to promote innovation and technological advances that would enhance the productivity of the economy. It also shifted resources from rural areas to major urban areas and others where stronger contributions to economic growth were expected. The government shifted public resources from the traditional small businesses in retail, wholesale, and others to new small venture businesses in sectors where venture businesses were expected to contribute to economic growth more dynamically, such as IT and high-tech industries.

The shift of government resources from the traditional sectors and regions to new ones had previously been difficult because the LDP relied on the traditional sectors for votes and money. LDP politicians and bureaucrats would have strongly opposed and thwarted the shift of government resources away from the traditional sectors. So it marks an important change in the LDP government's economic policy profile, no matter how small the magnitude of the changes in the distribution of government resources had so far been. Thus, during Koizumi administration, there was redistribution of government resources from traditional sectors and regions to modern ones.

The shift in economic policy was partly induced by the 1994 electoral reform which replaced the MMD system with a mixed system combining SMD and PR districts. Under the old MMD system, LDP politicians were able to win seats with a smaller number and percentage of votes than would be necessary under an SMD system. As a result, LDP politicians' main campaign strategies appealing to smaller segments of their constituencies – such as the building and maintenance of personal support organizations (*koenkai*) and the allocation of government resources to the construction, agriculture, and distribution sectors, and rural areas – made sense. Under the new mixed system with SMDs, however, candidates need to gain a larger number and percentage of votes. Consequently, they have to appeal to a wider range of constituencies, since appealing to the small segments of their constituencies may not generate sufficient votes to be elected.

This shift was also supported by the fact that the traditional sectors such as agriculture and rural regions experienced declining numbers of population and hence, declining numbers of voters. In contrast, the modern sectors such as high-tech, service industries, and urban areas experienced increased population and, hence, more voters. The LDP government led by Koizumi started efforts to cultivate and mobilize voters in the modern sectors with rising populations by crafting policies that appeal to those sectors.[6]

Social security was the only spending item that Koizumi was unsuccessful in cutting. Although he was unable to reduce spending, he significantly controlled the rate of growth of social security spending. There was significant upward pressure on Japan's social security spending because of the aging of the population as well as higher unemployment rates in recent years. Despite the pressure for spending increase in this area, Koizumi successfully contained the degree of spending growth. The slowdown of the growth in social security is apparent when compared to the rate of growth prior to his administration (see Table 9.1 and Figures 8.1 and 8.2).

Overall, the fiscal consolidation effort of the Koizumi administration is impressive all things considered. As a result of the administration's fiscal austerity between 2001 and 2006, Japan's total government spending growth slowed and then started a downward trend (Figure 9.1). The growth of government debt also slowed (see Figure 8.3). But whether gross government debt will be successfully reduced will depend on the ability of succeeding administrations to restrain government spending and whether economic growth will generate large tax revenues.

Reform of Government Programs and Institutions

We have so far looked at mostly quantitative changes in the amounts of total government spending under the Koizumi administration. We will now examine the administration's reform in specific government economic programs and institutions. Koizumi's fiscal consolidation and specific programmatic reforms went hand in hand to support his reform agendas, which were small government, deregulation, privatization, and liberalization. Koizumi executed more changes in government economic programs than can be seen in the quantitative changes in the amounts of government spending, particularly after his

---

[6] It should be noted that the shift of government resources away from traditional or rural sectors would be somewhat reversed later, after the LDP suffered a major loss in the 2007 upper house election, because the defeat was interpreted as a sign of voters' anger with the economic disparities created by Koizumi's economic reform.

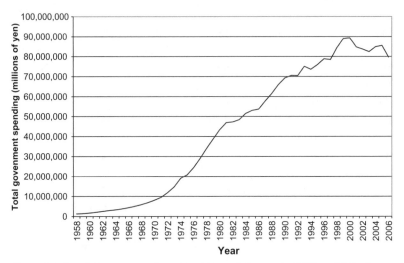

Figure 9.1. Total Government Spending (General Account), 1958 to 2006. *Source:* The data for 1958–2001 come from Statistics Bureau and Statistical Research and Training Institute, the Ministry of Internal Affairs and Communications, Nihon no Choki Tokei Keiretsu, [http://www.stat.go.jp/data/chouki/]. The data for 2001–2006 come from the Budget Bureau, the Ministry of Finance, Yosan/Kessan [http://www.mof.go.jp/jouhou/syukei/syukei.htm]. *Note:* The figures are actual expenditures at the end of each fiscal year, except for the year 2006 where the figures are those in the initial annual budget.

LDP won a landslide victory in the October 2005 lower house election. This victory gave Koizumi a solid public mandate to carry out his reform initiatives. Before the election, his reform attempts were often frustrated by the alliance of the LDP, bureaucracy, and client industries.

Prime Minister Koizumi's structural reform was directed at various government programs and institutions that underlay, justified, and buttressed the government's involvement in the private economy affecting the allocation of resources, economic decisions and activities, and ultimately the type of the economy Japan came to have. The specific targets of reform encompass a range of government institutions and programs firmly in place in postwar Japan – various government financial institutions; the FILP; the national postal services and PSS; public corporations in highway construction and others; government ministries and agencies and employment in the public sector; the fiscal relationship between national and local governments; and the structure of government budget accounts.

Many of these were the very features that had characterized Japan's political economic regime established and thrived under the LDP's one-party dominance. In this respect, Koizumi executed a great deal of changes to the old regime. The wide range of the government organizations and programs targeted demonstrates how large the Japanese government's involvement and intervention in the private economy had become, despite the fact that Japan's government spending levels and public employment were the lowest among industrial democracies.

Many of these targeted areas were interconnected to each other and affected the flow and allocation of economic resources in Japan. They together constituted a giant government-private system for the intermediation of financial resources. And the system partly mediated the political-economic patronage among the LDP, bureaucracy, and industry, and partly helped maintain the LDP government's political-economic regime. In this scheme of the circulation of resources, the government collected large amounts of money from the private economy in the form of postal savings and life insurance deposits, and used the funds to finance government programs (such as public works), then politically and discretionarily utilized the resource allocation to promote their political or economic goals as well as to achieve legitimate policy goals.

Japan's national postal services managed postal savings and life insurance and collected ¥330 trillion in deposits and contributions, which constituted a quarter of all individual financial assets in Japan, making it the largest financial institution in the country. Before the reform of 2001, the deposits collected through post offices nationwide automatically came under the control of the Trust Fund Bureau of the MOF. The money was then funneled to numerous government financial institutions, public corporations, and local governments through the FILP to fund government programs and make loans to public and private organizations to achieve government policy goals. The funds were used to promote policy goals in housing, social infrastructure and environment, welfare and education, small and medium businesses, agriculture and fisheries, roads, transportation, communication, industrialization, and international cooperation. This allocation of FILP funds was susceptible to the discretion of politicians and bureaucrats. In the early postwar period, when Japan had to rebuild the economy from scratch after the devastation of war but capital was scarce, the government's financial intermediation through the FILP helped build infrastructures necessary for economic reconstruction and development and promote economic growth. The government intermediation system played an important role in the history of Japan's economic development in that respect.

Critics argued that although the system contributed to Japan's reindustrialization process and emergence as the world's second largest economy by the 1970s, the system was maintained even after Japan had achieved a high level of economic development and its original objectives and missions were achieved. In fact, the amounts of funds the government allocated through the FILP dramatically expanded during the lost decade of the 1990s, as the government funded public works and various other government programs to spend its way out of the recessions.

Critics pointed out that the large amounts of the funds were used inefficiently, hurting Japan's resource allocation and the economy. The funds, if they were left in the private economy, would be more efficiently used by market actors to maximize profits. The government might use them to achieve certain legitimate policy goals, but the political allocation of economic resources was not necessarily made in a way to increase economic efficiency or equity. The government could also use the funds to advance their own political agendas. Politicians and political parties could, for instance, allocate the funds to their constituencies or client sectors in order to bolster their electoral strength without regard for the consideration of economic efficiency. Bureaucrats could allocate the funds to fund the public agencies and corporations they have built and controlled in order to increase their budgets, power, and reputation. Of course, not all funds were used politically and inefficiently. Some funds were used to support productive sectors, and some were used as a legitimate tool of fiscal expansion during recessions. But the LDP government often used the funds to boost its electoral strength and allocated them to public works and rural regions that were important electorally to the LDP.

The solution to the economic inefficiency created by this vast system of government financial intermediation was to reduce the funds the government absorbed from the private economy and used to fund government corporations and projects. This is exactly what Prime Minister Koizumi sought to achieve. He wanted to do this through multiple channels. First, he wanted to privatize Japan's national postal services, which had been organized as a government corporation in 2003 called the Japan Post to cut the flow of funds from the private economy to the government in the form of postal savings and life insurance premiums. Second, he wanted to abolish or privatize the government financial institutions that funneled the FILP funds to public corporations and targeted sectors, regions, and programs, so as to reduce the size of government financial intermediation. Third, he wanted to close or privatize the many public corporations that expended the FILP funds.

Koizumi was quite successful by the end of his term (2006) in reforming the government finance programs and institutions. He successfully legislated the privatization of the national postal services (in effect in October 2007). He legislated the closure or privatization of eight government finance institutions. He drastically reduced the FILP budget. He privatized the four highway public corporations. He privatized or abolished many other public corporations. He legislated the reduction of government budget special accounts used to run various government programs. He legislated the further reduction of government employees (both national and local government employees). He also initiated devolution from the national to local governments.

These reforms are impressive because each of them cut into the vested interests of powerful LDP politicians, bureaucrats, their client sectors, or all of them, who had served as veto players against Japanese prime ministers in the past. Each reform was opposed by some or all of veto players, and Koizumi's implementation of reform meant that he successfully overrode their opposition, which had always been very difficult under LDP rule.

The national postal services had a network of twenty-four thousand post offices nationwide. The national association of postmasters was one of the LDP's strongest and most crucial electoral support bases, showing a high level of cohesion and organization as a vote mobilization machine and commanding large numbers of organized votes. Many LDP politicians relied on their votes. As the postal services were run by government, they were able to keep open unprofitable post offices, particularly in rural and remote areas. In fact, over 71 percent of the post offices in the nation operated with a deficit in 2005 (*Mainichi Shimbun*, November 24, 2006), and when considered only in terms of mail delivery, 94.5 percent operated with a deficit. Rural residents favored these post offices because they were convenient, providing not only mail delivery but also savings and life insurance services, and, in their absence, the residents would need to travel far to receive substitute services. The LDP's electoral strength traditionally lay more in rural areas, and its government protected the postal services. LDP politicians opposed postal privatization, claiming that, if privatized, many unprofitable post offices in rural areas would be closed and therefore needed services would be denied to those living in rural areas. LDP politicians with expertise and influence in post and telecommunications policy were particularly powerful *zoku* politicians within the LDP. It would be difficult for any government or party leader to implement a policy opposed by them.

Postmasters opposed privatization vehemently for fear of losing business and their jobs because of a lack of profitability and harsh market competition. Postal workers would also lose their secure public employee status. LDP politicians had every good electoral reason to oppose privatization because they could earn the votes of postmasters and rural voters by doing so. Japanese bureaucrats (the Ministry of Internal Affairs and Communications, formerly, the Ministry of Posts and Telecommunications) would also oppose privatization or abolition of any public corporations and government programs, because they would lose power (less organizations and programs under their jurisdiction) and control over funds (budgets for their organizations and programs). Thus, postal privatization was opposed by the alliance of the LDP, bureaucracy, and client groups; in fact, the postal system was one of the best illustrations in Japan of how the iron triangle functioned.

When Koizumi came to power in 2001, the Japanese government ran eight government banks and public financial corporations: (1) Development Bank of Japan; (2) Central Cooperative Bank for Commerce and Industry; (3) Japan Finance Cooperation for Municipal Enterprises; (4) National Life Finance Corporation; (5) Japan Finance Corporation for Small and Medium Enterprise; (6) Agriculture, Forestry, and Fisheries Finance Corporation; (7) Japan Bank for International Cooperation; and (8) Okinawa Development Finance Corporation).

Most of these financial institutions were established in the 1950s and 1960s to support the implementation of the FILP by making long-term low-interest loans to achieve various government policy objectives supported by the FILP. They were under the control of the Japanese ministries, especially the MOF. Koizumi wanted to abolish or privatize these government financial institutions. Bureaucrats opposed it, because they would lose the government agencies they controlled. That would mean that they would lose agencies under their jurisdiction (less power) and budgets that would be allocated to them.

Moreover, Japanese bureaucrats had used these government financial institutions to secure their after-retirement employment by the practice of *amakudari*. Large numbers of government officials had traditionally taken executive positions at these financial institutions after retirement from their ministries. Thus, bureaucrats wanted to preserve the institutions, despite the wishes of Prime Minister Koizumi and other politicians to close or privatize them. It was often the case under LDP rule that, when bureaucrats opposed prime ministerial policy initiatives, LDP politicians who had expertise and influence in relevant policy areas also opposed and resisted the initiatives. This happened because LDP politicians and bureaucrats who shared expertise and influence in the same policy areas formed a formidable alliance and protected each other to preserve their vested interest.

Koizumi's restructuring of government financial institutions was met with intense opposition, but he managed to privatize or abolish them after the 2005 lower house election. Reduction of the FILP budget would be difficult for the same reasons, because, again, that would mean reduction of budgets that politicians and bureaucrats could use. But Koizumi drastically reduced the FILP budget during the five years of his tenure (Figure 9.2).

Privatization of the four highway public corporations similarly met with vehement opposition and resistance by LDP politicians and bureaucrats. The LDP's *zoku* politicians with expertise and influence in road construction had always been as powerful as those in postal services. The construction industry had traditionally been one of the LDP's most powerful and reliable vote-mobilization machines. Japan's construction industry had been large by international standards. And the government's spending on public works, such as road construction, had been the highest of all industrial democracies (easily two times higher), because the LDP government had customarily allocated large government resources to construction, particularly in rural areas. In return, the construction industry provided the LDP with votes and money. Japan's construction industry had been very well organized and had mobilized reliable organized votes for the LDP in elections. Furthermore, during recessions, the LDP government had almost always increased public works spending to stimulate the economy in a

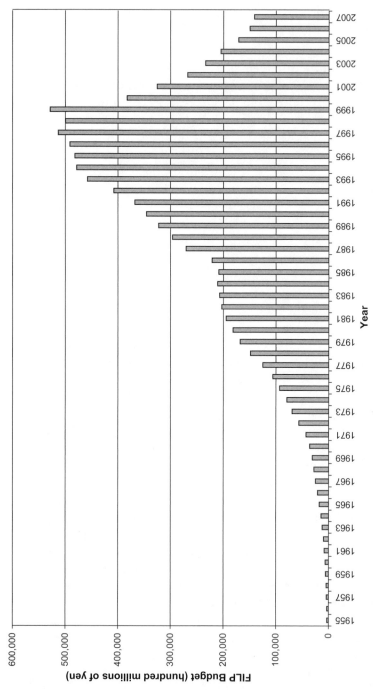

Figure 9.2. The Size of the FILP Budget, 1955–2007. *Source*: The data for 1955–2001 come from Statistics Bureau and Statistical Research and Training Institute, the Ministry of Internal Affairs and Communications, Nihon no Choki Tokei Keiretsu, [http://www.stat.go.jp/data/chouki/]. The data for 2001–2006 come from the Budget Bureau, the Ministry of Finance, Zaisei Toyushi [http://www.mof.go.jp/jouhou/zaitou/zaitou.htm]. *Note*: The figures for 1955–1968 are the actual amounts spent at the end of the fiscal year. The figures for 1969–2007 are initial budgets.

Keynesian fashion. As a result, LDP politicians' opposition would be strong against any measure that could lead to reductions in road construction spending.

The privatization of the highway public corporations was one of such measures that brought intense political resistance. Koizumi wanted to privatize the highway public corporations because they were a tool of wasteful and redundant road construction by LDP politicians, bureaucrats, and local governments. Many critics over the years pointed out that Japan's road system had been constructed without much consideration for economic efficiency or benefits. The Ministry of Construction (Ministry of Land, Infrastructure, and Transport after 2001) inevitably opposed privatization because its bureaucrats would not want to lose the source of power and control, budgets, and lucrative executive positions for them after retirement from the ministry. Road construction had also provided many jobs in rural areas. As a result, privatization was opposed not only by the construction industry but also by companies and workers in other sectors (e.g., farmers) and local governments.

The reform of these government financial institutions and programs would have been difficult for any Japanese prime minister to implement, because of the vested interests and political power of the alliance of the LDP, bureaucracy, and their client industries, as reviewed earlier, and because of various constraints on the power of the prime minister.

How successful was Prime Minister Koizumi in implementing these reforms? Koizumi was not very successful for much of his administration because the LDP's antireformers resisted the reforms. Koizumi had to make many compromises and concessions to gain their reluctant consent so that the substance of the reforms was watered down as a result. This environment changed after the 2005 lower house election, and Koizumi was fairly successful in implementing his reforms, following his LDP's historic electoral victory. When his postal privatization bills were rejected by the upper house as a result of the revolt of many LDP upper house members, Koizumi dissolved the lower house to ask for a public mandate on his reform. Although this dissolution and the high-handed approach that he took against the antireformers appeared controversial and was normally a violation of Japan's conventional consensual politics, it was received positively by the Japanese public. Koizumi successfully rallied the public around his reform, and his LDP gained an overwhelming landslide victory. After the election, no political opponents – be they LDP politicians or bureaucrats – were able to ignore the public mandate that Koizumi gained. The antireformers had no choice but to reluctantly approve his reform. As a result, Koizumi made significant progress – including postal privatization – in the last year of office.

Postal Privatization

As a result of Koizumi's reform, Japan's postal services were privatized and divided into four companies under a holding company (Japan Post) in October 2007 – three companies specializing in mail delivery, postal savings, and postal insurance, respectively, and another company running the post offices. Post offices handle mail, savings, and insurance by establishing contracts with the other three companies. The holding company will sell all shares of the savings and insurance companies by 2017.

The Koizumi administration was forced to make a series of concessions to the antireform alliance of LDP politicians, postmasters, and their other client groups to mitigate their opposition. As a result of the concessions, both postal savings and insurance companies are bound to continue their business contracts with all post offices for ten years after privatization and most likely after that as well. The financial costs of the maintenance of all three services at all post offices will be financed by a fund ranging from ¥1 trillion up to ¥2 trillion to be established from the sales of the shares of the postal savings and insurance companies; however, the holding company can buy back the shares. This was the administration's compromise to the LDP who wanted to ensure that all three services – postal savings, insurance, and mail – would be provided in rural areas and that post offices would not be forced to close by the savings and insurance companies' decision to terminate business with post offices. LDP politicians wanted to ensure that all three services would be offered at all existing post offices as long as possible.

The administration also compromised by agreeing to maintain the current post offices, at least one post office in each city, town, and village. This would make it difficult to close post offices in rural areas where the LDP drew many votes, even when closure makes economic sense as a result of unprofitability.

All employees (260,000) with the exception of nineteen thousand postmasters lost public employee status and the job security that went with it. Postal workers were previously public employees guaranteed lifetime employment. Now that postal services are privatized, it is easier for management to make layoffs when faced with the need to reduce labor costs and redundancy. This was a major change in the lifetime employment system that had dominated much of Japan's economy in the postwar period.

Critics argued that all the policy concessions that Koizumi made to mitigate the privatization opposition would undermine the performance of the privatized postal companies, as they would constrain the companies' economic decisions. The compromises would make it difficult for the post office company to restructure underperforming or unprofitable post offices. Postmasters would keep their public employee status, and it would be difficult for the company to lay them off even if they were redundant. These points are valid, but we also note that these privatized companies will be exposed to market competition (despite the constraints) and will have no choice but to run their companies efficiently (unless politicians decide to intervene again in the future). Most important, postal privatization will end the flow of funds from the private economy to government financial intermediation and inefficient programs and projects. This was the original goal of reform.

Restructuring of Government Financial Institutions

Koizumi enacted a significant restructuring of the eight government financial institutions that had represented a major part of the FILP. Two institutions will be privatized, one will be abolished, and five institutions will be consolidated into one public corporation. The Development Bank of Japan and the Central Cooperative Bank for Commerce and Industry will be privatized in 2008 (with a five- to seven-year transitional period). Japan Finance Cooperation for Municipal Enterprises will be abolished in 2008, and its functions will be continued by a new corporation to be founded by municipal governments. Four financial corporations – National Life Finance Corporation; Japan Finance Corporation for Small and Medium Enterprise, Agriculture, Forestry, and Fisheries; Finance Corporation; and Japan Bank for International Cooperation – will be consolidated into a single public finance corporation in 2008. The Okinawa Development Finance Corporation will be absorbed in the new public financial corporation in 2011.

As these reforms become effective in 2008, the national government will withdraw from the role as a financial intermediary in many areas of loan and financial programs, where such loans can sufficiently be provided by the private economy alone, but where the government institutions have supplied enormous amounts of loans for a long time. Businesses and others that had relied on the government banks will now be required to obtain funding from the private sector. This is a dramatic change in Japan's financial system. The size of the Japanese government's financial programs (formerly FILP programs) will be reduced significantly. The reform law requires that the total amount of loans outstanding as a percentage of GDP (as of 2005, ¥90 trillion, or 17.9 percent of GDP) be reduced 50 percent by the end of 2008.

The reform is significant because these public financial institutions made loans and ran other government financial programs using the enormous FILP budgets. The Koizumi administration was serious about retrenching the government financial system that had grown large enough to be called the Japanese government's "second budget." The magnitude of the reform can also be seen in the substantial reduction in the total amount of the FILP budget, as shown in Figure 9.2.

Privatization of Japan Highway Public Corporations

The four Japan Highway Corporations were privatized in October 2005. These highway corporations and their former national corporations had been criticized for wasting enormous amounts of government resources by building unprofitable and underutilized roads, highways, and bridges and for creating massive debt for the government and citizens. The excessive construction of roads had been conducted for decades. Highway and road construction was used by LDP politicians as a tool of distributive politics for electoral purposes and by bureaucrats related to road construction and local governments that wanted greater budgets and political power. Large road construction was also frequently used by the LDP government as a countercyclical tool during recessions in the postwar period. The purpose of privatization was to reduce the inefficient and wasteful construction of roads, highways, and bridges and reduce government debt created by the highway public corporations.

Koizumi succeeded in privatizing the highway public corporations; however, he was forced to compromise on some issues to the antiprivatization alliance of LDP politicians, bureaucrats, and the construction industry to mitigate their opposition. The compromise left room for politicians and bureaucrats to pressure the privatized highway companies to build roads even after privatization that they would not build on a rational economic analysis. Koizumi's privatization left open the possibility of continued government intervention, because the appointment of CEOs of the privatized companies needs to be approved by the Minister of Land, Infrastructure, and Transport. This may make it difficult for the privatized companies to refuse to build unprofitable roads demanded by politicians and bureaucrats. Another shortcoming of the reform was that it did little to restructure or reform what is called the highway companies' "family companies" that have monopolized the contracts for the provision of the services commissioned by the highway companies for decades. The efficiency and performance of the privatized companies will partly depend on how this potential for political intervention will be handled by the future governments, politicians, bureaucrats, and the private companies. In the long run, the privatized companies have a reasonable chance to gain independence and be run like other private corporations. But, at this moment, the possibility remains that it can go either way – the private companies may remain independent of political interference, pursue profits, and make decisions based on market logic; or politicians and bureaucrats may intervene in the private companies' decisions on road construction to achieve their political goals.

Closure or Privatization of Other Public Corporations

Koizumi closed or privatized 136 various public corporations and semipublic special corporations, including the New Tokyo International Airport Public Corporation, Japan Environment Corporation, Housing Loan Corporation, Japan National Oil Corporation in addition to the ones discussed earlier. Thirty-nine of the 136 corporations were transformed into incorporated administrative agencies rather than thoroughly privatized. These reforms significantly reduced government involvement and programs in many areas of the economy, as they were the ones that expended large government general and FILP budgets. The reform reduced the amount of the government budget allocated to the public and semi-public corporations by ¥1.8 trillion and cut the number of government employees.

The restructuring of these public and semipublic corporations was somewhat easier than the privatization of the postal services and highway corporations, because they did not adversely affect as large a segment of constituents and client groups of the LDP as postal services and highway construction. In the case of postal services and highway construction, the Koizumi administration faced large numbers of rural constituents, regions, companies, and organizations that had been some of the strongest electoral bases of the LDP in the postwar period. As a result, LDP politicians' opposition to reform was proportionately strong, and the administration had to overcome the strong opposition by the alliance of LDP politicians and their constituents and client groups. The other public corporations were not as important to the LDP politicians' voter base as those of the postal services and road construction; hence, LDP politicians' opposition was accordingly weaker. The administration did have to overcome serious opposition and resistance by government ministries and bureaucrats who did not want to lose their organizations, budgets, control, and sources of postretirement employment. But it did not have to face opposition by the united alliance of LDP politicians, government bureaucrats, constituents, and special interests.

A further restructuring of special public corporations and incorporated administrative agencies has been under way and will be forthcoming at the time of this writing. This will further reduce government intervention in the market economy.

Reforming the Relationship between the National and the Local Governments – Devolution

Prime Minister Koizumi initiated an effort to delegate policy-making power from the national to local governments, so that local governments could become more self-sufficient, fiscally responsible, and efficient. Devolution of policy-making power from the national to local governments also met with strong opposition by the alliance of LDP politicians and national bureaucrats. Japan has a unitary system in which power is concentrated in the national government and local governments do not have much power, in contrast to a federal system such as those in the United States and Germany, in which significant power is delegated from the national government to state governments.

To national bureaucrats, devolution meant a loss of power over policy and budgets. They did not want to concede power and budgets to local governments and opposed Koizumi's attempt at devolution. To LDP politicians, devolution similarly meant the loss of an important instrument of distributive politics directed toward their local districts. LDP politicians had devoted much effort to boosting their electoral strength by gaining government resources from the national government and allocated them to their local districts to woo individuals and groups that brought them votes (i.e., voters, local industries and businesses, local governments, and the local politicians who mobilized votes for national legislators). LDP politicians were able to use this tool, because government resources were controlled by the national government. Devolution would reduce or eliminate the usefulness of this instrument to LDP politicians, while local governments, governors, mayors, and local legislators would gain power at the expense of LDP politicians at the national level. As a result, both bureaucrats and LDP politicians at the national level opposed devolution.

Koizumi's devolution policy was only a beginning. The magnitude of change was very marginal and nominal. Koizumi transferred ¥3 trillion tax revenue sources from the national government to the local governments. In exchange, he implemented a ¥4.7 trillion reduction in government grants provided by the national government to local governments (2004–2006). The programs previously funded by the national grants are now run and financed by local governments. The size of government programs and revenue sources transferred as part of the devolution policy was small because of opposition from national bureaucrats and LDP politicians who did not want to lose their power and budgets. In addition, Koizumi also reduced the total amount of grants from the national to local governments to achieve small government and streamline spending and programs run by local governments.

But after Koizumi, there has been little progress in devolution under the succeeding administrations. The lack of progress reflects both resistance by national bureaucrats and politicians and the low priority devolution receives in the administrations' policy agendas.

FILP Budget Reduction Manifests the Combined Effect of Koizumi's Policies

Prime Minister Koizumi made resolute efforts to reduce the size of the FILP budget after coming into office. He reduced the FILP budget annually. Figure 9.2 shows the amount of the FILP budget between

1955 and 2007. The FILP budget had continuously expanded in the postwar period, except for a brief period in the second half of the 1980s when it leveled off. The FILP budget showed a dramatic increase throughout the 1990s, as the government used the FILP budget to increase government spending to stimulate the economy in recession. But the FILP budget was significantly reduced in the 2000s. The size of the FILP budget was ¥32 trillion in 2001, when Koizumi came to power. The amount was reduced to ¥15 trillion in his last year of office in 2006. This is a significant reduction in the FILP budget, which had peaked at ¥52 trillion in 1999. The FILP budget will decrease further as a result of Koizumi's restructuring of the government financial institutions and privatization of the postal savings discussed earlier.

Administrative Reform and *Amakudari*

Prime Minister Koizumi's attempt at administrative reform – the restructuring and downsizing of the government bureaucracy in terms of organizations, budgets, personnel – inevitably met with resistance from bureaucrats. From the perspective of bureaucrats, the more organizations, personnel, and budgets they have under their control, the more power, reputation, and job security they have. Thus, they would oppose administrative reform under most circumstances. In their opposition, they mobilized the support of their client LDP politicians with whom they shared common policy and political interests and had close relationships in relevant policy areas. These LDP politicians who had influence and expertise in certain policy areas also had much to lose from the restructuring and downsizing of government organizations and programs, because their political and policy power and resources would be adversely affected by the size of government organizations and budgets they influenced. Thus, Koizumi's administrative reform effort had to override opposition by the alliance of bureaucrats and LDP politicians.

Koizumi passed an administrative reform promotion law that required a 5 percent or higher reduction in the number of national government employees by 2011. Before the cabinet approval of the law, government ministries (justice, agriculture, health, labor, and welfare, and land) that were assigned to reduce employees resisted the reduction, but Koizumi overrode their opposition. The law also required a 4.6 percent or higher reduction in the number of local government employees. The employee reduction at the national and local levels will reduce government spending on wages and benefits for public employees. It will also turn the public wage system currently based on seniority into one based on merit and performance.

By contrast, the Koizumi administration made only marginal progress in reducing bureaucrats' practice of descent from heaven (*amakudari*). Many government officials still gain lucrative employment in numerous public and private corporations after retirement from their ministries. For instance, during the one year between September 2005 and August 2006, 42 percent (532 bureaucrats) of all 1,263 retiring high-ranking government bureaucrats took positions as CEOs and executives in public and semipublic corporations and incorporated administrative agencies after retirement (*Nihon Keizai Shimbun*, December 27, 2006). This grossly understates the current practice of descent from heaven because it does not include those who accepted positions in private corporations.

The difficulty of reform in this area is partly a result of opposition and resistance by bureaucrats who would lose their source of after-retirement employment and of power. Japan's powerful Japan Business Federation (*Keidanren*) recently announced its intention to prohibit its member corporations from accepting these bureaucrats. But it withdrew the proposal immediately when government bureaucrats expressed their reservations about the ban.[7]

Other Economic Policy Reforms

The Koizumi administration advanced many other policy reforms in addition to those mentioned above to pursue fiscal restraint and consolidation, cut back the size of government, make the Japanese economy more efficient and competitive, or make Japan's social security

---

[7] The succeeding Abe administration (2006–2007) was adamant about restricting the practice of descent from heaven but was forced to accept a much scaled-back reform because of opposition from bureaucrats and LDP politicians and Abe's lack of political skills and leadership. No effective measure to reduce the practice was adopted, as a result. The current Fukuda administration (2007–) has so far been much more sympathetic to bureaucrats' opposition, and no substantial restriction on descent from heaven is in sight.

and health care sustainable. A brief description of those other reforms follows.

Koizumi increased health care copayments and other health care burdens for aged citizens over sixty-nine years old and created a new health care program for citizens over seventy four years old to curb increases in health care costs. The new program will be managed by prefectures so as to give local governments an incentive to manage health care efficiently and reduce costs.

Koizumi implemented a 1.36 percent cut in the reimbursements of the costs of medical services and labor for doctors and health care institutions in 2006 to reduce rising health care costs (on top of 1.8 percent cut in the reimbursement of the costs of medicines and medical tools and materials; *Nihon Keizai Shimbun*, December 22, 2005). Reductions in these health care reimbursements have always been difficult for the LDP government to carry out, because the Japan Medical Association is a strong LDP electoral base. The LDP's *zoku* politicians who have influence over health and welfare policy always support doctors' opposition to reimbursement cuts, and they are some of the most powerful *zoku* politicians in the LDP. This alliance of physicians and powerful politicians is one of the reasons that Japan's health care costs have remained high. As a result, despite deflation since 1995 and declining general wages, the medical reimbursements had not been adjusted downward since 2002. But Koizumi overrode their opposition and carried out the spending cuts.

Koizumi increased pension contributions to make Japan's social security system sustainable. The contributions will gradually be increased from current 13.6 percent of income (shared evenly by employers and employees) in 2004 to 18.3 percent in 2017.

Under the Koizumi administration, the antimonopoly law was revised, and its enforcement was strengthened to reduce collusion and cartels. Previously, Japan's antimonopoly law enforcement had been lenient.

Koizumi initiated reform to introduce market competition in the provision of public services by establishing a system in which government offices and private companies compete for public services contracts.

The Koizumi administration passed the law requiring the government to reduce the size of government assets as a percentage of GDP by 50 percent by 2015. This was a further attempt to reduce the size of FILP and government in Japan's future economy.

Japan's government budget had thirty-one special accounts in addition to its general account. The special accounts had been set up separately from the general account to manage the national budget used for different policy programs. They were used for postal services, debt servicing, grants to local governments, the FILP, social security, and public works among others. The monitoring mechanism on the special accounts was much weaker than on the general account because of their complexity and, as a result, the special accounts had much wasteful or unrestrained spending. The special accounts were also one important medium of the FILP program and subject to the same criticisms leveled against the latter. The reform of the special accounts was part of Prime Minister Koizumi's reform of government financial intermediation.

Koizumi was able to pass a law in 2006 requiring a restructuring and rationalization of the special accounts. The law stipulated a reduction of the number of the special accounts by one-half to one-third by abolishing redundant accounts and consolidating the remaining or absorbing them in the general account by 2010. Subsequently it was decided to reduce the thirty-one special accounts to seventeen (*Mainichi Shimbun*, December 13, 2006). It also required the government to reduce the size of the special account budget by ¥20 trillion and allocate the generated fund for the servicing of the government's debt during the same period.

Koizumi attempted to terminate the earmarking of tax revenues from gasoline and automobile acquisition for road construction (the Government Special Fund for Road Construction: *doro tokutei zaigen* about ¥3.7 trillion). If successful, the funds would then be used for the general budget. This effort was met with intense opposition from local governments that did not want to see their road construction budgets drop and the LDP's road *zoku* politicians who wanted to maintain their source of power and budgets. Koizumi dropped the termination proposal at the end of his tenure. The succeeding Abe administration similarly announced the intention to terminate the program. But, again, this was met with opposition from local governments and LDP politicians, and they emasculated the reform. The Abe administration was forced to make serious concessions and agree to "build necessary roads" and only release the currently earmarked revenues for general budgets that are left over after building those necessary roads (*Mainichi Shimbun*, December 8, 2006). Of course, every new road in Japan is "necessary."

This case illustrates that the political influence of LDP politicians and road *zoku* politicians vis-à-vis the prime minister and party leadership remains strong. It illustrates that despite the reduction of their political power during the Koizumi administration, the LDP's *zoku* politicians can still override the prime minister's policy initiatives, depending on which prime minister they face and on the nature and magnitude of policy issues. In Abe's case, his lack of political skills and leadership contributed to the failure at reform.

Accounting for Koizumi's Success

Koizumi's success in achieving the reforms that previous prime ministers would have had difficulty achieving was contingent on several factors.

The first was the timing. The Japanese economy was in the worst condition in recent history, and everything the government had tried had failed by the time Koizumi came to office. The public was thus more receptive to different or unconventional policies and political leaders. This was likely the most critical factor in Koizumi's favor. Had the economy not been in such bad shape, even Koizumi would have had difficulty persuading the antireformers – the alliance of LDP politicians, bureaucrats, and client industries, and the public – that Japan's conventional policy and way of managing the economy would not work and would need to be changed. In fact, if the economy had not been in such bad shape and political leaders had not been so ineffective, Koizumi would not have probably been elected prime minister in 2001 in the first place. Note that he had previously been defeated in LDP presidential elections twice by very large margins.

Second, and related to the first factor, Koizumi was backed by the highest level of public support in history for most of his tenure. It made it difficult for the LDP – which opposed his reform and wanted to remove him – to replace him, because doing so would have been electorally suicidal for the LDP that experienced declining electoral strength. If Koizumi had not been publicly so popular, the antireform LDP would have easily removed him and his reforms would have been defeated or watered down so much as to be meaningless.

Third, Koizumi skillfully concentrated policy-making power in the prime minister's office, which enabled him to force his reforms through the LDP and override its opposition. For instance, in order to increase the chance of successfully legislating postal privatization in 2003, Koizumi generated an incentive structure combining retribution and reward for LDP politicians to support or not oppose postal privatization. Koizumi would propose privatization in the LDP presidential election, and would not appoint dissenters to be cabinet ministers. He would also not support the candidacy of dissenters in the next election. If he lost the presidential election, he would leave the LDP and dissolve the lower house under his new party with the campaign promise of privatization. These intentions would deter potential LDP dissenters from opposing privatization (Shimizu, 2005, chapter 6).

Power concentration was possible partly because of his great political and tactical sense and skills. But it was possible also because of the administrative reform that was designed by his predecessor Hashimoto and the 1994 electoral reform enacted by Prime Minister Hosokawa, both of which were already in place when Koizumi came to office. The administrative and electoral reforms shifted policy-making power away from the LDP and bureaucracy to the prime minister's office and his office as the LDP president. The two reforms created an institutional environment that would make it possible for the prime minister to take strong policy initiatives, if he wished to and enjoyed great public support.

Fourth, Koizumi was not a conventional LDP politician who had much stake in maintaining his power within the party. This made it possible for him to go against the LDP − not complying with the LDP's decision-making rules and procedures and disregarding the LDP's opposition to his reforms. If he had cared about his standing in the LDP, he would not have been able to shove his reforms into the face of the LDP. If anything, the more he confronted the LDP, the more popular he became among the public.

Fifth, Koizumi was also skillful in hammering out compromises and concessions with the antireform LDP. If one was to trust Koizumi's public comments, one would get the impression that he would not make compromises and concessions with the reform opposition. But, in reality, he made many significant concessions to the antireformers to weaken their opposition. This is what led critics to argue that although he may have achieved his reforms in form, they were watered down in substance as a result of his many policy concessions.

Sixth, Koizumi's reform initiatives were aided by the new policy-making style he built, in which he set the CEFP at the center of agenda setting and policy making. The CEFP was already in existence when Koizumi assumed power. It had been designed by Prime Minister Hashimoto and officially established in early 2001 under the Mori administration. This illustrates again how institutional change – Hashimoto's administrative reform – provided Koizumi with a foundation to take advantage of this new body in his reform attempts and make policy innovations.

The CEFP was managed by the administration's economic and fiscal minister, Heizo Takenaka. An economist, Takenaka generated policy proposals in consultation with other economists and business leaders. Koizumi and Takenaka made the proceedings of the CEFP open to the public. This made it difficult for the LDP's *zoku* politicians, bureaucrats, and special interests to openly interfere with Koizumi's reforms. This significantly weakened the ability of the antireformers to resist the reform initiatives (Shimizu, 2005).[8] From the start, Koizumi was determined to ignore the LDP's opposition in carrying out his policies, because if Koizumi gave LDP politicians significant say, they would successfully resist policies that hurt them or their clients.

Seventh, and finally, Koizumi was fortunate to win the 2005 lower house election by landslide. The election took place after his postal privatization bills were defeated by LDP upper house members' revolt and he subsequently dissolved the lower house. Very few observers originally thought that his LDP would win the election. Not many voters considered postal privatization important. Koizumi's approval rate recorded the lowest ever (37 percent) in a poll conducted in July between the lower and upper house votes (*Mainichi Shimbun*, July 18, 2005). Furthermore, in the same poll, 35 percent of respondents wanted the opposition Democratic Party (DP) to increase seats and only 25 percent wanted Koizumi's LDP to increase seats. Moreover, Koizumi practically expelled all of the thirty-seven LDP lower house members who voted against his privatization bills – this meant that his LDP would have to win thirty-seven additional seats just to maintain the same majority it had before the house dissolution. But soon after Koizumi dissolved the lower house, public opinion suddenly and

---

[8] In October 2005, however, Kaoru Yosano assumed control of the CEFP, and the center of economic policy making shifted back from the CEFP to the LDP. Thus, the strength of the CEFP is contingent on other factors, such as the prime minister's intention, willingness, and ability to set the CEFP at the center of policy making and the strength of the personalities involved. The CEFP also did not play a large role during the Abe administration. Neither has it under the current Fukuda administration.

dramatically changed. Public support for the Koizumi administration, LDP, and privatization increased significantly and, as a result, Koizumi and his LDP achieved a major victory.

In hindsight, we can say his political tactics and reform were supported positively by the public. It was not so much because the specific issue of postal privatization was on the minds of the voting public, but because it represented Koizumi's fight against the entrenched interests in Japan – the iron triangle – that had been tolerated in the past but was unable to provide economic growth and security. The public had had enough of the "old boys" system and Koizumi was the element of change. Koizumi took the gamble and events were on his side. Most of his reforms would have been shelved if the electoral outcomes had been different.

Koizumi: Lasting Influence?

Many of the reforms that Koizumi achieved were subject to the criticism that the integrity of the substance of his reforms was compromised because of the many concessions and compromises he made to mitigate the reform opposition. It is true that he made many concessions to win support for his reforms and, as a result, many of his reforms were toned down. But we note that the long-term direction Koizumi set for Japan's economy toward liberalization, deregulation, and a freer market economy will be difficult to reverse, especially in the face of the exigencies of the globalized economy calling for efficiency and international competitiveness. This does not rule out short-term policy swings that can occasionally happen as a result of changed political or economic conditions. Generally, once new institutions or systems are installed, it is difficult to reverse them because the transaction and transitional costs of doing so are prohibitively high.[9]

The privatized postal services, savings, and life insurance will be exposed to market competition and have no choice but to make their companies efficient and competitive. Consider the cases of Nippon Telegraph and Telephone and Japan Railway, which were privatized

---

[9] To illustrate, many politicians and political parties opposed electoral reform in 1994, and some politicians tried to reestablish the multimember district system after the mixed SMD-PR electoral system was installed; however, these efforts have failed and the mixed SMD-PR system has become a stable part of Japan's political institutions and is not likely to be altered in the near future.

in the 1980s. These former public corporations remain private and have performed much better after privatization. This is a general outcome when privatization takes place. National or public corporations perform better when privatized.

There is also criticism that the 40 percent reduction in national government employees (twenty thousand) was achieved by transforming government agencies and corporations into independent administrative agencies and therefore the actual size of the reduction is much smaller (*Mainichi Shimbun*, May 13, 2006). This ignores the fact, however, that those employees will lose their public employee status and be exposed to market competition and possibility of layoffs. Furthermore, there is general consensus among political parties that the government should contain spending on the employment costs of government employees at both the national and local levels as a whole and curb the number of public employees. Thus, policy reversal on reducing the number of public employees is not likely in the absence of some dramatic event.

Koizumi's success despite the opposition from the alliance of LDP politicians, bureaucrats, and their client industries and sectors is partly a result of a relative shift of policy-making power away from bureaucrats to politicians that took place in the second half of the 1990s and the 2000s.[10] Previously, Japanese bureaucrats were powerful and controlled policy making from policy conception to implementation (Johnson, 1982). Although LDP politicians were not powerless, they had difficulty carrying out policy that ran counter to bureaucrats' vested interests or that was opposed by them.

Yet, in the course of the 1990s and 2000s, politicians increased their policy-making power vis-à-vis bureaucrats. The power shift was partly a result of politicians' conscious effort to move policy-making power to where it should belong – elected officials (politicians), who have a public mandate to make decisions for voters, rather than nonelected officials (bureaucrats), who have no such mandate. Politicians had made such conscious effort ever since the non-LDP eight-party coalition government led by Prime Minister Hosokawa governed Japan in 1993. Politicians increasingly gained knowledge and expertise in policy issues over the years that had once been the monopoly of the bureaucracy. The power shift was also a result of bureaucrats' failure

---

[10] Politicians gradually increased power vis-à-vis bureaucrats throughout the postwar period, although the power shift was clearer in the late 1990s and 2000s.

and loss of respect by the public, especially the MOF, and the clear failure of public policy to end a decade of economic and financial distress.

Japanese bureaucrats would have resisted such a power shift under normal circumstances. But, since the 1990s, they were in a poor position to oppose such reform openly or legitimately. They had previously commanded much respect, reputation, and trust by the public for their competence. However, from the 1990s, a series of corruption scandals implicating high-ranking bureaucrats were brought to daylight, and their respect and trust were tarnished. Economic bureaucrats were also criticized for causing Japan's economic problems in the 1990s and for being incapable of salvaging the economy. Bureaucratic corruption had existed in the past, but, in the 1990s, the combination of corruption scandals and economic policy failure amplified the negative political conditions against bureaucrats and made it difficult for them to resist efforts by politicians to reduce their power.

Bureaucrats continue to retain power and attempt to resist further efforts to reduce their power or policies that run counter to their interests. And they enjoy monopoly of policy-making power on issues in which politicians have no interest. But, at least for now, politicians can set the policy agenda, determine the general framework or direction of policy, and have bureaucrats to make specific proposals within the framework. Bureaucrats may try to resist policy that goes against their interests; however, they are not likely to regain the power they once had against politicians.

Koizumi was able to cut into the vested interests of LDP politicians, bureaucrats, and client industries. This again does not mean that the alliance of the three actors has become entirely powerless – the iron triangle is weaker but not dead in Japan. Even under the Koizumi administration, efforts at deregulation to reduce the intervention and power of bureaucrats and politicians in some areas were successfully resisted by the alliance. To illustrate, a policy change to require license renewal of medical doctors was thwarted by the opposition of the Japan Medical Association, LDP politicians with influence in health and welfare policy, and bureaucrats of the Ministry of Health, Labor, and Welfare. An effort to extend the period of initial car inspection of new automobiles from three to four years was also foiled by the alliance of Ministry of Land, Infrastructure, and Transport bureaucrats, LDP politicians with political influence in this policy area, and car repair shops (*Nihon Keizai Shimbun*, April 15, 2005). Also, as mentioned earlier, the termination of the earmarking of the tax revenues from gasoline and automobile acquisition for road construction was successfully resisted by LDP politicians and the car and road industries.

Koizumi set the liberal-market course for Japan's economy. Succeeding policy makers or administrations may resist further progress in the future, but most of the reforms already made by Koizumi are not likely to be drastically reversed. In fact, in order to ensure that the direction toward a freer market economy will not be reversed, Koizumi enacted the Administrative Reform Promotion Law in 2006 to obligate succeeding administrations and policy makers to continue further market reform for the next five to ten years. The reform of government financial institutions, government agencies and employees, and special account budget discussed earlier was stipulated in this law. Institutional or organizational change, such as the privatization of the postal services and public corporations, will also be hard to reverse.

However, Koizumi's other accomplishments can potentially be reversed. Fiscal consolidation and austerity pursued by Koizumi can be easily reversed by politicians' and political parties' electoral concerns. In fact, there are already signs of some policy change that can slow down Japan's fiscal consolidation. Just before the end of his tenure (June 2006), Prime Minister Koizumi established a fiscal consolidation plan (to be observed by succeeding prime ministers) to reduce government spending in the next five years and achieve primary balance surpluses by 2011. But the size of concrete spending cuts was scaled back and the contents and methods of the cuts were made obscure by the LDP's opposition.

The succeeding Abe administration's efforts at spending cuts were also much more moderated than during the Koizumi administration, partly because of the large increases in tax revenues resulting from economic recovery that started in 2005. The spending cuts were resisted also because of the LDP's electoral concerns. The LDP faced an upper house election in the summer of 2007 and feared that it would not be able to win the election with fiscal austerity. Prime Minister Abe's LDP suffered a historic defeat in the upper house election. Not only did his LDP-CGP coalition government lose the majority in the upper house, the opposition DP replaced Abe's LDP as the largest party in the house.

The LDP's defeat was a result of several factors – Abe's lack of political skills and leadership; multiple money scandals surrounding his cabinet members, which severely diminished public support for him; the revelation that Japan's Social Security Agency had amassed fifty million cases of unidentified social security payments that it had received from citizens over the years as a result of its negligence; and the fact that Japanese voters remained discontented with their economic insecurity and disparity. This last point is important because it signifies less public support for liberalization policies. The economic insecurity and disparity has been attributed to Koizumi's economic reform (hence, the LDP) by the media, public, and opposition parties. Public discontent was magnified by the money scandals by Abe's cabinet ministers and the Social Security Agency scandal.

The DP capitalized on these events and dramatically increased seats in the election at the expense of the LDP by promising to take policy measures to protect the economic well-being of citizens and redress economic disparities. These policy measures could entail increasing redistributive government spending on economically dislocated people and regions, potentially implying retreats from fiscal austerity and from Koizumi's reforms that emphasized market competition and economic competitiveness and efficiency. In the face of the electoral results overwhelmingly supporting the DP's policy, the LDP is now under pressure to consider adjusting its previous economic policy positions set by Koizumi. Prime Minister Fukuda, who succeeded Abe, has expressed his intention to tone down Koizumi's economic policy.

The future of Japan's economic policy will be affected by many political and economic factors, and policy will experience short-term, although most likely minor, policy swings. In the long run, there currently seems to be wide consensus among business, political parties, and the public that Japan needs a free market economy to ensure economic prosperity. The public, however, is concerned about the economic insecurity and disparity and, in a somewhat contradictory way, expects the government to redress the economic insecurity and disparity. At the time of this writing, it appears that the general direction of economic policy established by Koizumi is likely to remain, although the voice for more redistribution and social protection that has gained some currency among the public, media, and political parties will put countervailing pressure on liberalization policy in the short- to medium-term.

Finally, the future fiscal conditions of the Japanese government depend on whether or not Japan will have a strong political leader (such as Koizumi) who can overcome strong spending pressures created by politicians' electoral concerns, on economic conditions and resulting tax revenues, and on whether Japan can successfully continue to make its economy efficient and competitive, which would contribute to the government's fiscal balance.

10

Japan's Corporate Governance, Labor Practices, and Citizens' Social and Economic Life at the Beginning of the New Century

Introduction

The economic problems of the 1990s and 2000s had an impact not only on the Japanese government's economic policy, politics, and political outcomes but also on broader aspects of Japanese society and life. Although many factors were attributed to Japan's economic problems, policy makers, politicians, and observers argued that the structural features of the Japanese economy were an important cause of the problems. Japan's corporate governance, financial system, labor market practices, and the clientelistic relationships between government and industry were considered sources of economic inefficiency, impairing the performance of the Japanese economy.

Japanese corporations themselves also felt the need to restructure their business and management and regain competitiveness and efficiency to improve their performance, as many of them suffered poor performance, debt, excessive investment and capacity, low rates of returns, redundancy, and high production costs. Private corporations, particularly those in the export sector, were the first ones to acknowledge the need for change and to initiate reform, because they were exposed to international competition and had no other choice but to change if they wanted to survive in the market economy. They were thus much more forthcoming in executing their own changes than politicians, bureaucrats, and their constituent industries and sectors that had been accustomed to favorable government policy and protection provided by politicians and bureaucrats. These traditional constituents' first inclination was to hang on to their entitlements and ride out the economic recessions with help from the government. But other private corporations that realized they would need to

235

change sought their survival and revival in their own reform, especially because those that had not received as much government protection believed that the government's discretionary economic policy created resource allocation inefficiencies and hurt the performance of the national economy. In their view, Japan's highly regulated economy was an important cause of economic inefficiency. Subsequently, Japan's private corporations reconsidered their conventional Japanese-style practices in corporate governance and labor relations and made changes, thereby improving their performance by the mid-2000s.

Japanese workers were naturally affected by private corporations' reform in corporate governance and labor market practices. Japanese workers, as we have seen in Chapter 2, had conventionally enjoyed a high level of job security and continuous improvement in their standard of living throughout the postwar period before the 1990s. But change in their companies forced change in their career and socioeconomic life, and they were required to forego benefits they had long received from the conventional Japanese-style management. This affected not only their current socioeconomic life but also their expectations about their future.

Thus, the Japanese-style management and labor market practices much celebrated during the 1980s no longer exist in their original form. But Japanese corporations' reform also has not been a complete denial of the traditional Japanese way. Corporate leaders still find much value in Japanese-style practices today, such as lifetime employment, cooperative management-labor relations, and even cross-shareholding. So do many workers. Thus, continuity exists in Japan's economy and society along with change. In time, Japanese companies and workers will find a new Japanese way of business – Japanese business and labor practices will be closer to American-style corporate governance and labor market practices than before but will be far from being the same.

This chapter outlines various changes that Japanese corporations have implemented and how they have affected the lives of Japanese workers and people. It illustrates what has changed and remained. The chapter then examines socioeconomic issues that, in tandem with the changes in corporate governance and labor market practices, affect Japan's economy, government policy, and Japanese lives. It reviews notable changes in what was considered a Japanese way of the economy and business. It shows that these changes create socioeconomic difficulties as well as political ones for Japan in the new century.

What Are Japanese Companies Like Now?

Many aspects of the Japanese economy changed from the second half of the 1990s. Faced with protracted multiple recessions and stagnant corporate performance in the 1990s, Japanese companies had to reconsider what was considered the Japanese way of management and labor practices that had produced favorable economic results in the past. And, indeed, in the second half of the 1990s, Japanese companies started gradually changing the way they operated their business to regain competitiveness and performance.

Faced with economic stagnation and the need to make economic adjustments, Japanese companies first had to restructure to reduce labor costs and economic waste. Before the 1990s, major Japanese companies rode out many recessions including the two oil crises in the 1970s without resorting to layoffs as a common practice. Whenever they faced recession and needed to lower production costs, they always found ways to achieve it without relying on layoffs. Even when they had to remove redundant workers, they transferred them to their subsidiaries or subcontractors to support their continuous employment. The previous recessions were relatively short and almost never resulted in an actual drop in real GDP. As a result, Japanese companies were able to ride them out without relying mainly on layoffs.

Japanese companies believed that the benefits of retaining their long-term workers outweighed its costs, as it gave both employers and employees the incentive to invest in job training and the upgrading of workers' job skills and knowledge, and that it promoted human capital formation and enhanced their productivity and ultimately company performance. The retention of core workers also saved the companies the cost of losing workers' loyalty and devotion and of having to hire and train new workers when the economy recovered. Companies found it more beneficial to make adjustments to economic fluctuations by other means while retaining workers, as their long-term core workers were long-term investments and assets. Also, Japan's relatively flexible wage adjustments and workers' willingness to cooperate with their employers during economic hardships helped companies reduce production costs without layoffs (e.g., reduced bonuses, reduced compensation for overtime work, nationwide wage coordination and restraint cooperatively achieved by Japanese employers and labor unions since 1975). In addition, Japanese companies and workers believed that the retention of core workers was the norm. That is one of the reasons that Japan's unemployment had been low before the 1990s.

As the recessions protracted and their performance stagnated, Japanese companies started restructuring in the second half of the 1990s. The magnitude of the recessions and stagnation overwhelmed their capacity to reduce costs without restructuring their management and labor practices.

First, they started letting go of employees systematically for the first time in recent history. They still made every effort to find them new employers before laying them off and to monetarily compensate for the workers' losses to ease their financial difficulty. But they did start using layoffs as one of the means of restructuring. As a result, for instance, the number of workers employed by Japanese banks declined from the peak of 460,000 in 1994 to 300,000 in 2004 (*Nihon Keizai Shimbun*, December 31, 2004). Fuji Heavy Industries Ltd. (of which Subaru is the automobile section) decided in 2005 to let seven hundred employees go for the first time in its history since the foundation in 1953 (*Nihon Keizai Shimbun*, November 6, 2005). But its method of layoff was still such that the company invited early retirement applications from employees and offered them additional retirement bonuses (on top of regular retirement bonuses) and new employment elsewhere. Other major corporations have taken similar approaches to restructuring redundant workers, inviting voluntary early retirement with the offer of additional retirement bonuses and new employment.

Second, Japanese companies started gradually reducing their long-observed practices of lifetime employment and the system of seniority-based promotion and wage increases. Before the 1990s, major companies (although not all of them) provided employees with lifetime employment, and employees were promoted based on seniority and given wage increases annually. But the economic stagnation and poor performance of the 1990s led many companies to reform those employment and wage systems in the second half of the decade. The reform of corporate governance and labor management had two broad points: (1) the reduction or abolition of the seniority wage system, and the introduction of a performance-based wage system; and (2) the reduction of workers employed with lifetime employment ("regular workers"), and companies' increasing reliance on "nonregular workers" (temporary and part-time workers) without lifetime employment.

Table 10.1. Use of lifetime employment and/or seniority wage by Japanese companies

Year of surveys	1999	2002	Change (2002–1999)
Lifetime employment + Seniority wage	68.2%	53.7%	−14.5%
Lifetime employment + Merit wage	20.1%	29.1%	9.0%
No or limited lifetime employment + Merit wage	9.6%	16.7%	7.1%

Source: Policy Research Institute (2003); Miyajima et al. (2003).

Table 10.1 shows the results of two surveys of Japanese companies conducted by the Policy Research Institute of the MOF in 1999 and 2002 (Policy Research Institute, 2003; Miyajima et al., 2003). Overall, these results combined with other evidence illustrate three characteristics about current Japanese corporate governance and labor market practices.

First, many Japanese companies have indeed made changes to their employment and wage systems. In particular, many companies replaced their seniority wage system with a merit-based wage system. They have also reduced or terminated many generous benefits they used to previously provide their employees, such as housing subsidies and spouse benefits, in order to economize on labor costs (although these are not measured in the surveys).

Second, and at the same time, a large majority of companies still maintain the practice of lifetime employment. Thus, the Japanese-style management in this area still has remained, illustrating the continuing strong belief among corporate managers in the benefits of lifetime employment. There have been changes, however. Companies now limit lifetime employment to selected numbers of core workers and hire more part-time or temporary workers without lifetime employment. Many Japanese companies also still consider their own employees to be main stakeholders.

The results show that 53.7 percent of companies still maintain both lifetime employment and the seniority wage system in 2002. The percent of companies offering these benefits declined 14 percent from 1999, but the majority of the companies still practice both lifetime employment and the seniority wage system. This indicates the resilience of Japanese-style management and labor practices. If we set aside the wage system, 82.8 percent of companies continued to practice lifetime employment in 2002. And an additional 11.4 percent of companies partially use lifetime employment.

In contrast to the resilience of lifetime employment, the wage system has experienced more change. In 2002, 29.1 percent of companies use a merit-based wage system while maintaining lifetime employment. This is an increase of nine percentage points from 1999. If we add to this the companies that use merit-based wages but no lifetime employment, 45.8 percent of companies use a merit-based wage system in 2002. This is an increase of sixteen percentage points from 1999, when the percentage of companies offering a merit-based wage system was 29.7 percent. The ratio of companies that mainly use both nonpermanent employment and merit-based wage is 16.7 percent in 2002, which represents an increase of seven percentage points from 1999. Thus, there is a significant decline in the use of the seniority wage system, but, at the same time, Japanese companies still maintain lifetime employment, at least, for their core workers. These trends are consistent with anecdotal cases of companies such as Canon and Toyota.

Canon decided to apply merit-based wage to all its employees, but the goal of the reform was partly to make possible its preservation of the practice of lifetime employment even during economic downturns (*Yomiuri Shimbun*, January 9, 2005). As we will see later in this chapter, the numbers and percentages of nonregular workers in Japan who do not have lifetime (or permanent) employment have been increasing steadily. The numbers and percentages of Japanese workers with lifetime employment are on the decline. But Japanese companies still grant lifetime employment to their core regular workers, because they believe that it is beneficial for human capital formation and corporate performance. For instance, the chairman of the Japan Business Federation (*Nippon Keidanren*), Japan's largest peak organization of employers, remarked that Japan's recent economic recovery was due to the fact that employers had maintained Japanese-style management that valued employees and long-term employment (*Nihon Keizai Shimbun*, January 11, 2006). Companies (e.g., Sumitomo Trading) that adopted merit-based wage have also partially readopted seniority wage to better train young workers without compromising their ability to cooperatively work with their colleagues (*Nihon Keizai Shimbun*, March 1, 2006). We see here an instance of the stickiness of local, informal institutions (i.e., Japanese-style management) in the midst of institutional change induced by more universal imperatives of today's globalized economy (e.g., trade openness, capital mobility, international competition). That is, the globalized economy may impose similar pressure on national economies to move toward a free market economy, but different countries with different informal practices and norms may respond to the universal pressure in distinct or culturally influenced ways.

Third, cross-shareholding in Japan decreased during the 1990s recessions, but has recently started increasing again to guard against hostile takeovers, and a large majority of Japanese companies still conduct cross-shareholding. Cross-shareholding by Japanese companies has been a major feature of industrial organization in Japan. Japanese companies mutually held shares of other companies that were either their main banks or their group companies or that they had close long-term transactional relationships with. They practiced cross-shareholding for the purposes of preventing hostile takeovers, maintaining stable long-term business relationships with other companies, and sharing business risks. Cross-shareholding permitted corporations to plan and conduct business and projects with a long-term view without worrying about short-term stock prices or quick profits normally demanded by shareholders, because these mutually held shares were stably owned by Japanese companies for a long time.

After the 1990s economic crises started, cross-shareholding was criticized for being one of the causes of Japan's economic problems, because, it was argued, Japanese corporations did not have an effective monitoring mechanism on their economic decisions and activities that would normally be provided by outside shareholders and market, as their group companies and banks held their shares. It has been cited as a factor for excessive, highly speculative investments in assets during the bubble and poor economic decisions by Japanese companies in general (e.g., Lincoln, 2001). It also has been speculated that this is a factor in low returns on investments in Japan.

Since the collapse of the bubble, Japanese companies (especially banks) had reduced cross-shareholding by selling shares of group companies, main banks, and others that they had close long-term transactional relationships with. In 2003, cross-shareholding accounted for 24.3 percent of the monetary value of all shares traded in Japan (Cabinet Office, 2006). Yet the evidence shows that cross-shareholding is still practiced by a large majority of Japanese companies and has in fact continuously increased since 2004. The results of the same surveys of Japanese companies mentioned earlier (Policy Research Institute, 2003; Miyajima et al., 2003) show that, in 2002, 83.2 percent of companies still practiced cross-shareholding. The percentage declined from

88.4 percent in 1999, but it remains high. When asked why they practice cross-shareholding, over 70 percent of the companies answered that they mutually hold shares with other companies to maintain stable, long-term business relationships, around 30 percent answered "to prevent hostile takeovers," and over 10 percent answered "to realize corporate activities based on a long-term view" (the companies chose up to two answers in the surveys). In addition, cross-shareholding by Japanese companies has been on the rise again ever since 2004. In 2006, ¥12.8 trillion worth of stocks were cross-shareholding, representing a 30 percent jump from ¥9.8 trillion in 2004 (*Nihon Keizai Shimbun*, January 23, 2007). Thus, the pattern in cross-shareholding also shows that there has been change in Japanese management, but a great deal of continuity also exists.

New Corporate Governance Institutions

Japanese corporations are now facing a more competitive and transparent environment in which they are increasingly being required to be more sensitive to shareholders. Japan is moving away from a stakeholder system to a shareholder system.

Stricter Enforcement of the Antimonopoly Law and Reduced Collusion

A distinctive feature of Japanese business – collusion and bid-rigging – still exists but has decreased as a result of the recent revision of the law and the government's concerted efforts to enforce the antimonopoly law more strictly than previously. An indication of a decrease of collusion is seen in the decreased ratio of final winning bid prices to the projected final project prices planned by governments in the results of the bidding for public works commissioned by the national and local governments. Although the average rates vary between the national and local governments and across industries and areas, the reported average rates had previously been over 95 percent, but they are now in the 80 percent range (*Nihon Keizai Shimbun*, February 22, June 13, and July 18, 2006). The decline in the percent range shows that companies cannot collude as easily as in the past so that companies offering lower prices win bids. As a result, the government pays prices lower than projected. Widespread collusion, particularly in the construction industry, previously had been considered a source of high prices and economic inefficiencies. Construction companies and others that won government projects made more profits (illegally and unethically) than they should because of collusion. Fair public bidding without collusion usually produces competitive contracted prices and lower prices, whereas collusion makes it possible for participating companies to keep contracted prices high. Collusion had also bred an environment for bureaucratic corruption, by which government employees received bribes from bidding companies in exchange for information on the projected project prices planned by governments, so that the latter can win bids with the highest prices.

The stricter enforcement of antimonopoly law by the government has made it more difficult for contracting companies to collude than previously. As of this writing, news stories reporting suspected or actual cases of collusion still keep coming in, involving Japanese companies, prefectural governors, and government and public corporation officials. But this is also a result of the government's heightened enforcement and determination to penalize collusion. As a result, more companies and industries are deterred from colluding. In fact, companies that have previously engaged in collusion are now afraid to collude, because the revised antimonopoly law gives confessing companies leniency in penalty and many companies have actually come forward to avoid or reduce penalty; hence, the increase in the number of prosecuted or reported cases of collusion in recent years.

Collusion may not completely cease to exist.[1] But it will continue to decline in frequency and magnitude, and there will be much greater fairness in private corporations' competition for government projects.

The Japanese government has also been trying to reduce the number of government projects contracted through "discretionary contracting" (i.e., the contracting of government projects without public bidding competition) and increase the share of government projects contracted through public bidding to increase fairness and transparency, reduce the monetary costs of government projects, and reduce room for bureaucratic corruption. But progress has so far been slow. Discretionary contracting was a major source of bureaucratic corruption,

---

[1] As we write in late 2007, it has been revealed that the vice minister of the Ministry of Defense (the very top bureaucratic official of the ministry) had received bribes for over ten years from a defense contractor and was arrested.

because it provides room for government employees to discretionarily give government contracts to companies in exchange for bribes or other favors. It has also been a source of the high costs of government projects.

Breakdown of the Conventional Corporate Group Relationships and Increased Foreign Direct Ownership

There have been many small- and large-scale mergers of well-known companies across conventional boundaries of corporate groups and nationality. This reflects companies' desire and need to increase competitiveness by streamlining redundant sections, operations, and employees between multiple companies and by increasing market shares. This is the area of corporate governance that has clearly changed in Japanese-style management after the lost decade. One of the features of Japanese-style management used to be the importance of *keiretsu* relationships among firms (conglomerates or corporate groups). Japanese companies tended to have transactions within their corporate groups with which they had stable, long-term relationships. Similar long-term relationships also existed between major corporations and their subsidiaries and subcontractors. This was considered one of the factors that made difficult the market entrance by foreign companies and products in Japan.

But mergers across *keiretsu* boundaries are now commonplace. For instance, about twenty major banks that had existed in Japan before the lost decade have been merged into three "mega-banks" and three other group banks. Japanese business based on the *keiretsu* structure used to be relatively closed to both domestic and foreign firms outside the *keiretsu* groups, but mergers and joint ventures between Japanese and foreign firms are also now commonplace. Foreign ownership of (formerly Japanese) companies has also increased. And as a result of the liberalization of the financial markets, foreign financial institutions (particularly life insurance companies) are now major market actors in Japan and formidable competitors for Japanese companies. Foreign ownership of company shares also accounted for 23.7 percent of all stocks in Japan in 2004. Foreign direct investment in Japan also reached over ¥4 trillion (*Nihon Keizai Shimbun*, June 22 and June 29, 2005). Allowing market competition in the Japanese economy is a slow, gradual process. But, in the long run, the economy will incrementally move toward further liberalization of markets and more competition.

The role of foreign investors, especially, is a radical change in Japan's system of corporate governance and one that was encouraged by Koizumi.

New, Receptive Attitudes toward Investment in Stocks and Mutual Funds

There has been change in Japanese people's attitudes toward bank and postal savings and investment in stocks. Japanese individuals used to predominantly save their money in bank or postal savings accounts more than invest in stocks or mutual funds. But, since 2004, Japanese consumers have increasingly invested in mutual funds, and the amount invested in mutual funds has drastically increased and marked the highest in 2006 (almost ¥47 trillion: *Nihon Keizai Shimbun*, July 18, 2006). There is a shift of large amounts of money from bank and postal savings accounts to mutual funds. More than half of the stocks traded in the Japanese stock markets were traded by individuals in 2005 (53.2 percent between January and October: *Nihon Keizai Shimbun*, January 17 and November 10, 2005). The increased investment in stocks is attributable to economic recovery and increasing stock prices, low interest rates on savings, and the sales of mutual funds by banks that was liberalized in 1998.

Increased Transparency and Openness

The level of transparency in corporate activities and balance sheets has been greatly improved. The country learned an important lesson about the adverse effects of nontransparency from its experience with the bubble economy, the collapse of the bubble economy, and the massive nonperforming loan. The requirements for information disclosure by corporations have been made more stringent, and Japanese corporations are much more forthcoming in disclosing their business and financial information. This took place simultaneously with their much increased desire and willingness to acquire capital from the equity market. Japanese companies now rely more on equity finance, cater much better to shareholders, and concern themselves with their stock prices. They are exposed to greater pressure from shareholders than before. Improvements in transparency and openness have also taken place in government, and as a result, Japan is a much more open society than it was a decade ago.

Adverse Consequence of Restructuring for Japanese Workers: Increase of "Nonregular" Workers and Personal Financial Fragility and Instability

Despite some continuity in Japanese corporate governance and labor market practices, there is one type of change that has had grave impact on the lives of workers and families and on the future economic stability of Japan; that is, Japanese companies' increasing reliance on "nonregular" workers, such as temporary and part-time workers.[2] This has negatively affected workers and families, because it increases their job and financial insecurity and results in lower wages often without health care or social security benefits. Japan's income inequality and poverty rates have both increased significantly in recent years and are now some of the highest among industrial democracies. Thus, the Japanese are now or have the potential to be exposed to an income gap between the rich and poor and low income. Aside from the increases in income inequality and poverty rates, this will also have grave consequences for Japan's economic future, because the decline in the occupational and financial well-being of workers has had adverse effects on Japan's fertility rates, which in turn fuels population decline and the aging of Japan's population.

Japanese companies started restructuring in the second half of the 1990s, faced with protracted recessions and falling profits. They had had redundant workers as a result of the recessions and their practice of lifetime employment. As we have seen earlier, many Japanese companies and managers still express their belief in the economic benefits of lifetime employment and have maintained the practice for their core workers. Japanese companies restructured, instead, by increasing their reliance on nonregular workers (temporary and/or part-time workers) while preserving lifetime employment for their core workers. In Japan's business and labor environment with weak worker protection, temporary and part-time workers have provided companies with a means to reduce labor costs, as those workers' wages are much lower than regular workers and companies do not have to pay for those workers' health care and social security. Nonregular workers have also allowed Japanese companies to increase their ability to adjust to economic fluctuations.

Figure 10.1 shows the number of nonregular workers (temporary and/or part-time workers) from 1993 to 2004. The number rose

---

[2] The impact of this change was noted in the *Economist* (2008) and the *Wall Street Journal* (Yuka, 2008).

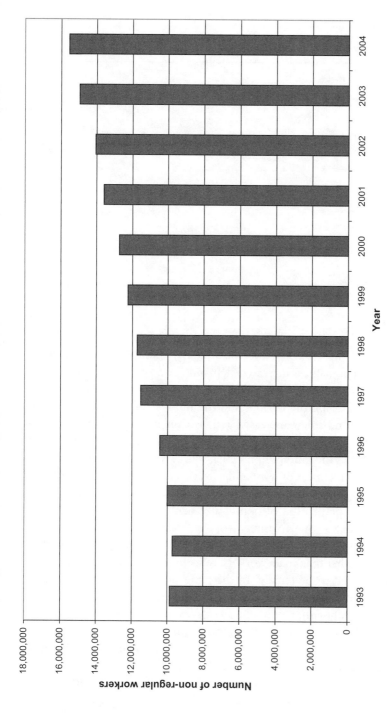

Figure 10.1. The Number of "Nonregular Workers" in Japan (Men and Women Combined). *Source:* The Labor Market Policy Research Commission (2005).

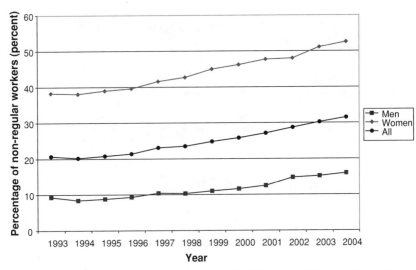

Figure 10.2. Ratio of Nonregular Workers to Total Employed Workers. *Source:* The Labor Market Policy Research Commission (2005).

annually since 1995. These workers increased from 9,710,000 in 1994 to 15,550,000 in 2004. Needless to say, these increases are not a result of companies' increased demand for more workers in general that would normally occur during economic booms – Japan was in recessions during the period, and the number of jobs was declining. Japanese companies' increased reliance on nonregular workers and decreased reliance on regular workers is illustrated in Figure 10.2, which shows the ratio of nonregular workers to total employed workers. The percentage of nonregular workers to total workers increased from 20.2 percent in 1994 to 31.5 percent in 2004. In the most recent survey, the percentage of nonregular workers increased to a high of 33.0 percent – one in three workers (*Mainichi Shimbun*, March 2, 2007). The percentage of nonregular workers among female workers is much higher than male workers, reflecting the pattern that part-time workers tend to be female. In the same survey, as of 2006, increases in nonregular workers still exceed those for regular workers (men and women combined), despite the fact that recent economic recovery has increased Japanese companies' demand for workers.

Nonregular workers face not only job insecurity but also much lower wages than regular workers. Figure 10.3 reports wage disparity between male regular workers and male part-time workers in terms of average hourly wages. In 2002, part-time workers' wages were only 39 percent of regular workers' wages. And the disparity increased over

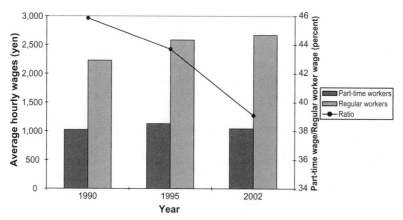

Figure 10.3. Wage Disparity between Male Regular Workers and Male Part-Time Workers (Average Hourly Wages). *Source:* The Labor Market Policy Research Commission (2005).

the three-year period illustrated in Figure 10.3. In 2005, male non-regular workers' wages were only 60 percent of male regular workers' (*Nihon Keizai Shimbun*, March 28, 2006). (*Nihon Keizai Shimbun*, March 28, 2006). In addition to lower wages, nonregular workers usually do not receive health care or social security benefits that are provided by employers for regular workers.

Nonregular workers and unemployed workers have been increasing, particularly among young people. The Japanese government has kept track of increasing numbers of young nonregular workers and unemployed workers ages fifteen to thirty-four, classifying them as "freeters" (roughly, part-time and temporary workers or those who are unemployed and wish to gain such nonregular jobs) and "NEET" (Not in Education, Employment, or Training). The grim financial and employment conditions among young workers (unemployment, low wages, and job insecurity) are considered one of the causes of Japan's recent low fertility rates, fueling population decline. Japan's fertility rates had already been low and the source of continuing concern about the future.

Increasing Income Inequality and Poverty: Japan Is Not the Egalitarian Society that It Was

Before the 1990s recessions, Japan was applauded for achieving economic growth without sacrificing income equality. In contrast, in many newly emerging countries, economic growth was often accompanied by increases in income inequality. In the 1990s and the start of the new century, however, Japan's income distribution has become increasingly unequal, and its poverty rates high. Japan has, for now at least, become a country with one of the highest income inequality and poverty rates among OECD countries.

The increases in inequality and poverty were a result partly of the recessions that forced companies to rely less on regular long-term workers and more on nonregular temporary or part-time workers and partly the result of the increase in the aged population and change in family structure. Now that the economy is performing better and companies are hiring more regular workers, there is a chance Japan's income distribution and poverty rates will improve if the country can maintain a favorable economic performance. However, it will be difficult for Japan to fully recover the low levels of income inequality and poverty Japan enjoyed in the past. If anything, the government's policy has moved more toward neoliberal market reform that usually has the effects of increasing inequality and poverty.

In 2001, Japan had the fourth highest income inequality of all OECD nations in the ninth-to-first decile ratio next only to Mexico, Turkey, and the United States (Table 10.2) and the third highest in the median-to-first decile ratio next to Mexico and the United States (Forster and d'Ercole, 2005; Burniaux et al., 2006). Japan's relative poverty rates in 2001 were the fourth highest of all OECD nations (next to Mexico, the United States, and Turkey) (Table 10.3). Because late-developing or newly emerging economies such as Mexico and Turkey usually experience higher income inequality and poverty rates than mature industrial countries, Japan and the United States are the top two highest-ranked countries (among OECD nations) in terms of income inequality and poverty rates.

Japan might claim that its income inequality and poverty are lower than the United States; however, the United States has had the highest income inequality and poverty for being the most advanced economy in the world. So the United States' being worse is hardly a relief. Japan's income inequality in terms of Gini coefficients is the eighth highest in 2001, next to Mexico, Turkey, the United States, Portugal, Italy, Greece, and the United Kingdom. But this is not reassuring, because these countries are either newly emerging economies or countries known to be unfriendly to low-income workers and families. What is worse, Japan was the only OECD country other than Mexico and

**Table 10.2. Income inequality:
Ratio of the ninth to first decile
earnings of equivalized
disposable income in 2001**

Mexico	9.3
Turkey	6.5
United States	5.5
Japan	4.9
Portugal	4.8
Italy	4.8
Greece	4.5
Ireland	4.2
United Kingdom	4.1
Unweighted average	4.1
Spain	4.1
Canada	3.8
Germany	3.6
France	3.5
Austria	3.2
Finland	3.2
Luxembourg	3.2
Netherlands	3.1
Belgium	3.0
Czech Republic	3.0
Sweden	2.8
Norway	2.8
Denmark	2.7

Note: The ratio of the ninth to first decile
earnings of equivalized disposable income
after taxes and transfers (adjusted for the number of persons in the household).
Source: Förster and Mira d'Ercole (2005).

Turkey that experienced a decline in average real disposal household
income between 1995 and 2000, even though real GDP per capita
increased over that period, and the average real income decline mainly
affected workers in the bottom two deciles of the income distribution
(Forster and d'Ercole, 2005).

It is debatable whether income inequality is always bad and equality
is always good. However, postwar Japan was not an unequal society
with high poverty rates. In fact, Japan was known for achieving rapid
economic growth while maintaining a high level of equity. Around
1970, Japan had one of the lowest levels of income inequality among
OECD countries, next to Sweden, Norway, and the Netherlands

Table 10.3. Relative poverty rates in 2001; Ratio of the median to first decile earnings of equivalized disposal income in 2001

Mexico	20.3
United States	16.9
Turkey	15.9
Japan	15.3
Ireland	14.9
Portugal	13.7
Italy	13.7
Greece	13.3
Spain	12.5
United Kingdom	10.7
Unweighted average	10.4
Canada	10.3
Germany	9.8
Austria	8.6
Netherlands	7.9
France	7.0
Finland	7.0
Norway	6.3
Belgium	5.8
Luxembourg	5.5
Denmark	5.3
Sweden	4.6
Czech Republic	4.3

Note: The percentage of the population with equivalized disposable income below 50 percent of the median income.

Source: Förster and Mira d'Ercole (2005).

(Saywer, 1976). And, during the period, Japan's equality was still increasing. But in 1984, Japan's inequality measured by the ninth-to-first decile ratio was the eighth highest and the seventh highest in 1994. In 2001, Japan's inequality climbed to the fourth. Japan's relative poverty rates was the seventh highest in 1984 and 1994; however, Japan moved to the fourth place in 2001 (Burniaux et al., 2006).

Moreover, all of these increases in income inequality and poverty had taken place before the Japanese economy hit the real bottom in the early 2000s and before the numbers and percentages of non-regular workers (temporary or part-time workers) with half as much income as regular workers increased significantly as a result of Japanese companies' restructuring. The latest data point for the OECD data for Japan compared above is 2000. Thus, it is reasonable to assume that Japan's income inequality and poverty rates have deteriorated further between 2001 and 2006 than the OECD data in 2000 suggest, in the absence of improvements in the economic condition of workers and of change in the government's redistributive policy during the period.

An additional problem is that the rise in income disparity has been especially sharp among young workers, though higher unemployment among young workers is common to many industrial nations. As discussed earlier, unemployment and temporary/part-time work are particularly high among young workers in Japan. Many of them are those who graduated during the 1990s recessions and could not find regular employment because of the recessions. When new graduates did not find work immediately on graduation, it became difficult for them to find stable jobs later, because Japanese companies traditionally employed only new graduates, and there was not a job market for those who had been out of school or for mid- and senior-level workers.[3] Furthermore, as Japan's basic pension scheme requires twenty-five years of contributions, it may be difficult for some of these young workers to be eligible for social security pensions in old age and may increase the chance of poverty.

As Japan's economic growth improved starting in 2003, companies have had stronger demand for employees and increased the employment of regular workers with lifetime employment to secure talented workers by offering attractive labor conditions. As the economy continues to perform well, Japan will see some reductions in the percentage of nonregular workers. Income inequality and poverty may even decline to a certain extent.

Nonetheless, income equality and poverty rates are not likely to decline to the pre-1990s levels. Japanese companies want to maintain greater flexibility to adjust to economic fluctuations and so will rely on nonregular workers more than before the 1990s recessions. There is evidence that this strategy has been successful. As a result of companies' increased reliance on nonregular workers and decreasing reliance on

[3] In recent years, Japanese companies have started hiring those who are not new graduates or who are mid- or senior-level workers. So the job market for these workers exists now. But the majority of hires are still with new graduates, and the market for non–new graduates is still very small.

regular workers with lifetime employment, the speed of labor adjustment by Japanese companies has significantly increased in recent years (Cabinet Office, 2006). Many companies now use performance-based wage systems so that income disparity will remain even among workers of the same company as well as between regular and nonregular workers. The income gap will not be easily narrowed, because Japan has a minimal welfare regime and the redistributive effect of Japan's welfare and tax systems is the smallest among OECD countries – even smaller than that of the United States (d'Ercole, 2006).

Because of the traditional lack of the Japanese government's interest in state provision of welfare (except for a brief period in the early 1970s), major policy changes to drastically ameliorate the disparity problems will not be forthcoming. It has been the government's policy to maintain a small welfare state ever since the early 1970s; a welfare system based more on self-help and family support.

The LDP government has started taking some policy measures to assist low-income industries, regions, and workers and families after the LDP suffered a major defeat in the July 2007 upper house election. One of the reasons for the defeat was voters' anger with economic disparity and difficulty. The government will continue to take some measures along these lines, as long as voters remain discontented concerning disparity and economic insecurity enough to cause an electoral backlash. In the long run, however, the Japanese government's main means of promoting citizens' well-being will continue to be through the promotion of the general economy and industries and regions and through reliance on family support (instead of directly assisting the economically dislocated individually). The LDP government's distributive government spending (pork barrel) for depressed industries and regions serves to redress economic difficulty and disparity to a certain extent, if those sectors and regions coincide with the dislocated segments of society. Yet, Nordic-type direct assistance and generous or universalistic welfare provision will not happen in Japan.

Prime Minister Abe (2006–2007) repeatedly made it clear (as did Koizumi) that his administration had no intention to achieve greater equality in outcomes. And his declared support for measures to reduce inequality was, for the most part, rhetoric and electoral. Prime Minister Fukuda (2007–), who came to power after the LDP's devastating electoral loss, has, of course, stated that the government should "pay attention to the inequality issue and correct what needs to be corrected." But he also has made it clear he will not reverse the market reforms started by Koizumi (Fukuda was Koizumi's chief cabinet secretary after all). There are, of course, politicians who are interested in greater equality, whether from genuinely ideological positions or for electoral concerns. But there are no visible would-be leaders in the largest LDP or second-largest DP who support outright welfare expansion and alternation of Japan's traditional welfare policy. Politicians and much of the public feel that the country cannot finance more generous welfare programs than the internationally modest welfare system currently in place.

In addition to income disparity between individual workers and households, Japan has also been experiencing rising income inequality between urban and rural prefectures. Since 2002, the income gap between urban and rural prefectures has widened according to the most recent data for 2004 (*Mainichi Shimbun*, March 6, 2007). This is considered at least partly a result of the large-scale retrenchment of public works under the Koizumi administration since 2001. Before Koizumi's retrenchment, large chunks of public works and government resources had gone to rural prefectures (where the LDP's electoral strength was traditionally great), and the economies of those rural areas were dependent on public works funded by the government, especially during economic downturns. This regional disparity is also a characteristic of Japan's recent economic recovery. Although urban areas with growing industries, businesses, and factories have experienced an economic boom, it largely has not spread to rural areas because they lack these types of industries and businesses. A similar gap also exists between large and small corporations. Big corporations have enjoyed the benefits of economic expansion, but small firms who are often the former's subsidiaries and subcontractors have not experienced the same benefits, partly because the latter's profit is squeezed by the former's efforts to reduce production costs. As a result, the benefits of the recent economic expansion are distributed unevenly in Japan.

Thus, economic disparity in Japan is increasing in many areas and on different levels. Japan's golden period, in which there was a relatively high level of income equality and many people enjoyed job and financial security and felt that they were middle class, is over. And it is difficult to picture a future economic environment in which Japan will again achieve the previous level of income equality. Income inequality has increased in virtually all countries that carried out neoliberal market reform, and no country has yet reversed the trend.

Decline of Population and Birth Rates, Population Aging, and Their Effects

Most industrial countries have experienced aging population, slow-down in population growth, and low fertility rates.[4] People live longer because of medical advances. As the economy matures, people have fewer children. And more women work than before, get married and have children at older ages, or do not marry or have children at all, contributing to lower fertility rates. The United States is one of the few exceptions that still maintains strong population growth, partly because of inflows of immigrants and relatively high fertility rates. However, most countries face demographic challenges. The problems of aging and low population growth are and will remain the most serious in Japan compared to all industrial economies.

Japan's population growth has slowed down significantly over the years, and actually started its descent in 2005 for the first time. The working population (current employees plus those looking for jobs) started declining in 1999 (*Nihon Keizai Shimbun*, January 28, 2005). Population decline is projected to continue, and Japan's total population is projected to decline to 89.9 million in 2055, compared to the 2005 population of 127 million (National Institute of Population and Social Security Research, 2006) (Figure 10.4). Thus, unless boosted by higher fertility rates or inflows of immigrants, Japan will experience a 30 percent decline in population from 2005 to 2055. This will be a major drain on the Japanese economy.

The aging of the population is the most severe in Japan of all industrial countries. People now live longer. The Japanese have the highest life expectancy in the world (85.6 for women and 78.6 for men in 2004: OECD, 2006). Japanese families are having fewer and fewer children. The fertility rates (1.25 per woman for 2005) are the lowest of OECD countries (except for East European countries and South Korea) (see Table 10.4). This is a decline from 1.54 in 1990. The OECD average in 2004 was 1.62 (the United States was 2.05). In Tokyo, the fertility rate is only 0.98 (*Mainichi Shimbun*, June 1, 2006).

The National Institute of Population and Social Security Research projects that Japan's fertility rates in 2055 will remain at 1.26 with the

---

[4] Ebertstadt (2004) provides a detailed discussion of population trends in Asia and the United States, arguing that many Asian economies will face severe demographic issues in the coming decades, in contrast to the United States.

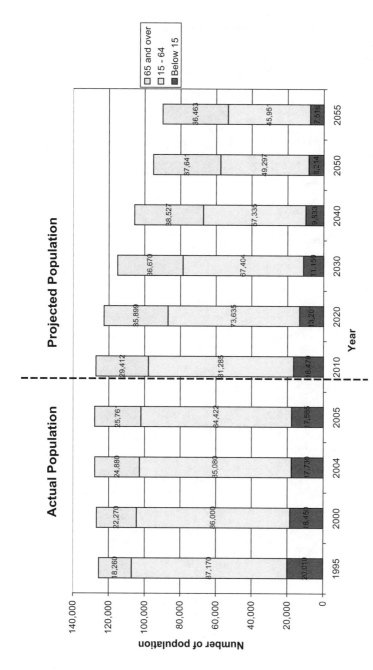

Figure 10.4. Total Population Projection. *Source:* The National Institute of Population and Social Security Research (2005); the Labor Market Policy Research Commission (2005).

Table 10.4. Fertility rates: Number of Children Born Per Female

Year	1990		2004
Average	1.86	Average	1.62
Mexico	3.35	Turkey	2.21
Turkey	3.07	Mexico	2.20
Iceland	2.30	United States	2.05
Sweden	2.13	Iceland	2.04
New Zealand	2.12	New Zealand	2.01
Ireland	2.11	Ireland	1.93
Slovak Rep.	2.09	France	1.91
United States	2.08	Norway	1.83
Poland	2.04	Finland	1.80
Norway	1.93	Denmark	1.78
Australia	1.91	Australia	1.77
Czech Rep.	1.89	United Kingdom	1.76
Hungary	1.84	Sweden	1.75
United Kingdom	1.83	Netherlands	1.73
Finland	1.78	Luxembourg	1.69
France	1.78	Belgium	1.64
Canada	1.71	Canada	1.53
Denmark	1.67	Austria	1.42
Belgium	1.62	Switzerland	1.42
Netherlands	1.62	Portugal	1.40
Luxembourg	1.61	Germany	1.36
Korea	1.59	Italy	1.33
Switzerland	1.59	Spain	1.32
Portugal	1.57	Greece	1.29
Japan	1.54	Japan	1.29
Austria	1.45	Hungary	1.28
Germany	1.45	Slovak Rep.	1.24
Greece	1.39	Poland	1.23
Spain	1.36	Czech Rep.	1.22
Italy	1.33	Korea	1.16

Source: The OECD (2006).

lowest scenario projection of 1.06. One reason for the low projected fertility rate is the projection that 23.5 percent of all Japanese women born in 1990 will never get married. In contrast, only 5.8 percent of women born in 1955 did not get married (National Institute of Population and Social Security Research, 2006). In 2005, only 36 percent of females between eighteen and thirty-four years old were married (*Mainichi Shimbun*, December 20, 2006).

Japan's population will grow old and become "grayer" as a result of the low fertility rates and population decline. In 2006, people sixty-five years old and older represented 20.7 percent of total population in Japan, compared to 19.5 for Italy, 18.6 percent for Germany, 16.2 percent for France, 16.0 percent for the United Kingdom, and 12.4 percent for the United States (*Mainichi Shimbun*, September 17, 2006). By 2055, however, the aged population will reach 40.5 percent in Japan (National Institute of Population and Social Security Research, 2006).

The OECD (2006) calculates an alternative age-dependency ratio – population aged sixty-five and over as a percentage of population aged twenty to sixty-four – to measure the extent of population aging by expressing it as a percentage of aged citizens presumably dependent on current workers between twenty and sixty-four. These statistics are presented in Table 10.5. Japan's ratio in 2000 was 28 percent – already one of the highest close to Sweden at 30 percent, Italy at 29 percent, and Belgium and France at 28 percent ratio. Japan's ratio, however, is projected to grow to 72 percent in 2050 – only next to the highest projection for Spain at 73 percent, and Italy will be the third highest at 71 percent. The ratios of the other countries that currently have high rates – Sweden, Belgium, and France – will not grow nearly as much as Japan's ratio. The ratios in 2050 will be 43 percent for Sweden, 50 percent for Belgium, and 58 percent for France. Their population aging will be much milder than Japan's. In 2050 Japan, approximately 1.4 current workers will support one aged citizen, whereas, in 2000, 3.6 current workers supported one aged citizen. In contrast, in the United States, 2.6 current workers are projected to support one aged citizen by 2050, whereas, in 2000, 4.8 current workers supported one aged citizen.

Women, Work, and Birth Rates

Japanese society will be forced to become a friendlier place for women, because of the declining population and the need to increase fertility rates, population, and the workforce. Japan needs to stem the decline of the population to maintain a vital economy and economic growth and to finance social security pensions and health care for a growing aged population. To do that, Japan must maintain and increase its population and labor force, which means that Japan must increase birth

Table 10.5. Age-dependency ratio: Population aged sixty-five and over as a percentage of population aged twenty to sixty-four

Year	2000		2050
Average	23	Average	51
Sweden	30	Spain	73
Italy	29	Japan	72
Belgium	28	Italy	71
Japan	28	Korea	68
France	28	Greece	64
Spain	27	Portugal	63
Greece	27	Czech Rep.	60
United Kingdom	27	France	58
Portugal	27	Slovak Rep.	57
Germany	26	Poland	56
Norway	26	Austria	55
Austria	25	Germany	54
Switzerland	25	Finland	52
Finland	25	Ireland	50
Hungary	24	New Zealand	50
Denmark	24	Belgium	50
Luxembourg	23	Hungary	50
Czech Rep.	22	Australia	48
Netherlands	22	United Kingdom	47
United States	21	Norway	45
Australia	21	Canada	45
Canada	20	Sweden	43
Poland	20	Switzerland	43
New Zealand	20	Luxembourg	40
Iceland	20	Iceland	40
Ireland	19	Denmark	39
Slovak Rep.	19	Netherlands	39
Korea	11	United States	39
Turkey	10	Mexico	35
Mexico	9	Turkey	31

Source: The OECD (2006).

rates. Japan must create a working, social, and economic environment in which it will be much easier for women to marry and have children. In the past, Japan's traditional views expected women to stay home as housewives and care for family and raise children. The society had a typical male breadwinner model, as was the case with many Catholic continental European countries (e.g., Germany, France, and Italy). Japan was very similar to these continental European countries, in that the norm was for men to earn income, and their companies were to provide welfare benefits for them and their family.

As a result, it was difficult for Japanese women to pursue both careers and family. The common belief was that women who wanted to become or remain core permanent workers more or less had to give up having family and children. Japanese companies operated on the assumption that female workers quit work when they got married. In such a male-dominant corporate environment, even women who gave up marriage and family had difficulty staying in their companies and be considered indispensable workers. There was strong social and corporate pressure on women to resign. In addition, men worked long hours, and their wives could not rely on them to help with childrearing and housework, making it difficult for women to consider pursuing full-time and/or permanent careers while raising children.

In recent years, more and more women have wanted to pursue professional careers. As a result, the age of marriage has become higher, more women have not gotten married or have chosen to have fewer or no children; therefore, Japan's fertility rates have been suppressed.

The economic problems of the 1990s and 2000s created an additional obstacle to Japan's fertility rates and population growth. The economic problems and change in corporate governance and labor practices made companies utilize and rely more on nonregular workers, such as part-time and temporary workers. Wages for these nonregular workers are significantly lower than for regular workers. In most cases, companies do not provide the nonregular workers with health care, social security, and other fringe benefits. And the rate of nonregular workers is much higher among young workers who are at an age when one usually gets married and starts a family.

These less-than-desirable employment and financial conditions have made young workers postpone marriage and childrearing or even discourage them from getting married and having children. These conditions have had a negative impact on Japan's birth rates and population growth. In order to increase birth rates and population, Japan needs to create a societal and corporate environment favorable to women's pursuit of careers and family. It also needs to mitigate unemployment, and employment and financial instability and uncertainty among young workers. Even if it turns out to be difficult to force companies to hire more young workers and provide them with full-time permanent jobs, Japan needs to improve the economic and employment well-being of nonregular workers, for instance, by providing them with health care and welfare benefits and by implementing active labor market policy to give them job (re)training to upgrade their job skills and knowledge so that they can find stable regular jobs. But since Japanese companies' increasing reliance on non-regular workers has been exactly due to the latter's lower labor costs (wages and benefits) in the first place, it will not be easy to require companies to provide higher wages and generous benefits. Furthermore, given Japan's minimal welfare regime and the relative lack of government desire to expand welfare along with the dominance of neoliberal economic thinking, it will be difficult to expect the government to provide larger welfare.

To improve birth rates and population growth and maintain the influx of workers into the labor market, Japan needs, above all, to encourage women's participation in the labor market by creating a favorable corporate and labor environment for them. At the same time, Japan needs to encourage women to have family and children while pursuing their careers by providing them with more advanced maternity practices and benefits and with systems that will make it easy for women to work and raise children at the same time, such as day care facilities and flexible working hours.

Thus, Japan's labor market will be a friendlier place for women than previously; however, Japan's conservative values in gender equality have not shown much progress. In a 2005 poll, for example, 48.9 percent of respondents opposed the statement that "Men should work outside, and women should protect home," whereas 45.2 supported it (*Kyodo Tsushin*, February 5, 2005). The majority of males supported the question. Irrespective of attitudes, Japan needs to maintain the size of population and workforce in order to sustain their standards of living and maintain a vigorous economy; hence, it has to become a friendlier place for females. Attitudes will adjust in time to reality.

In fact, both the government and private corporations have started to put in place measures to increase female labor market participation and fertility rates, and will continue to do so until they can mitigate population decline. The government has decided to increase child benefits. It has also decided to increase maternity leave benefits and to subsidize companies that provide day care facilities to their employees. It has decided to subsidize companies that take certain measures to improve the labor conditions of part-time workers (70 percent of part-time workers are female). It is now considering providing part-time workers with social security pensions. More corporations now offer more generous maternity leave options, flexible working hours, and day care facilities located at the place of work (*Kyodo Tsushin*, January 3, 2005; *Nihon Keizai Shimbun*, January 14, August 15, 2005, October 16, November 13, 2006; *Asahi Shimbun*, February 14, 2006; *Yomiuri Shimbun*, April 26, 2006; *Mainichi Shimbun*, December 15, 2006).

In addition, the government has begun the effort to mitigate the problem of the decline of the labor population by encouraging near- or after-retirement workers to work longer. The government has required that Japanese companies extend their retirement age or continue to employ employees who have passed their retirement age. Most companies have followed these requirements with a large majority of companies opting to employ workers after reaching the traditional retirement age. Japanese companies now expect a decline of the workforce and are more willing than before to provide measures to create a working environment and conditions that will put them in a good position to secure talented female and old workers.

Immigration is Not an Immediate Solution for Workforce Decline

Other than increasing fertility rates, allowing greater immigration would be an alternative approach to the problem of the decline of the population and workforce. But, for the moment, the Japanese government is not likely to drastically loosen its strict immigration policy. Japan has always had a very strict immigration policy. It is difficult for non-Japanese nationals to obtain citizenship, permanent residence, or work visas. Even when one is married to a Japanese citizen, naturalization is time-consuming.

The stringent policy results from the sentiment common among policy makers and publics that immigrants would disrupt the social fabric and order of their highly homogeneous society. The Japanese feel that non-Japanese would not understand not only the Japanese language but also intricate and unique Japanese mentality and culture. As a result, the Japanese government has allowed a very limited inflow of immigrants. It has allowed the immigration of Japanese descendents raised in Latin American countries such as Brazil and Peru. And now it is considering also allowing highly skilled workers to work in Japan, such as old-age care nurses, who are in short supply domestically because of the aging population. But at least for now, the government is reluctant to allow greater immigration. It will, over time, allow more immigration because of necessity, but it will be gradual and incremental.

Japan's Welfare Regime: Implications for the Economy and People Today and in the Future

Japan has had one of the smallest government welfare states of all industrial economies of North America, Europe, and the Pacific. Welfare spending by the U.S. government has been known to be very low by international standards, but Japan's welfare spending is at least as low as the U.S. level. This is a mixed blessing for Japan.

On the one hand, the current welfare system is not as enormous and encompassing as that of many West European countries. As a result, welfare retrenchment will be somewhat easier in Japan than in Scandinavian or some continental European countries, where governments provide high levels of social security transfers and public services. Politicians generally have difficulty retrenching expansive entitlement programs, because the number of recipients who are accustomed to generous welfare provision is large, and thus pose an obstacle to policy makers as vested constituents (Pierson, 1994). Japan's public welfare is meager, and both the size of adversely affected recipients and the magnitude and range of retrenchment are smaller. Thus, Japanese politicians have a little more leeway in reforming welfare system, as they face less serious electoral repercussions. In addition, although Japan faces large projected increases in welfare spending because of aging, which is a serious problem, the magnitude of the increases would be even more pernicious if Japan had the high level of social security and other welfare provision that we find in many European countries.

On the other hand, despite the low level of welfare spending, the Japanese government still expects large increases in social security payments and health care costs for the elderly. As of 2002, 69.9 percent of total government spending on social security, health care, and welfare was for the aged (*Yomiuri Shimbun*, June 3, 2005). This poses a serious problem because Japan's aged population is large and will grow larger and faster than in other industrial countries, and the number of workers who will finance the elderly's social security and health care will shrink at the current rate of child birth and immigration. Thus, Japan's welfare spending for the elderly will increase greatly, but it will not have sufficient workers to finance the spending. The financial burdens of welfare and health care for the elderly on workers will grow, but the welfare benefits those current workers will receive when they become old will decrease. Japan thus faces a severe generational disparity.

Furthermore, meager welfare provision means that Japanese people who face bleak financial or employment conditions are not sufficiently protected. These individuals will not likely be salvaged in the future, because the government already faces financial difficulty just with the current, modest level of welfare provision when aging has not yet advanced nearly as much as it will in the near future. This will become a vicious circle. The unemployed or poor will receive insufficient public assistance and in turn will not have a family or, if they have a family, they will have fewer children. This exacerbates Japan's already low fertility rates and aging problem.

In the face of declines in birth rates and population, aging, and changing labor market practices and increasing income inequality and poverty, the financial sustainability of Japan's social security and health care is not easy to achieve without serious cuts in benefit levels and hikes in pension and health care contributions. These demographic and economic trends alone make sustainability a difficult task.

Sustainability faces additional problems because of the failure of many workers and employers to make social security contributions or join legally required social security schemes. This has led not only to shortfalls in revenues from social security contributions but also to citizens' and employees' distrust in Japan's social security system. The nonpayment to social security is in turn a result of economic difficulties, people's distrust in Japan's social security system, and poor enforcement of contribution collection by the government.

Japan's Welfare in Comparative Perspective

The Japanese government's welfare spending is one of the lowest among all industrial nations. In terms of spending levels, Japan has a residual welfare regime along with liberal market economies of Anglo-Saxon countries (Esping-Andersen, 1990). But it also shares certain features of Catholic conservative welfare regimes of continental European countries in terms of occupation-specificity of social security, traditional values of family and community support, and the male breadwinner model (Esping-Andersen, 1997).

Figure 10.5 shows government welfare spending as a percentage of GDP in 2001 in terms of in-cash transfers (income support and

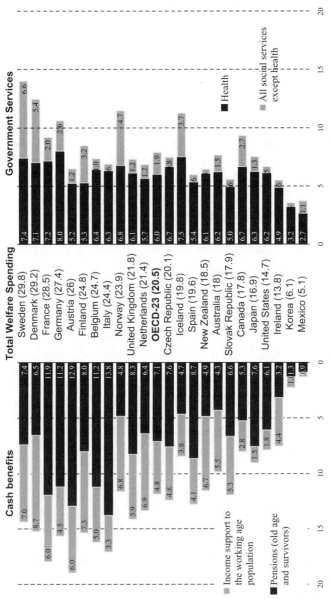

Figure 10.5. Government Welfare Spending as a Percentage of GDP by Policy Areas (2001). *Note:* Numbers in the middle in parentheses are total welfare spending. *Source:* OECD Social Expenditure database: http://www.oecd.org/els/social/expenditure and http://www.oecd.org/dataoecd/56/21/35632949.xls Reprinted with minor modifications with permission.

old-age pensions) and public services (health care and all other public services, such as education and day care facilities). Japan's overall welfare spending was the fifth lowest (16.9 percent) among the OECD countries, after Mexico, South Korea, Ireland, and the United States. Japan has relatively sizable old-age pensions and health care spending (both slightly above the OECD averages), because of a large aged population and the national health services. The Japanese government, however, provides little income assistance for poverty alleviation (the third lowest, even lower than the United States) and for nonhealth public services.

The residual (minimal) nature of the Japanese government's social spending is evident not only in total government spending, but also in the meagerness of social security benefits paid to recipients. Table 10.6 shows the replacement ratios of old-age social security benefits in OECD countries around 2004 (net replacement ratios at average earnings after taxes and social security contributions as a percentage of individual preretirement earnings). This is a statistic that indicates approximately what percentage of preretirement income retirees receive from social security in old age. Japan's figure is 39.2 percent, the second lowest of all OECD nations, second only to Ireland. This 39.2 percent statistic means roughly that when the Japanese citizen reaches old age, they have to either scale back their living expenses, supplement their social security pensions with other sources of income such as private pensions or savings, or have their children look after them as the traditional Japanese commonly did in the past. Three-generation households used to be common in traditional Japan but, today, the number of nuclear families has increased, and more old parents live by themselves.

Table 10.7 shows unemployment net replacement ratios around 2004 (average of net replacement rates over sixty months of unemployment, unemployment benefits plus additional social assistance, for four family types and two earnings levels). This indicates, approximately, what percentage of previous income is subsidized by unemployment insurance when people lose jobs. Japan's unemployment replacement ratio is the tenth lowest (57 percent). Excluding newly emerging economies, only Australia, Canada, Italy, Spain, and the United States have lower unemployment replacement ratios. Japan's low replacement ratio means that social protection for people out of job is weak, and their economic difficulties are alleviated less.

Table 10.6. Net replacement ratios of old-age social security benefits at average earnings in 2004

Average	71.2
Greece	110.1
Turkey	104.0
Hungary	97.8
Netherlands	96.8
Luxembourg	96.6
Denmark	95.7
Austria	90.9
Spain	88.2
Portugal	86.7
Iceland	84.2
Poland	82.3
Italy	77.9
Slovak Rep.	72.9
Finland	70.7
Belgium	66.5
Sweden	65.6
Switzerland	64.9
Czech Rep.	64.4
Korea	63.6
France	63.1
Norway	61.8
Canada	58.6
Germany	58.0
Australia	56.4
United States	52.4
Mexico	45.1
New Zealand	41.4
United Kingdom	41.1
Japan	39.2
Ireland	38.5

Note: Net replacement ratios at average earnings after taxes and social security contributions as a percentage of individual pre-retirement earnings.

Source: The OECD (2006).

These numbers show that the social security benefits the Japanese people receive when they become old or unemployed are meager by international standards. Japan's high income inequality and poverty rates reviewed in the previous section result partly from this relative

Table 10.7. Average of net replacement rates over sixty months of unemployment in 2004 (unemployment benefits plus additional social assistance)

Average	57
Mexico	..
Turkey	..
Switzerland	81
Denmark	78
Finland	73
Iceland	73
Netherlands	73
Sweden	73
Germany	73
Luxembourg	71
Ireland	70
New Zealand	66
Austria	64
Portugal	63
United Kingdom	63
Belgium	62
France	62
Norway	60
Czech Rep.	60
Poland	59
Japan	57
Australia	52
Spain	50
Canada	50
Korea	43
Slovak Rep.	40
Hungary	31
United States	31
Greece	25
Italy	5

Source: The OECD (2006).

absence of social assistance for the elderly, low-income workers and families, and the unemployed. Income inequality and poverty exist in all OECD countries. But, in most other countries, especially Scandinavian and continental European countries, inequality and poverty are rectified by social assistance to much larger extents than in Japan.

As a result of low public assistance, Japanese citizens' welfare in old age or unemployment depends on support from family and relatives to a larger extent than most other OECD countries. Furthermore, because of the large social stigma attached to the receipt of welfare benefits, the takeup rates of poverty assistance in Japan are likely very low. With low public social protection, it is no wonder that Japan's income inequality and poverty deteriorated during the last fifteen years of financial and economic distress when people's income decreased, more people were unemployed, and corporations reduced their regular workers and depended increasingly on nonregular workers with much lower wages and benefits.

Before the 1990s, the Japanese welfare system worked reasonably well, because Japan had robust economic growth for much of the postwar period and unemployment was very low. People experienced steady rises in their income and standards of living, and most people had stable jobs. The Japanese people's social security and health care depends heavily on private sources. These were provided by their employers for company employees, teachers, and government employees, and by the government for the self-employed. Thus, Japan's welfare is occupationally segregated (as in many continental European countries), and people's social and economic well-being (including social security and health care) depends on their employment status. This system works relatively well if unemployment is low and people are employed. Japan's welfare system is based on the assumption that somebody in each family is employed. Most of the time, it meant that men (husbands) held jobs and earned income, and wives and children received welfare benefits such as health care through men's companies.

These assumptions do not necessarily hold for every worker and family any longer as a result of the economic problems in the 1990s and the first few years of the new century. More Japanese became unemployed, or more people had nonregular jobs that did not provide them with social security and health care. They are eligible to participate in the National Health Insurance and National Basic Pensions provided by the government, but their benefit levels are lower.

Furthermore, Japan's modest welfare system worked reasonably well in previous times when aged parents lived with their children and the latter took care of the former. Traditionally, children supporting aged parents was common. Consequently, aged Japanese were able to get by even with humble social security pensions. But today, nuclear families have increased, more and more old-age citizens live by themselves, and social security pensions are the only source of income for some of them. The National Institute of Population and Social Security Research projects that in 2025, the percentage of aged-citizen-only households where only aged citizens (sixty-five years old and over) live by themselves without their children or others will reach 13.7 percent of Japan's entire households, compared to 6.5 percent in 2000. The percentage of the households headed by those sixty-five years old and over will reach 37.1 percent compared to 23.8 percent in 2000, and 56.4 percent of them will be headed by citizens seventy-five years old and over (*Mainichi Shimbun*, August 25, 2005).

In the past, traditional Japanese families (three generations or more) were probably better able to cope with one family member's loss of employment, because they were more likely than nuclear families to have multiple income earners. Japan also used to have tightly knit neighborhoods and communities where giving and receiving help was probably easier than today's much more anonymous society.

The number of single-mother families exposed to economic difficulties is also on the rise in Japan. This is a relatively recent phenomenon since Japan had low divorce rates for a long time. But divorce has been on the rise, although divorce rates are still low compared to other industrial economies. The number of single-mother households was 1.23 million in 2003, representing a 28 percent increase from 1998. Their average income in 2003 was 40 percent of that of the average household. Over 80 percent of the single mothers had jobs, but half of them only had temporary or part-time jobs. Their unemployment rate in 2004 was also almost twice as high as that of the average household (*Nihon Keizai Shimbun*, June 1, 2005). Nevertheless, the Japanese government has reduced income assistance benefits to this group as a result of its fiscal consolidation effort started under the Koizumi administration and plans to reduce benefits further (*Mainichi Shimbun*, December 24, 2006).

Overall, Japan's welfare system was built on certain foundational premises – traditional family support, community support, self-help, low unemployment, a robust economy, stable long-term employment, generous welfare benefits provided by private companies, and a growing and young population. In fact, private sector unions supported welfare retrenchment and the maintenance of the residual welfare state in the 1970s, when the LDP government initiated retrenchment after the first oil shock and the onset of slow economic growth convinced the government and business of the need to curb government spending. These workers' welfare was provided mainly by their companies, so they did not show interest in universalistic, public welfare (Shinkawa, 1993).

When these premises held, Japan's welfare system worked reasonably well. But these premises have weakened today. And Japan's welfare system has not adapted to the new conditions. More precisely, the government has little intention to reform the welfare system in such a way as to protect the newly vulnerable, dislocated people in the near future. On the contrary, the government has sought to retrench welfare spending almost across the board since the Koizumi administration in order to curb government spending and reduce deficit and debt. The Koizumi and succeeding Abe administrations' policy solution to inequality and poverty was to promote economic growth by creating a free market economy (and thus reducing social protection) and let the strong economy thus achieved create jobs for the dislocated and improve their living standards – a typical neoliberal (neoconservative) prescription much along the lines of U.S. President Reagan's "trickle-down" effect.

The current prime minister, Fukuda, also will not make serious change to Japan's minimal welfare. In fact, no leader in the LDP or DP would change it. Although the JCP and SDP might, they are too small to control the government. Japan's residual welfare regime is historically and firmly institutionalized and enjoys the support of conservative and centrist party politicians.

Despite these bleak statistics, it is also true that Japan's income inequality and poverty are not yet as bad as they could be. First, Japan's unemployment is still low by international standards, meaning more people have jobs than may be the case in other countries. Second, relative poverty rates and income inequality are measured relative to the rest of the population. Japan is an affluent country and, as a whole, people have high standards of living. So Japan's inequality and poverty do not mean the same thing as those in developing nations or developed nations with lower per capita income or standards of living. In absolute terms, the Japanese, poor or unemployed, are better off than the poor or unemployed in developing nations.

Nevertheless, increasing inequality and poverty represent a significant change to the Japanese people, who used to believe that Japan was an egalitarian society. Various recent opinion polls show that 60–75 percent of the Japanese respondents feel that income inequality increased during the five years of the Koizumi administration (*Yomiuri Shimbun*, April 18, 2006; Kyodo Wire, January 27, 2006). In 1987, 75 percent of the respondents to surveys indicated they belonged to the middle class, whereas only 20 percent indicated that they belonged to the lower class. The situation dramatically changed by 2006, when 54 percent answered they belonged to the middle class and 37 percent to the lower class (*Nihon Keizai Shimbun*, February 5, 2006). Aside from the objective accuracy of their own perception, the fact is that more Japanese feel their socioeconomic conditions lag behind the wealthy.

Expected Economic and Social Difficulties in the New Century

Japan's population decline and aging have serious implications for its economic and social conditions in the future. If no effective measure is taken to facilitate higher fertility rates, labor participation, or labor productivity, the population decline will reduce the size of Japan's labor force, cause economic stagnation, and lower people's living standards. The Labor Market Policy Research Commission of the Ministry of Health, Labor, and Welfare projects that the population decline will reduce Japan's labor force population from 66.4 million in 2004 to 56 million in 2030, if no effective policy measure is taken against the recent negative trends in the labor market we have reviewed. Furthermore, the decline in labor force population will suppress annual real economic growth rates to 0.6 percent during the period from 2015 to 2030 (currently 1.3 percent between 1999 and 2004 – note that Japan was in recession during this period), assuming that labor productivity growth stays around 1.5 percent annually (currently 1.7 percent during 1999–2004) (Labor Market Policy Research Commission, 2005). The model simulation assumes that the recent trends in the labor market – corporations' increasing reliance on temporary and part-time workers, a large wage gap between regular and nonregular workers, high rates of unemployment, job insecurity, and nonregular workers among young Japanese populations, reductions in corporations' investment in human capital formation, and so on – will suppress labor productivity. Economic stagnation and personal financial insecurities could push down Japan's low fertility rates even further, fueling the decline of the population and workforce and economic stagnation. It potentially can be a vicious cycle, unless some of the trends are reversed.

Low economic growth – in conjunction with aging and low fertility rates – will make it difficult for Japan to sustain the current levels of social security and health care benefits because there will be more senior citizens to support and the labor force that will support them will be smaller. Low economic growth will also limit government resources as will the need to service the current high level of gross government debt. Benefit levels may need to be scaled back. Or the social security and health care contributions made by current workers may need to be drastically increased. Most likely, both will need to be implemented.

The Japanese government has already carried out both benefit reductions and cost increases in recent years. In 2004, it legislated a gradual increase in the contribution rate to the Employees' Pension Insurance from current 13.6 percent of annual income (evenly shared by employers and employees) to 18.3 percent by 2017, and a gradual increase in the monthly contribution rate for the National Pension Insurance system from ¥13,300 per month to ¥16,900 by 2017. The premise was that the government would not need to increase these rates after 2017. It also legislated benefit cuts and restraint by introducing a system of automatic benefit adjustments that would automatically reduce benefits in response to reductions in the working population (who pay pension contributions) and increases in life expectancy and by reducing the net replacement ratio from current 59.7 percent to 50 percent for the Employees Pension system. The premise was that the government would be able to maintain this replacement ratio in the foreseeable future. The reform also increased the government's burden share of the National Pension Insurance from current one-third to one half by 2009. The government also increased health care copayments for company employees and aged citizens as well as cut the reimbursements for doctors' labor costs and prescriptions in the past several years. It also increased cost burdens for old-age care.

Yet, the latest data for fertility rates and population decline have already rendered the government's projection too optimistic. With the new data taken into account, there will be a need for further benefit reductions or cost increases. Before the new data for fertility rates became available, it was projected that Japan's social security payments (pensions, health care, and other welfare) will increase from ¥90 trillion in 2006 to ¥141 trillion in 2025 – a 57 percent increase (Ministry of Health, Labor, and Welfare, 2006). The costs of taxes and social security contributions people have to pay to fund social security will jump from current ¥82.8 trillion in 2006 to ¥143 trillion yen in 2025 – a 72 percent increase. These projections have turned out to be "optimistic" in light of a newest estimate for Japan's future fertility rates. The original projections were estimated based on the projected 2050 fertility rate of 1.39 as of 2002; however, the most recent fertility rate projection for 2055 is 1.26.

With the current rate of decline in fertility rates, the financial burdens of social security on workers and corporations can be larger. Higher social security burdens on workers and employers – be they taxes or contributions – can impair the competitiveness and efficiency of Japan's economy. They can reduce workers' incentive to work and corporations' incentive to invest and employ workers. They can thus induce further economic stagnation which in turn will feedback and increase social security spending.

Not only are future projections for social security spending dismal for Japan; the Japanese government already faces great difficulty in managing the current social security system. There are an extremely large number of people who have failed to pay into social security; there are a large number of companies who have failed to provide their employees with social security which is legally mandated; and there will be a large number of current workers who will not be eligible to receive pensions when they reach old age. There is also a severe generational inequity in social security burdens and benefits between current recipients and workers. As a result of the government's failure to collect social security contributions from many current workers and companies and the inequities in the system, people's trust in the future sustainability and viability of the social security system has become low. This could potentially contribute to a further increase in the number of workers and companies that do not pay into the social security system.

The contribution requirement of Japan's National Pension Insurance is steep – one must make contributions for twenty-five years to be eligible for old-age benefits. It is therefore important to ensure workers continue to pay into the system throughout their professional life. As of 2003, about twenty-two million self-employed, students, and other noncompany employees participated in the National Pension Insurance. Of this group, over ten million people (50 percent) during the two years of 2002–2004 failed to pay contributions for more than one month. This number does not include people who were exempted from payment due to insufficient income or unemployment or the people who had failed to make the payment before 2002. Of the ten million, 3.3 million people did not make any contributions at all for a twenty-four-month period (*Yomiuri Shimbun*, October 10, and November 17, 2004).

Furthermore, another government investigation revealed that about 30 percent of all corporations legally mandated to provide employees with social security insurance (firms with more than five employees) did not do so in 2005. As a result, 2.7 million workers were not registered as participants in the Employees' Pension Insurance (*Mainichi Shimbun*, September 15, 2006). The government also estimated in 2004 that the number of people who already were or would be ineligible to receive basic pensions was eight hundred thousand. This number did not include ineligible people at ages sixty to sixty-five, so the actual number could be higher.

The large number of noncontributing people and corporations is problematic. It not only reduces the government's receipts based on social security contributions but also suggests a large number of people will not be eligible to receive old-age pensions. These people will likely have to receive income assistance from the government when they reach old age, and push up the government's social security spending that is already high as a result of the aging and decline of the population.

Another source of problems facing Japan's social security is severe generational inequity in the benefits and costs that people receive and pay. Japan's social security is the most generous to current aged citizens – they receive high benefits, and their contributions were relatively low when they were contributing workers. When they were workers, Japan's population was young, aging was not severe, Japan's economic growth was high, and government tax revenues increased annually and were abundant. So there were many current workers to support a small aged population, and government had abundant revenues and could be generous in social security provision. There are also currently enough workers to support the aged. But as a result of an aging, declining population, and slow economic growth, today's young workers will have to pay weightier contributions, whereas the benefits they will receive in their old age will have to be significantly moderated. One estimate by the government shows that today's Japanese at sixty and over will receive ¥56 million more social security (and public services and benefits from public investments) in their lifetime from the government than the social security contributions (and taxes) they paid to the government. In contrast, the Japanese who were born after 1983 will receive ¥39 million less social security (and public services and benefits from public investments) than the contributions (and taxes) they will have paid to the government. The benefit gap between these two generations is ¥96 million (Cabinet Office, 2004).[5] It is not easy for the government to justify the inequity and convince current, young workers to bear the heavy burdens to support aged citizens and only to receive much more modest benefits when they reach old age.

As a result of all these existing or future problems with social security, many Japanese do not trust the sustainability of their social security system. A poll shows that 59 percent of the respondents believe the system will be bankrupt in the near future. Distrust is higher among younger generations. Seventy-seven percent of the respondents in the forties answered that it will be bankrupt (*Mainichi Shimbun*, September 17, 2006). It will not be easy for the government to convince Japanese workers to continue to support the social security system, especially when there are currently so many people and corporations that do not pay into the system. In 2004, it was revealed that many politicians – including Prime Minister Koizumi, his cabinet ministers, opposition party leaders and members, and many others – had failed to pay social security contributions for years. This invoked public criticism, particularly because politicians were legislating the social security benefit cuts and contribution hikes of 2004. The chief cabinet secretary and the leader of the DP ended up resigning because of their nonpayment.

On top of everything else, Japan's Social Security Agency lost the trust of Japanese citizens in 2007, when it was revealed the agency had amassed fifty million cases of unidentified social security payments that it had received from citizens over the years because of its negligence. Japanese citizens understandably associated the government with the agency's negligence and failure and penalized the governing LDP in the 2007 upper house election.

There is a chance that the pessimistic picture painted about the future financial problems of Japan's social security is somewhat exaggerated. The Japanese government – particularly the MOF – has in the past run systematic campaigns for fiscal austerity since the 1970s by propagating desperately critical conditions of government finance. The government certainly succeeded in running such campaigns and

---

[5] These estimates do not calculate the benefits and costs of social security alone, and include the benefits and costs of public services and investments as well as social security.

persuading political parties and publics to support fiscal austerity in the 1980s and successfully eliminated fiscal deficit by 1990. The MOF has always been fiscally conservative, and there is a possibility that the pessimistic scenarios about social security are part of its campaign to get government finance back in shape which has significantly deteriorated during the lost decade. If this is the case, Japan may successfully cope with the financial problems of social security. However, there is also no doubt that Japan's social security will face financial difficulties. Therefore, the Japanese government's successful response to the problems is imperative.

Overview

Much has changed in the Japanese economy since the 1990s. Much of the change in corporate governance and labor market practices has been an adaptive shift by the Japanese economy to rise above the economic stagnation of the 1990s and the first half of this decade. These reforms are similar to the neoliberal reform of the British and American economies in the 1980s. As a result of restructuring and corporate governance reform, Japan's major corporations have become lean and regained competitiveness and resilience, although small and medium businesses and corporations lag much behind major corporations in economic recovery. The major corporations are poised to continue relatively good performance in the foreseeable future.

In contrast to the recent good performance by major corporations, Japanese workers and families do not face a rosy picture. They will have to get used to lower job security and harsher job competition. Improvements in their living standards will be harder to come by than before the 1990s, as a result of slower economic growth, changes in corporate governance and labor practices, a declining labor force, and the aging population. They will also have to bear increased burdens of social programs. And they will have to expect lower benefits for themselves.

Despite some notable shifts that we observe in Japan's economy and society, it is not likely that the pace and magnitude of change will remain the same. Japanese corporations and people have made the changes that were necessary to renovate their malfunctioning economy, and their approach has worked well enough to put the economy on the recovering track. In the absence of further economic or societal urgency, it is not likely that they will continue their reform toward an American-style free market economy as rapidly as in the past. Japanese corporations and people probably feel that their Japanese way of business and life, which ceased working well in the 1990s, has started working again modified with some efficiency-enhancing changes. Japan will continue incrementally to adopt systems and practices that have worked well in other industrial economies; however, Japan will keep parts of the Japanese way that continue to function in the new environment.

There will be a societal or political force toward restoring economic equity which has been reduced as a result of economic reform. If the public sentiment against decreased equity remains strong and if a political party can capture significant electoral gains by capitalizing on the sentiment, politicians will try to advance policy measures to redistribute wealth by political means and increase equity. This is essentially what happened in the 2007 election and in its aftermath. This force toward greater equity will be met with resistance by the economic rationality of Japan's major corporations that want to maintain competitiveness by containing labor costs. The outcome of the clash of interest between corporations and workers is uncertain. But as long as the Japanese continue to be Japanese, corporations and workers will work out a compromise that will either please both maximally or displease both minimally. The result will still be their own – it may be different from their old way, but still a new Japanese way.

Finally, one thing that we can say with certainty is that Japan will continue its deregulation and liberalization that has been pursued in the decade. As a result, there will be increased openness and competition in the economy. Japan's economy will become more liberal over time. This is so because deregulation and liberalization now have strong support in Japan. Major corporations are particularly adamant proponents. Deregulation and liberalization have also become dominant policy ideas among policy makers – politicians and bureaucrats. Politicians and bureaucrats will still try to block certain types of deregulation and liberalization if they impair their political power or the economic interests of their client industries and sectors. Nonetheless, they have accepted the general policy direction toward deregulation and liberalization.

11

Japanese Political Economy in the First Decade of the New Century

Introduction

The financial and economic distress that characterized Japan's economy for fifteen years has been largely resolved; however, Japan has not yet returned to stable, broad-based growth and price stability as of late 2007. Although the majority of observers both inside and outside of Japan regard Japan to be growing at a "moderate" rate,[1] there continue to remain problems with the reliance on the export sector, weak balance sheets of the large number of small financial institutions, weak consumption spending by the household sector, and the low levels of measured inflation. Hence, to conclude that Japan has achieved sustainable economic stability and growth is premature as of late 2007. But, at the same time, it appears that Japan's economy will continue to grow moderately, and a return to the economic and financial distress of the 1990s is unlikely.

Many changes have taken place in Japan in the past two decades. But Japan is not finished with change. Change and reform are still ongoing, and Japan will continue to change until it reaches a new equilibrium where its political-economic regime stabilizes. It is not a straightforward task to project how Japan will change and how it will affect its politics and economy in the coming future. Nonetheless,

---

[1] The Bank of Japan's October 2007 "Outlook for Economic Activity and Prices" stated: "Japan's economy is expanding moderately.... The pace of improvement in the household sector; however, has remained slow relative to the strength in the corporate sector. From the second half of fiscal 2007 [April 1, 2007 to March 31, 2008] through fiscal 2008 [April 1, 2008 to March 31, 2009], the economy is likely to continue its sustained expansion, although there are uncertainties regarding overseas economies and global financial markets. A virtuous circle of growth in production, income, and spending is expected to remain in place" (Bank of Japan, p. 1).

some projections can be offered with a reasonable degree of confidence. This last chapter reviews the direction in which Japan's politics, liberalization policies, and economy are likely to go in the next several years and beyond.

Economic Reform and the Economy

Japan's economic reform will continue. The government will continue to advance deregulation, liberalization, and privatization. It will continue to introduce more market principles and competition in the economy. Japanese companies will continue to reform their corporate governance and labor market practices until they find a combination of systems that stably work well and enable them to survive market competition. Major companies, particularly, will make a successful transition, although small and medium-sized businesses and rural economies to date lag behind in their efforts to make necessary changes to become competitive.

Reform and change by the government and private corporations, however, will not result in a complete departure from the Japanese way of politics and business. Japan will not be another American-style liberal market economy. Nonetheless, the changes will push the Japanese economy toward an open and competitive economy. It will be a much more deregulated economy than that before the 1990s.

How much more liberal Japan's economy will become depends on (1) its performance in producing favorable economic outcomes and (2) the extent of the political backlash against market reform implemented since the Koizumi administration.

With regard to the first factor, if the Japanese economy starts performing well to the satisfaction of corporations, politicians, bureaucrats, and workers, Japan's market reform will slow. Reform involves transaction and transition costs, and human beings tend to be content with what they have, as long as it works sufficiently well. When things work fine, they have a much lower incentive to execute change. The characteristics of an economic environment that would slow the pace of reform include the following: the elimination of any deflation potential; the ability of Japan's key industries and financial firms to become internationally competitive; and resolution of the problems of aging, low fertility rates, the social security system, and their strain on the economy. Reform will not cease, however. These issues will require continued efforts by the Japanese government and companies to upgrade the economy and technology, so, in this sense, Japan's economy will continue its incremental evolution.

If Japan's economy still underperforms, however, Japan will pursue further market reform. At this point, it appears Japan's economy has achieved a degree of stability that accelerated market reform on the scale during the Koizumi administration is not likely. Japan will continue to recover and grow at moderate rates. In this environment, the pace of reform is likely to slow. It will mean less enthusiasm for market reform, especially on the part of the public.

Regarding the second factor, if the Japanese economy creates further income inequality and more economically dislocated workers and families, industries, and regions, there will be a backlash against market reform. Political parties will then try to champion the cause of the dislocated to enhance their electoral prospects. Political parties have actually already started efforts to court voters by proposing larger social protection by the government and the redistributive measures to mitigate the economic hardships experienced by low-income workers and families, small and medium-sized businesses, farmers, rural economies, and still depressed sectors.

In the 2007 upper house election, the DP significantly increased seats and became the largest party in the house by promising more redistributive policies against Prime Minister Abe's LDP that had supported a continuation of market reform started by Koizumi. The electoral results led many LDP politicians to demand that the LDP government change its economic policy on market competition and fiscal austerity and conduct a more expansionary and redistributive economic policy to protect dislocated sectors, regions, and households. They fear that the LDP would otherwise suffer a major loss in the next lower house election and lose control of government to the DP.

There remains a reasonable consensus among political parties on the general need for deregulation and liberalization to build a competitive economy. They are also aware of the need to reduce gross government debt by trimming budgets. As a result, the major parties (LDP, DP, and CGP) will not abandon market reform and fiscal consolidation completely. Nor will they support policies to revert Japan's economy back to what it was before market reform. However, some slowdown and even a slight policy reversal in Japan's market reform and fiscal consolidation seem inevitable, in the presence of public discontent with negative side-effects of market reform and political parties' electoral concerns.

Political parties' flirtation with a more expansionary fiscal policy and larger social protection will continue at least until the next lower house election likely in 2008. Whether it will continue thereafter depends on the outcome of the election, the direction of public opinion at that time, and the ingenuity and ability of political leaders and policy makers in convincing the public of the need for market reform and fiscal consolidation.

Currently, the DP (the second largest party in the lower house and the largest in the upper house) is best positioned to gain electorally from criticizing the LDP government for tolerating income inequality and poverty for the sake of market reform, and will capitalize on the situation to promote its electoral strength in its pursuit of gaining control of government. LDP politicians have no choice but to match the DP's redistributive policy platforms for electoral concerns and, at least in pretense, rush to the rescue of the economically dislocated. Japan's new mixed SMD-PR electoral system introduced in 1994 makes an alternation of political parties in government easier than the previous MMD system, which had kept the LDP in power for decades. A shift in votes can translate into a larger shift in parties' seat shares under the new system. This should make political parties more vulnerable to electoral pressures from the public.

In addition, the size of non-party-identifiers (voters who do not support any existing party or independent voters) has hovered around 50 percent of the entire population of voters in the past decade. This group can significantly influence electoral outcomes. They are swing voters, who change their votes for political parties election by election, and it is important for parties to mobilize their support if they want to win elections. Political parties have no choice but to court public opinion as long as they wish to win elections and gain control of government in light of the new electoral system that makes them susceptible to public opinion and the presence of the large percentage of swing voters. In this regard, the important factors to affect the direction of government policy and the economy are how serious and widespread the economic dislocation of workers and families will be and how much the dislocated will be mobilized by political parties in elections. At the time of this writing, public opinion that Koizumi's market reform created income disparities and economic difficulty has not disappeared. This will move political parties slightly toward more social protection and redistribution.

The negative attitude about the effects of market reform, however, is countered by political and economic actors that benefit from and support market reform. They include business owners and other wealthy classes that increased their income by taking advantage of opportunities provided by deregulation and a freer market economy, major corporations that see their future in an open economy and market competition and support liberalization, and relatively affluent local governments in urban areas that have prospering companies in their regions and are beneficiaries of economic recovery and of reduction in government redistribution of wealth from urban to rural areas. They oppose a reversal of market reform, deregulation, and liberalization.

The balance between market winners and those who have not been well served by market reform will determine the direction of public opinion, which, in turn, will influence political parties' economic policy positions in the next several years. As of late 2007, those who see more negative consequences of market reform have swayed public opinion. At the same time, Japan cannot afford to cease market reforms. Japan must improve its labor productivity and rate of return on savings to counter the effects of a declining workforce and graying population. Demographics is the final trump card that prevents Japan from stopping or returning to the past.

In sum, there will be a slight policy adjustment, if not some reversal, because of public discontent with the negative side effects of reform and the LDP's electoral defeat. Political parties are currently more willing to change policy and allocate government resources to reducing the gap between the rich and poor and between urban and rural areas. The bureaucracy (except for the MOF) is trying to capitalize on this opportunity and increase their ministries' budgets. For now, Japan's reform and fiscal consolidation will slow down. There will be a slight policy shift to allocate more government resources to rural areas and active labor market policy to improve the well-being of the unemployed and low-income workers and households. Still, such redistribution will be done in a way not to grossly impair economic efficiency. The Japanese feel that they cannot revert back completely to their traditional distributive policy that caused much misallocation of economic resources. But political parties feel that market reform should be balanced against the goal of more equity.

Demographic and Socioeconomic Challenges

The resolution of the socioeconomic problems emanating from the aging and decline of the population discussed in the previous chapter will not be easy. There is, however, an element of optimism in Japan's prospects for a reasonable resolution of the problems. The optimism is inferred from the history of Japan's past adaptation to major socioeconomic or political crises. Although past performance is not always a reliable indicator of the future, Japan has in the past shown great capacity to meet crisis situations and events and ride them out successfully. Japan has shown resilience to crises, which was buttressed by the patience and perseverance necessary to achieve adaptation and adjustment.

The ability to adjust and adapt is not unique to Japan, but Japan has shown a resistance to crisis in the past. Such past resilience is observed in Japan's industrial and military catchup with the West after the Meiji Restoration in 1868, observed in Japan's emergence from the ashes of World War II, and observed from Japan's adaptation to the end of the fixed exchange rate system and oil crises in the 1970s. It is uncertain whether Japan will overcome the new economic problems with as great success as in the past because the demographic changes and resulting socioeconomic problems are a new and huge challenge for Japan. There is concern that the younger generations of Japanese who have grown up in affluence may lack the level of perseverance possessed by previous generations who endured poverty and war devastation. Nonetheless, Japan certainly has the potential to overcome the new challenges.

Change takes a long time and is gradual in Japan. It is partly because of Japan's consensual decision making, conservatism, and desire for security, stability, predictability, and certainty. So Japan's change – be it economic or political – will continue to be slow and gradual. But Japan has shown a willingness to make necessary changes in the face of crises in the past. We believe that Japan will make necessary changes to mitigate the negative economic consequences of the aging and declining population. Japan will try efforts to increase fertility rates first. It also will try to enhance the productivity of its economy, so that high economic productivity will compensate for the decline of the workforce. The government has already started taking measures to increase the productivity of the economy and will continue to do so. In fact, the demographic challenges are the primary reason why

Japan's market reforms will continue to some degree – this is the only way that Japan can increase productivity to offset the effects of a grayer population.

Japan will also encourage greater female participation in the workforce and render the labor market a more friendly place for females. This dramatic social-economic change will have far reaching impacts on Japanese society, but in ways that are not easy to predict at this point. If these approaches do not work or are insufficient, Japan may resort to increasing immigration. Immigration, however, will not be its first choice.

Generational Replacement

Economic and demographic difficulties are not the only source of change in Japan. Generational replacement of politicians and voters is also under way. The Japanese government and economy for most of the postwar period were managed by politicians and bureaucrats who had experienced World War II and economic hardships in the first half of the twentieth century. Because of their wartime experience and resolve not to repeat the same mistake, politicians on the issues of national security and diplomacy tended to be dovish, pacifist, and pro-America, and to support the national security arrangement provided by the U.S. military forces with Japan's limited Self-Defense Forces. That is, they were content to continue restricting Japan's defense spending and commitments, while relying on the U.S. forces to provide Japan's national security. The LDP has always had its share of hawkish and nationalistic politicians who wanted to see a more assertive Japan in international politics and to revise the "constitution imposed by the United States" and have stronger military forces. These politicians' nationalistic voices were, in the past, successfully contained by the majority of pro-peace politicians.

The traditional politicians, however, are gradually fading away from the main stage of Japanese politics. They are getting old and being replaced by young politicians who did not experience World War II or economic hardships before Japan's rapid economic growth. The young politicians are more willing to assertively take a stance on controversial political issues and agendas, such as constitutional revision and deployment of the Self-Defense Forces overseas for multinational peacekeeping efforts. These issues have been more or less taboo in postwar Japan because of their negative association with Japan's war and aggression.

Shinzo Abe was the first prime minister who was born after the end of the war. Although his ideology was in no way representative of that of the entire population of young politicians, he was an openly nationalistic politician. He actively pursued nationalistic agendas such as the revision of the constitution (which prohibits Japan's possession of armed forces, use of force, and participation in collective security arrangements); promotion of patriotism and nationalism; and the construction of an educational system that would promote nationalism among Japanese children and students and that would increase the national government's control over education. He openly visited the Yasukuni Shrine, when a prime minister's visit almost always invited criticism and protest from the neighboring Asian countries (although he did not do so during his term as the prime minister in order to avoid criticism and protest from China and South Korea). Abe wanted to promote patriotism and glorify Japan and openly questioned the validity of historical allegations made against wartime Japan of aggression, such as comfort women, when he knew that such statements would invoke foreign governments' protest. Abe also did not register opposition or reservations when an LDP leader repeatedly announced that Japan should consider the possibility of acquiring nuclear weapons, which used to be unthinkable before this decade.

Previously, these signs of nationalism would have been viewed with alarm and antipathy by the Japanese public and received serious criticism by the media. According to recent polls, however, more of the public and young politicians are less averse to these issues. There is a shift in public opinion, as the memory of the war has become more distant and the number of the Japanese who did not experience the war has increased. This will not cause an immediate radical departure in Japan's foreign or national security policy from its previous pro-peace positions. In the long run, however, it will have an altering effect on foreign and national security policy. Japan's participation in multinational peacekeeping efforts and constitutional revision will continue to remain on the policy agenda, and there will be slow and gradual change in foreign policy.

Developments in North Korea are a wild card for Japan's foreign policy in the future, and China's military goals in Asia will also influence Japanese foreign policy. Japan will likely become a more "normal" nation in terms of political involvement in the world, but at the same time, Japan will continue to attach great importance to not alienating its Asian neighbors because its economic interests in preserving good relationships with them are too large.

This more open debate about Japan's foreign policy is reflective of another impact of the generational replacement of politicians and voters. Young politicians are less constrained by the informal rules, norms, and practices that were established by their senior politicians under the LDP's one-party dominance. Such generational replacement of politicians and citizens will alter the features of Japan's politics and economy, as old politicians fade away, though the speed of change will be slow. Japanese politics and policy making have and will become more open and transparent. Political deliberations and decisions that used to be made in behind-the-scene deal-making among political parties are now conducted openly in the Diet or in public. Open criticism of party leadership by backbenchers used to be strongly discouraged in the past, but now, it is common. Politicians' accountability to the public will continue to increase. Young politicians are more willing to debate policy issues openly and to make decisions by using majority rule (neither of which was really the case under LDP rule), rather than being constrained by consensus or unanimity rule. Politicians will also be more attentive to public opinion, making them more responsive to the public.

Power of the Prime Minister: Lasting Influence of Koizumi

Koizumi changed Japan's policy making and generated a great deal of policy innovations, many of which would have been difficult under previous prime ministers. But it does not mean that the new features of policy making that he introduced will remain firmly in Japanese politics under all future prime ministers. This is because the politics and policy-making process observed during his administration were more a result of his personal attributes and his political skills and boldness (plus the political and economic conditions surrounding his administration) than a result of a more fundamental change of Japanese politics.

No doubt, some features of the Koizumi administration will remain. The Koizumi administration set the precedent that a prime minister can advance his policy initiatives strongly and successfully in the midst of strong policy opposition by his own party, core supporters, the bureaucracy, or client industries and sectors. Thanks to the revision of the cabinet law that gave the prime minister more power and the precedent Koizumi set, future prime ministers will be able to enjoy greater agenda-setting power than previously.

However, possibility of strong prime ministerial leadership is contingent on public support as well as their political skills and audacity to successfully weave their way through the veto points in the policy-making process and dominate over the policy opposition. Koizumi's successful postal privatization and other reforms after the September 2005 election were assisted crucially by the luck that he had in leading his LDP to a landslide victory in the 2005 lower house election and by the fact that the public had had enough of the LDP "old boys" approach to policy making. The victory was partly a result of his keen political sense and tactics. But it also was partly luck, because the LDP's victory was not originally expected at all when he dissolved the lower house. In the future, a prime minister's policy initiatives will be thwarted if he does not have a clear public mandate or lacks the political skills and audacity to silence the policy opposition. A prime minister's party can always replace him if he does not wield large enough public support but tries to impose his policy opposed by the party. The party's support for the prime minister depends on whether good electoral prospects are expected under his leadership and whether the party has an electorally viable alternative to replace the prime minister.[2]

Koizumi had a conducive political and economic environment in which to advance drastic economic reforms – Japan's economy was in a deep recession, policy measures over a ten-year period had failed to return the economy to sustainable growth, and, as a result, the public was ready for larger change in policy. Koizumi enjoyed high public support. It will be difficult for a future prime minister to replicate these conditions in normal times and gain approval for policy changes of similar magnitude.

In sum, the policy-making process observed under the Koizumi administration is more "Koizumi's politics" than "a new Japanese

---

[2] Although the LDP wanted to replace Koizumi, it was unable to, because he was enormously popular among the public (an electoral asset for the LDP) and the party did not have an equally electorally viable replacement. Although the LDP suffered defeat in the 2007 upper house election under Prime Minister Abe's leadership, it was unable to immediately unseat him, because it did not have an alternative candidate who could clearly improve on Abe's dismal performance.

politics." It was also a case in which the individual attributes of a prime minister mattered much, which had not happened often in Japanese politics. At the same time, one should be careful not to attribute the many changes introduced by the Koizumi administration solely to personality and a special set of circumstances, because real and lasting changes in Japan's economic and political institutions did take place.

Koizumi's successor, Prime Minister Shinzo Abe, did not even come close to Koizumi's standard during his short tenure from September 2006 to September 2007. Abe's policy initiatives were effectively neutralized by his LDP; for example, the LDP was successful in blocking the termination of the earmarking of tax revenues for road construction and the institution of a new legal framework to effectively restrict descent from heaven by bureaucrats. The old LDP was able to reassert itself to some degree under Abe, because Abe was more conciliatory to the LDP and its factional and intraparty dynamics than Koizumi. Abe lacked the political skills and boldness to advance his own policy initiatives in the face of the LDP's opposition. He originally enjoyed very high public support when he took the office, so he had a chance to take strong policy initiatives. But public support declined significantly because of his lack of leadership and political skills. Multiple money scandals involving his cabinet members also were revealed and damaged his approval ratings. What decisively diminished public support for him was the revelation that Japan's Social Security Agency had amassed fifty million cases of unidentified social security payments that it had received from citizens over the years as a result of its negligence. On the devastating loss in the 2007 upper house election, he resigned after one year in office without achieving much more than his nationalistic agendas, which was possible mostly because of his LDP's overwhelming two-thirds majority in the lower house achieved by the previous Koizumi administration in the 2005 lower house election. Thus, Abe's case was one in which the lack of political skills and experience limited his policy-making leadership.

Abe's successor, Prime Minister Yasuo Fukuda, has been in office for a short period of time. He has been much more conciliatory and accommodative to bureaucrats and LDP politicians than Koizumi, showing that the kind of strong power exercised by Koizumi is contingent on the prime minister's personality and preferences and his will and political skills to exercise it. Fukuda is a typical consensus-oriented LDP politician and is not likely to pursue his own policy opposed by the LDP by forcefully overriding policy opposition as Koizumi did.

Fukuda supports the general direction of market reform established by Koizumi. However, as a result of the July 2007 elections in which the public expressed concern over the growing economic insecurity in Japan and expressed the frustration that economic reform has been carried too far, Fukuda has had no choice but to tone down market reform and fiscal austerity and take policy measures to reduce economic difficulty experienced by low-income households and struggling industries and rural areas. That means being more responsive to LDP politicians' demands for redistributive policy and fiscal expansion. This is because the DP with redistributive electoral platforms dramatically increased seats in the 2007 upper house election, and the LDP that had kept its support for market reform reduced seats. LDP politicians fear that LDP would also lose the next lower house election and lose control of government, unless some measures to correct the negative side effects of market reform are adopted.

The DP and opposition parties have become an effective veto player since the LDP-CGP coalition government lost majority control in the upper house in 2007. Although the LDP-CGP government still controls the lower house, it cannot pass any bill in the upper house unless it obtains cooperation from the DP. The DP won the election by proposing redistributive economic policy. As a result, the LDP-CGP government needs to make economic policy concessions in a redistributive direction to pass its bills in the upper house.

The Japanese prime minister now has much enhanced power of agenda-setting. So Fukuda will probably propose his own policy initiatives. But because of his consensual style, they are not likely to be ones that run counter to the interests of LDP politicians, bureaucrats, or client industries. For that matter, he will have difficulty pursuing his policy opposed by the opposition DP, because the DP is now the largest party in the upper house.

The Bureaucracy in the New Japan

The political power of the once renowned Japanese bureaucracy vis-à-vis the executive branch and politicians has declined in the past decade.[3] The bureaucracy is still very active in policy making and is

---

[3] Slower, smaller-scale increases in politicians' policy making power vis-à-vis bureaucrats had taken place over a longer stretch of time during the postwar period. But the recent increase in politicians' relative power is a discrete shift and more unambiguous.

essential in the management of the government and economy, including the drafting of policies and legislative bills and the implementation
of government policy. However, because of the changed political institutions starting in the 1990s and the changes and precedents made
by the Koizumi administration, the politicians – the prime minister, cabinet ministers, and other legislators –have gradually increased
dominance over the bureaucracy in setting the policy agenda and the
direction of policy making and in making the final decisions over
contested or difficult issues.

Politicians' efforts to gain policy-making power away from bureaucrats started when the Hosokawa administration came to power in
1993. The revision of the cabinet law and other administrative reform
of 2001 partly laid the foundation for the prime minister's increased
power vis-à-vis bureaucratic ministries. Numerous bureaucratic corruption cases and mismanagement of the economy in the 1990s also
did not help bureaucrats avert the slide of their power. But what
made the power shift unambiguous was Prime Minister Koizumi,
who advanced many reforms that ran counter to the vested interests
of bureaucratic ministries and their client industries and sectors by
overriding their opposition. Many reforms were about deregulation –
the reduction of government intervention in the economy to increase
the efficiency and competitiveness of the economy. As such, they were
designed to reduce the regulatory power of bureaucratic ministries and
allow a greater role for market forces. To bureaucratic ministries, the
reforms meant the reduction of their power and budget. Bureaucrats
tried to thwart Koizumi's reforms, but Koizumi resolutely overrode
their opposition on a variety of issues such as budget cuts, closure or
privatization of public corporations, and reductions of the number of
government employees. In the process, the precedent was established
that politicians can set policy agendas and lead the policy-making process. Bureaucrats are still and will remain indispensable policy makers,
and their power will not drastically dwindle. But it will be difficult for
the bureaucracy to reassert itself to the role it played before the late
1990s.

Deregulation and the decline of the bureaucracy's power vis-à-vis
politicians, however, do not mean the decline of Japan's industrial policy. The Japanese government is still very active today in identifying
industries with great growth potential, promoting their development
by allocating government resources to them and by coordinating with
the private sector, and guiding the economy toward economic growth.

Since the second half of the 1990s (the Hashimoto administration), and particularly since the Koizumi administration, the governing LDP has promoted deregulation and the restructuring of the bureaucracy. One might think that these reforms must have led not only to the reduction of the Japanese bureaucracy's size and power but also to have restricted its ability to guide the economy through industrial policy. Deregulation has certainly reduced the numbers of policy areas in which the bureaucracy has regulatory power and has lessened the extent of the bureaucracy's regulatory power. However, the bureaucracy still actively guides the economy – it does so in a different way now than it did before.

Deregulation is by now a policy direction relatively widely accepted in Japan with the caveat that there is concern about how far it should go and who should bear the costs of deregulation. Bureaucratic ministries still adamantly resist deregulation but also know that this is the direction the Japanese economy needs to take in order to regain economic competitiveness and growth. They do not voluntarily agree to reduce their power, jurisdiction, and budgets or relinquish certain government regulations they control. But at the same time, the bureaucracy is aware that the competitiveness and efficiency of the Japanese economy need to be improved, and that it is hard to achieve it without deregulation and liberalization. They recognize market forces as a more likely approach to competitiveness and efficiency than the old style form of regulation.

As a result, many government ministries now find their raison d'être in finding ways to increase Japan's economic competitiveness and efficiency and guiding the economy in the direction that allows Japan to achieve sustained economic growth. That is, they guide Japan's deregulation and strategically assist the development of industries with large growth potential. The Japanese government, for example, has been shifting its resources to high-tech industries at the forefront of the world economy. The government's method of industrial promotion by cooperating with the private sector is also still much alive. So, in this respect, the Japanese bureaucracy's role of guiding the economy has not changed significantly.

Politicians along with their policy advisors have so far been the ones that set the deregulatory direction of economic reform and even decide the general contents of reform. However, bureaucrats still exert great influence in Japan's economy. They still set the specifics of Japan's competitiveness policy and economic reform, as well as identify industries they believe Japan should strategically promote and devise specific measures to promote them. They can affect the shape of Japan's economic reform also by not agreeing to certain deregulatory measures (e.g., their refusal to cooperate with the Koizumi administration's devolution, which restricted the extent of devolution). The bureaucracy has become active in encouraging venture businesses in high-tech areas and assisting small businesses that have lagged behind large corporations in economic recovery. It also has made efforts to revitalize traditional commercial areas that had decayed in the past decades. Although the bureaucracy will not engage in unilateral industrial development, it will remain active in assisting and cooperating with private corporations to promote Japan's industries and economic growth.

Politicians' power has increased, and bureaucrats' has decreased. But both actors are still important and need each other, as they mutually benefit by working together. Politicians' policy making and management of the economy would be a more daunting task if they alienated bureaucrats. So they will remain close allies and continue to protect each other in most issue areas. Although Koizumi determinedly and successfully overrode bureaucratic opposition during his term, succeeding Abe was more conciliatory to bureaucrats. And now, Prime Minister Fukuda is even more sympathetic to bureaucrats and manages the government based on cooperation with bureaucrats. The Japanese bureaucracy will remain one of the important actors in policy making and economic management.

Public Opinion, Policy Competition, and Potential for Change in Government

Japanese politics now has some new features. Public opinion matters now more than before. Political parties compete with each other based on policy programs and are more responsive to the public. The continuation of these trends in the future is not unconditional, however. Political parties' responsiveness to public opinion depends on the presence of relatively close competition between the two largest parties. It is conditional on the continuing electoral and parliamentary strength of the DP (or any future second largest party) and a reasonably close power balance between the DP and LDP.

Political parties now have to be sensitive to public opinion for three reasons. First, under the new mixed SMD-PR electoral system, a shift in votes can translate into a larger shift in parties' seat shares. It makes an alternation of political parties in government easier than the previous system that kept the LDP in power for so many years. This makes political parties sensitive to shifts in public opinion.

Second, candidates and political parties now need to appeal to larger numbers and percentages of voters under the new system in order to win seats than they did under the old system (technically, this results from the reduction in the number of representatives elected from each district). Organizing *koenkai* supporters and mobilizing client industries and networks of local politicians in their districts are not sufficient to ensure reelection any more, and candidates need to appeal to larger segments of their constituents – unorganized or regular voters that their organization and networks cannot cover.

Third, the size of non-party-identifiers is large who do not support any existing party and who change their votes for political parties from election to election. They have constituted about 50 percent of the entire population of voters in the past decade, and can affect electoral outcomes greatly. Their large size makes it necessary for political parties to mobilize their votes by crafting policy platforms that appeal to them.

These factors make political parties more attentive to public opinion and more vulnerable to electoral pressures from the public. Political parties have no choice but to court public opinion as long as they wish to win elections and gain control of government. Because political parties pay attention to public opinion, the public can now affect the direction and nature of government policy more than before. Political parties' sensitivity to public opinion is clearly shown in their response before and after the recent upper house election, in which the DP proposed more redistributive policy to woo the public during the campaign, and the electoral results moved the LDP's economic policy in the same redistributive direction after the election. It shows that the Japanese public can now move government policy significantly. It also means that government policy (what the government can do) can be seriously affected by electoral conditions. In this sense, public opinion can play a role in deciding the shape of the future Japanese economy.

However, the increased importance of public opinion in Japanese politics is contingent on a continuing electoral and parliamentary environment where the second largest party (currently, the DP) is large enough to potentially pose an electoral threat to the largest party (currently, the LDP). If the DP's electoral strength were not large enough to pose a threat to the LDP-CGP coalition government's rule, the LDP would have less incentive to be responsive to public opinion. But if the DP is large enough, a shift in public opinion can potentially vote the LDP out of power and the DP in power. In this case, the LDP will have no choice but to be responsive to public opinion. Currently, the DP has grown large enough to electorally threaten the LDP, so the LDP heeds public opinion; hence, at least temporary policy adjustments in the LDP's market reform and fiscal austerity have been made. In this environment, LDP politicians feel that they cannot ignore the equity issue even though it runs counter to the market reform policy currently in place.

At its electoral strength in late 2007, the DP has a reasonable chance of seizing control of government and replacing the LDP. An alternation of political parties in government is possible in the not-so-distant future, especially because the LDP's electoral strength has declined over the years and the LDP would not have as many seats as it does now without the CGP's electoral cooperation. Despite Prime Minister Koizumi's personal popularity among the public during his tenure, the LDP has become increasingly dependent on the votes mobilized by the CGP, which has been the LDP's coalition partner since 1999. But it also will not be easy for the DP to maintain the electoral strength it showed in the 2007 upper house election.

If government change continues to be a viable possibility, policy competition among political parties will remain active, and the parties will try to win votes by generating better policies or policies that appeal to voters. In this scenario, the business of Japanese politics will be conducted based on policy issues more than during the days of the LDP's one-party dominance. In this environment, unorganized Japanese citizens (such as consumers) or those not part of the mutual support system of politicians, bureaucracy, and client industries will play a role in shaping Japan's future. In the past, the interests of these groups tended to be neglected by politicians. But it also has a potential cost, in that political parties may have difficulty implementing policies that are necessary but not popular among the public. Market reform and fiscal austerity potentially fall into this category. If politicians' electoral concerns keep them from implementing policies necessary for Japan or its economy, this will have an adverse impact on Japan's future.

In contrast, if the LDP (or any other party) regains electoral strength sufficient to give it a stable parliamentary majority, the party will not have to be overly sensitive to public opinion. In this case, the party can afford to pursue policies it wants, even when they are opposed by the public, because voter revolt may not be sufficient to threaten the party's control of government.

The LDP is not likely to regain the electoral strength it once had – except for one possible scenario. That is, there can be another round of party realignment, in which parties split and merge. Not being able to project the possibility of the regaining of electoral strength to keep it stably in power, the LDP may decide or try to absorb part of another party, such as the DP, to enlarge its size. If this happened, the LDP would be able to reestablish its electoral strength. Alternatively, part of the LDP may decide to leave the LDP to form a new party with part of the DP. The DP has many former LDP members, who could cooperate with LDP defectors if they left the LDP. If this happened, the two major parties (the LDP and DP) could split and merge into three parties.

Parts of the DP also may consider party realignment. The DP is comprised of former members of the LDP, DSP, and SDP with a wide range of policy positions from the right to left. As such, the DP contains policy differences within it (particularly, on the issues of constitutional revision and defense), which increase the possibility of policy disagreement serious enough to make the party's cohesive policy making difficult. If DP politicians cannot reconcile their policy differences, they may decide to split and either form a new party or join another existing party.

The possibility of further party realignment depends on many idiosyncratic factors at the levels of individual politicians, political parties, and their supporters. In any event, the basic trend in party competition will still be toward the formation of two large political parties. Japan's new mixed-member electoral system gives advantages to large parties and disadvantages to small parties. For now, the LDP will try to boost electoral strength, because it is more economical to try to strengthen a party that is already the strongest of all parties than to instigate the DP's breakup and party realignment. The LDP under Koizumi started this effort to woo and co-opt new growing industries, like high-tech, IT, and M&A, as the populations and prosperity in its traditional electoral bases (such as agriculture, small businesses in distribution, and construction) had declined over the years. The new industries could provide a growing source of votes and money. Koizumi aimed to cultivate new socioeconomic interests by advancing deregulation and liberalization, which would benefit new, growing

industries and consumers (i.e., largely unorganized individual voters). Koizumi's reduction of government redistribution of economic
resources from urban to rural areas was also construed partly as a way
to boost LDP support in urban areas where the LDP had traditionally
been weaker.

A Final Note

Japan has been in transition since 1980. Japan reached the highs of
economic and political stability in the 1980s only to collapse into
economic, financial, and political distress in the 1990s. Japan began
to emerge from the distress under the leadership of Koizumi and by
2005 appeared to have passed a turning point. The journey has been
remarkable. In the process, Japan's economic and political institutions
have adjusted to the new environment. A new Japan is emerging –
one whose economy is more open and transparent and one whose
political institutions are more competitive and responsive to the public.
Japan continues to face difficult changes internally and externally. The
demographic changes and the unraveling of the old social contract that
promised relative equality and security will continue to shape Japan's
economic and political institutions. The passing of the old generation
and the desire to become a more normal nation combined with threats
from North Korea and China will further shape Japan's international
role.

It would be premature to conclude that Japan will fail to adjust and
become a less competitive force in the world. In fact, there is more
reason to be optimistic than pessimistic about Japan's prospects. Japan
will remain a fascinating case study of economic and political development. Hopefully, Japan will provide in the near future a case study
of a country that successfully revitalized its economy from stagnation
and adjusted to the economic challenges created by population aging.

References

Aberbach, Joel D., and Robert D. Putnam (1981). *Bureaucrats and Politicians in Western Democracies*. Cambridge, MA: Harvard University Press.

Aoki, Masahiko (1988). *Information, Incentives, and Bargaining in the Japanese Economy*. New York: Cambridge University Press.

Aoki, Masahiko (2001). *Towards Comparative Institutional Analysis*. Cambridge, MA: The MIT Press.

Aoki, Masahiko, and Hugh Patrick (1994). *The Japanese Main Bank System: Its Relevance for Developing and Transforming Economies*. New York: Oxford University Press.

Bank of Japan (2001). *The Role of Monetary Policy under Low Inflation: Deflationary Shocks and Policy Responses*. Institute for Monetary and Economic Studies. *Monetary and Economic Studies* 19(S-1): 1–450.

Bank of Japan (2007, October). *Outlook for Economic Activity and Prices*. Bank of Japan.

Benston, George J., and George G. Kaufman (1997). "FDICIA after Five Years." *Journal of Economic Perspectives* 11(3): 139–158.

Bernanke, Ben S. (2003). "Some Thoughts on Monetary Policy in Japan." Presented to the Japan Society of Monetary Economics, Tokyo, Japan (May 31). Available at http://www.federalreserve.gov/boarddocs/speeches/2003/20030531/default.htm.

Blomstrom, Magnus, Byron Gangnes, and Sumner La Croix, eds. (2001). *Japan's New Economy*. Oxford: Oxford University Press.

Borio, C. E., V. N. Kennedy, and S. D. Prowse (1994, April). "Exploring Aggregate Asset Price Fluctuations across Countries." *BIS Economic Papers* No. 40. Basle, Switzerland.

Burdekin, Richard C. K., and Pierre L. Siklos, eds. (2004). *Deflation: Current and Historical Perspectives*. Cambridge: Cambridge University Press.

Burniaux, Jean-Marc et al. (2006). "Labour Market Performance, Income Inequality and Poverty in OECD Countries." *OECD Economics Department Working Paper* No. 500. Paris: OECD.

Cabinet Office (2004). *Nihon keizai 2004: Jizoku-teki seicho no kanosei to risuku*. December. Tokyo: Author. Available at http://www5.cao.go.jp/keizai3/2004/1219nk/keizai2004pdf.html.

Cabinet Office (2006). *Nenji Keizai Zaisei Hokoku-sho/Keizai Zaisei Hakusho*. [Annual Report on Japanese Economy and Public Finance/Economic Survey of

Japan] Tokyo: Author. Available at http://www5.cao.go.jp/j-j/wp/wp-je06/06–00000pdf.html.

Calder, Kent E. (1988). *Crisis and Compensation: Public Policy and Political Stability in Japan*. Princeton, NJ: Princeton University Press.

Calder, Kent E. (1990). "Linking Welfare and the Developmental State: Postal Savings in Japan." *Journal of Japanese Studies* 16(1): 31–59.

Cargill, Thomas F. (2001). "Monetary Policy, Deflation, and Economic History: Lessons for the Bank of Japan." *Monetary and Economic Studies* (Special Issue), 19(February): 113–134.

Cargill, Thomas F. (2005), "Is the Bank of Japan's Financial Structure an Obstacle to Policy?" *IMF Staff Papers* 52(2): 311–334.

Cargill, Thomas F. (2006). "Japan's Economic and Financial Stagnation in the 1990s and Reluctance to Change." In Magnus Blomstrom and Sumner La Croix, eds., *Institutional Change in Japan*. London: Routledge.

Cargill, Thomas F., and Gillian Garcia (1982). *Financial Deregulation and Monetary Control*. Stanford, CA: Hoover Institution Press. Published in Japanese by the Toyo Keizai Shimposha Company, Tokyo, Japan, 1983.

Cargill, Thomas F., and Gillian Garcia (1985). *Financial Reform in the 1980s*. Stanford, CA: Hoover Institution Press.

Cargill, Thomas F., and Federico Guerrero (2007). "Japan's Deflation: A Time-Incon-sistent Policy in Need of an Inflation Target." *International Finance* 10(2): 115–130.

Cargill, Thomas F., and Michael H. Hutchison (1997). "Macroeconomic Policy in Japan: International and Comparative Perspectives." In M. Fratianni, D. Salvatore, and J. von Hagen, eds., *Macroeconomic Policies in Open Economies*. Westport, CT: Greenwood Press.

Cargill, Thomas F., Michael M. Hutchison, and Takatoshi Ito (1997). *The Political Economy of Japanese Monetary Policy*. Cambridge, MA: MIT Press.

Cargill, Thomas F., Michael M. Hutchison, and Takatoshi Ito (1998). "The Banking Crisis in Japan," In G. Caprio Jr., W. C. Hunter, G. G. Kaufman, and D. M. Leipziger, eds., *Preventing Bank Crises: Lessons from Recent Global Bank Failures*. Washington, DC: The World Bank.

Cargill, Thomas F., Michael M. Hutchison, and Takatoshi Ito (2000). *Financial and Central Bank Policy in Japan*. Cambridge, MA: MIT Press.

Cargill, Thomas F., and Thomas Mayer (1998). "The Great Depression and History Textbooks." *The History Teacher* 31(4): 441–458.

Cargill, Thomas F., and Hugh Patrick (2005). "Response to Economic and Finan-cial Distress in Korea and Japan." *2005 Korea's Economy*. Washington DC: Korea Economic Institute.

Cargill, Thomas F., and Elliott Parker (2003). "Why Deflation Is Different." *Central Banking* 14(1): 35–42.

Cargill, Thomas F., and Elliott Parker (2004a). "Price Deflation, Money Demand, and Monetary Policy Discontinuity: A Comparative View of Japan, China, and the United States." *North American Journal of Economics and Finance* 15(1): 125–147.

Cargill, Thomas F., and Elliott Parker (2004b). "Price Deflation and Consumption: Central Bank Policy and Japan's Economic and Financial Stagnation." *Journal of Asian Economics* 15(3): 493–506.

Cargill, Thomas F., and Shoichi Royama (1988). *The Transition of Finance in Japan and the United States*. Stanford, CA: Hoover Institution Press.

Cargill, Thomas F., and Naoyuki Yoshino (2003). *Postal Savings and Fiscal Investment in Japan: The PSS and the FILP*. Oxford: Oxford University Press.

Colignon, Richard, and Chikako Usui (2001). "The Resilience of Japan's Iron Triangle." *Asian Survey* 41(5): 865–895.

Commons, John R. (1934). *Institutional Economics*. New York: Macmillan.

Council on Economic and Fiscal Policy (2005, February 15). "Saishutsu-Sainyu Ittai Kaikaku ni tuite." Available at http://www.keizai-shimon.go.jp/minutes/2005/0215/item1.pdf.

Curtis, Gerald L. (1988). *The Japanese Way of Politics*. New York: Columbia University Press.

Curtis, Gerald L. (1999). *The Logic of Japanese Politics: Leaders, Institutions, and the Limits of Change*. New York: Columbia University Press.

d'Ercole, Marco Mira (2006). "Income Inequality and Poverty in OECD Countries: How Does Japan Compare?" *Japanese Journal of Social Security Policy* 5(1): 1–15.

Doi, Takero, and Takeo Hoshi (2003). "Pay for the FILP." In Magnus Blomstrom, Jennifer Corbett, Fumio Hayashi, and Anil Kashyap, eds., *Structural Impediments to Growth in Japan*. Chicago: University of Chicago Press.

Economist (2005). "Land of the Rising Price." December 17th.

Economist (2008). "Sayonara, Salaryman." January 5th–11th.

Ebertstadt, Nicholas (2004). "Power and Population in Asia." *Policy Review* 123(Feb./Mar.): 3–27.

Epstein, David, and Sharyn O'Halloran (1999). *Delegating Powers: A Transaction Cost Politics Approach to Policy Making under Separate Powers*. Cambridge: Cambridge University Press.

Esping-Andersen, Gosta (1990). *The Three Worlds of Welfare Capitalism*. Princeton, NJ: Princeton University Press.

Esping-Andersen, Gosta (1997). "Hybrid or Unique? The Japanese Welfare State between Europe and America." *Journal of European Social Policy* 7(3): 179–189.

Feldman, Robert Alan (1986). *Japanese Financial Markets: Deficits, Dilemmas, and Deregulation*. Cambridge, MA: MIT Press.

Fisher, Irving (1933). "The Debt-Deflation Theory of Great Depressions." *Econometrica* 1(4): 337–357.

Förster, Michael, and Marco Mira d'Ercole (2005). "Income Distribution and Poverty in OECD Countries in the Second Half of the 1990s." *OECD Social, Employment and Migration Working Paper No. 22*. Paris: OECD.

Frankel, Jeffrey A. (1984). *The Yen/Dollar Agreement: Liberalizing Japanese Capital Markets*. Cambridge, MA: MIT Press.

Freedman, Craig (1999). *Why Did Japan Stumble?* Cheltenham, UK: Edward Elgar.

Freedman, Craig (2006). "Post-War Japan." *Centre for Japanese Economic Studies*. Sydney, Australia: Macquarie University.

Friedman, Thomas L. (2000). *The Lexus and the Olive Trees*. New York: Anchor Books.

Friedman, Thomas L. (2005). *The World Is Flat*. New York: Farrar, Straus, and Giroux.

Friedman, Milton, and Anna J. Schwartz (1963). *A Monetary History of the United States*. Princeton, NJ: Princeton University Press.

Fujii, Yoshihiro (2004). *Shibarareta Kinyuu-Seisaku: Kensho Nihon Ginko*. Tokyo: Nihon Keizai Shimbun-sha.

Fujiki, Hiroshi, Kunio Okina, and Shigenon Shinatsuka (2001). "Monetary Policy under Zero Interest Rate: Viewpoint of Central Bank Economists. *Monetary and Economic Studies* 19 (February): 89–130.

Fukui, Haruhiro (1970). *Party in Power: The Japanese Liberal Democrats and Policy-Making*. Berkeley: University of California Press.

Garrett, G., and C. Way. (1999). "Public Sector Unions, Corporatism, and Macroeconomic Performance." *Comparative Political Studies* 32(4): 411–434.

Gourevitch, Peter (1986). *Politics in Hard Times: Comparative Responses to International Economic Crises*. Ithaca: Cornell University Press.

Haley, John O. (1992). "Consensual Governance: A Study of Law, Culture, and the Political Economy of Postwar Japan." In Shumpei Kumon and Henry Rosovsky, eds., *The Political Economy of Japan, Vol. 3: Cultural and Social Dynamics*. Stanford, CA: Stanford University Press.

Hall, Peter A., and David Soskice (2001). *Varieties of Capitalism: The Institutional Foundations of Comparative Advantage*. New York: Oxford University Press.

Hamada, Koichi, and Akiyoshi Horiuchi (1987). "The Political Economy of the Financial Market." In Kozo Yamamura and Yasukichi Yasuba, eds., *The Political Economic of Japan, Vol. 1: The Domestic Transformation*. Stanford, CA: Stanford University Press.

Hamada, Koichi, and Akiyoshi Horiuchi, eds. (2004). *Ronso: Nihon no Keizai Kiki: Choki Teitai no Shinin wo Kaimei Suru*. Tokyo: Nihon Keizai Shimbun-sha.

Hayami, Masaru (2000). "Price Stability and Monetary Policy." Presented to the Research Institute of Japan, Tokyo (March 21).

Hetzel, Robert (2003). "Japanese Monetary Policy and Deflation." Federal Reserve Bank of Richmond. *Economic Quarterly* 89(3): 21–52.

Hirose, Michisada (1981). *Hojokin to Seikento*. Tokyo: Asahi Shimbun-sha.

Hirose, Michisada (1989). *Seiji to Kane*. Tokyo: Iwanami Shoten.

Hoshi, Takeo, and Anil K. Kashyap (2001). *Corporate Financing and Governance in Japan*. Cambridge, MA: MIT Press.

Hoshi, Takeo, and Takatoshi Ito (2004). "Financial regulation in Japan: A sixth year review of the Financial Services Agency." *Journal of Financial Stability* 1: 229–243.

Hoshi, Takeo, and Hugh Patrick (2000). *Crisis and Change in the Japanese Financial System*. Boston: Kluwer Academic Publishers.

Ihori, Toshihiro (2001). "Shakai Shihon Seibi (Kokyo Toshi) no Yakuwari." Report. Chiho Keizai no Jirutsu to Kokyo Toshi ni kansuru Kenkyu-kai. June. Policy Research Institute, the Ministry of Finance. Tokyo, Japan. Available at http://www.mof.go.jp/jouhou/soken/kenkyu/zk052/zk052b.pdf.

Ihori, Toshihiro, et al. (2002). "90 Nendai no Zaisei Unei: Hyoka to Kadai." *Financial Review* (July): 36–68.

Ishi, Hiromitsu (2000). *Making Fiscal Policy in Japan: Economic Effects and Institutional Settings*. New York: Oxford University Press.

Ishii, Kanji (2007). "Equity Investments and Equity Investment Funding in Prewar Japan: Comments on 'Were Banks Really at the Center of the Prewar Japanese Financial System?'" *Monetary and Economic Studies* 25(1): 77–88.

Ishikawa, Masumi, and Michisada Hirose (1989). *Jiminto: Choki Shihai no Kozo*. Tokyo: Iwanami Shoten.

Ito, Takatoshi (1992). *The Japanese Economy*. Cambridge, MA: MIT Press.

Ito, Takatoshi (2004). "Inflation Targeting and Japan: Why Has the Bank of Japan not Adopted Inflation Targeting?" *NBER Working Paper No. 10818* (September).

Johnson, Chalmers (1982). *MITI and the Japanese Miracle*. Stanford, CA: Stanford University Press.

Kamada, Koichiro (1993). "The Real Value of Postal Savings Certificates." *Monetary and Economic Studies* 11(2): 59–96.

Kane, Edward (1981). "Accelerating Inflation, Technological Innovation, and the Decreasing Effectiveness of Banking Regulation." *Journal of Finance* 36(2): 355–367.

Karube, Kensuke, and Tomohiko Nishino (1999). *Kensho Keizai Shissei: Darega Naniwo Naze Machigaetaka*. Tokyo: Iwanami Shoten.

Kindleberger, Charles P. (1996). *Manias, Panics, and Crashes: A History of Financial Crisis*. New York: John Wiley & Sons, Inc.

Krugman, Paul. (1998). "It's Baaack: Japan's Slump and the Return of the Liquidity Trap." *Brookings Papers on Economic Activity* 2: 137–187.

Krugman, Paul (2002). *The Return of Depression Economics*. New York: W. W. Norton.

Kuwayama, Patricia (2000). "Postal Banking in the United States and Japan: A Comparative Analysis." *Monetary and Economic Studies* 18(1): 73–104.

Kuznets, Simon (1971). *The Economic Growth of Nations*. Cambridge, MA: Harvard University Press.

The Labor Market Policy Research Commission of the Ministry of Health, Labor, and Welfare (2005). "Jinko Gesho-ka ni okeru Koyo/Rodo Seisaku no Kadai." July 27. Available at http://www.mhlw.go.jp/houdou/2005/07/dl/h0727-2a.pdf.

Lacker, Jeffrey M., and John A Weinberg (2007). "Inflation and Unemployment: A Layperson's Guide to the Phillips Curve." Federal Reserve Bank of Richmond. *Economic Quarterly* 93(3): 201–228.

Lee, Chung H. (1992). "The Government, Financial System, and Large Private Enterprises in the Economic Development of South Korea." *World Development* 20(2): 187–197.

Lee, Chung H. (2002). "The State and Institutions in East Asian Economic Development." *Journal of the Korean Economy* 3(1): 1–17.

Lee, Chung H. (2006). "Institutional Reform in Japan and Korea: Why the Difference?" In Magnus Blomstrom and Sumner La Croix, eds., *Institutional Change in Japan*. London: Routledge.

Lijphart, Arend (1999). *Patterns of Democracy: Government Forms and Performance in Thirty-Six Countries*. New Haven, CT: Yale University Press.

Lindgren, Carl-Johan, Gillian Garcia, and Matthew I. Saal (1996). *Bank Soundness and Macroeconomic Policy*. Washington, DC: International Monetary Fund.

Lincoln, Edward J. (2001). *Arthritic Japan: The Slow Pace of Economic Reform*. Washington, DC: Brookings Institution Press.

Mackay, Charles (1980). *Extraordinary Popular Delusions and the Madness of Crowds*. New York: Harmon Books. (Originally published in 1841.)

McCallum, Bennett. (2003). "Japanese Monetary Policy, 1991–2001." Federal Reserve Bank of Richmond. *Economic Quarterly* 89(1): 1–31.

Ministry of Finance (various years). Japanese government budget data. Available at http://www.mof.go.jp/jouhou/syukei/syukei.htm.

Ministry of Health, Labor, and Welfare (2006). "Shakai Hosho no Kyufu to Futan no Mitoshi." May. Available at http://www.kantei.go.jp/jp/singi/syakaihosyou/dai18/18siryou2.pdf.

Minsky, Hyman P. (1982). "The Financial Instability Hypothesis: Capitalistic Processes and the Behavior of the Economy." In C. P. Kindleberger and J. P. Laffargue, eds., *Financial Crises: Theory, History and Policy*. Cambridge: Cambridge University Press.

Miyajima, Hideaki et al. (2003). "Shinten suru Koporeto-gabanansu Kaikaku wo Ikani Rikai suruka." Policy Research Institute, The Ministry of Finance: *Financial Review* (December): 156–193.

Mochizuki, Mike Masato (1982). *Managing and Influencing the Japanese Legislative Process: The Role of Parties and the National Diet*. Ph.D. diss., Harvard University, Cambridge, MA.

Mulgan, Aurelia George (2002). *Japan's Failed Revolution: Koizumi and the Politics of Economic Reform*. Canberra, NSW: Asia Pacific Press.

Nakao, Takehiko (2002). "Nihon no 1990-nendai ni okeru zaisei seisaku no keiken: Baburu hokai-go no nagabiku keizai teimei no nakade." PRI Discussion Paper Series No. 02A-11. Policy Research Institute, the Ministry of Finance. Tokyo, Japan, February.

The National Institute of Population and Social Security Research (2006). *Nihon no shorai suikei jinko*. December. Tokyo: Author. Available at http://www.ipss.go.jp/pp- newest/j/newest03/newest03.asp.

Noland, Marcus, and Adam Posen (2002). "The Scapegoats for Japanese Deflation." *Financial Times*. December 6th.

Organization for Economic Cooperation and Development (OECD) (various years). *Economic Outlook: Statistics and Projections*. CD-ROMs. Paris: OECD.

Organization for Economic Cooperation and Development (OECD) (2006). *Society at a Glance: OECD Social Indicators*. Paris: OECD.

O'Hara, Maureen, and David Easley (1979). "The Postal Savings System in the Depression." *Journal of Economic History* 34(3): 741–753.

Ohkawa, K., and Harvey Rosovsky (1973). *The Economic Growth of Japan*. Stanford, CA: Stanford University Press.

Okazaki, Tetsuji (1998). "Nihon no Zaisei Seisaku to Makuro Keizai: Rekishi-teki Pasupekutibu kara no Saihyouka." *Financial Review* (October).

Okazaki, Tetsuji (2007). "The Evolution of Corporate Finance and Corporate Governance in Prewar Japan: Comments on 'Were Banks Really at the Center of the Prewar Japanese Financial System?'" *Monetary and Economic Studies* 25(1): 89–94.

Okina, Kunio (1999). "Monetary Policy under Zero Inflation: A Response to Criticisms and Questions Regarding Monetary Policy." *Monetary and Economic Studies* 17(3): 157–199.

Okina, Yuri (2000). "Recent Developments Surrounding Japan's Postal Savings Business and Its Future Position in the Financial System." *Japan Research Review* (July).

Patrick, Hugh and Henry Rosovsky, eds. (1976). *Asia's New Giant: How the Japanese Economy Works*. Washington, DC: The Brookings Institution.

Pempel, T. J. (1990). *Uncommon Democracies: The One-Party Dominant Regimes.* Ithaca, NY: Cornell University Press.

Pempel, T. J. (1998). *Regime Shift: Comparative Dynamics of the Japanese Political Economy.* Ithaca, NY: Cornell University Press.

Pierson, Paul (1994). *Dismantling the Welfare State: Reagan, Thatcher and the Politics of Retrenchment in Britain and the United States.* New York: Cambridge University Press.

Policy Research Institute (2003). "Shinten suru Koporeto-gabanansu Kaikaku to Nihon Kigyo no Saisei–Hokoku-sho." The Ministry of Finance. June. Available at http://www.mof.go.jp/jouhou/soken/kenkyu.htm and http://www.mof.go.jp/jouhou/soken/kenkyu/zk063/furoku02.pdf.

Richardson, Bradley (1997). *Japanese Democracy: Power, Coordination, and Performance.* New Haven, CT: Yale University Press.

Sakakibara, Eisuke (1991). "The Japanese Politico-Economic System and the Public Sector." In Samuel Kernell, ed., *Parallel Politics.* Washington DC: Brookings Institution.

Sakamoto, Takayuki (1999a). *Building Policy Legitimacy in Japan: Political Behavior beyond Rational Choice.* Basingstoke, UK: Macmillan/New York: St. Martin's Press.

Sakamoto, Takayuki (1999b). "Explaining Electoral Reform: Japan versus Italy and New Zealand." *Party Politics* 5(4): 419–438.

Sako, M. (1997). "Shunto: The Role of Employer and Union Coordination at the Industry and Inter-Sectoral Levels." In M. Sako and H. Sato, eds., *Japanese Labour and Management in Transition: Diversity, Flexibility and Participation.* London: Routledge.

Sato, Seizaburo, and Tetsuhisa Matsuzaki (1986). *Jiminto Seiken.* Tokyo: Chuo Koron-sha.

Sawyer, Malcolm (1976). "Income Distribution in OECD Countries." *Economic Outlook* Paris: OECD, pp. 3–36.

Schoppa, L. J. (2001). "Japan, the Reluctant Reformer." *Foreign Affairs* 80(5): 76–90.

Schumpeter, Joseph A. (1942). *Capitalism, Socialism and Democracy.* New York: Harper & Brothers.

Shiller, Robert J. (2005). *Irrational Exuberance* (2nd ed.). Princeton, NJ: Princeton University Press.

Shimizu, Masato (2005). *Kantei Shudo: Koizumi Junichiro no Kakumei.* Tokyo: Nihon Keizai Shimbun-sha.

Shinkawa, T. (1993). *Nihon-gata fukushi no seiji-keizai-gaku* [The Political Economy of Japanese-Style Welfare]. Tokyo: Sannichi Shobo.

Souma, Toshiyuki, and Yoshio Tsutsui (2005). "Recent Competition in the Japanese Life Insurance Industry." *Osaka University Discussion Paper No. 637* (June). Available at http://www.iser.osaka-u.ac.jp/library/dp/2005/DP0637.pdf.

Suzuki, Yoshio (1980). *Money and Banking in Contemporary Japan.* New Haven, CT: Yale University Press.

Suzuki, Yoshio, ed. (1987). *The Japanese Financial System.* Oxford: Clarendon Press.

Tanaka, Hideaki (2004). "Zaisei Rule: Mokuhyo to Yosan Manejimento no Kaikaku." In Aoki Masahiko and Tsuru Kotaro, eds., *Nihon no zaisei kaikaku: Kuni no katachi wo dou kaeruka.* Tokyo: Toyo Keizai Shimpo-sha: 295–363.

Tett, Gillian (2003). *Saving the Sun.* New York: HarperCollins Publishers.

Teranishi, Juro (2007). "Were Banks Really at the Center of the Prewar Japanese Financial System?" *Monetary and Economic Studies* 25(1): 49–76.

Toya, Tetsuro (2006). *The Political Economy of the Japanese Financial Big Bang*. Oxford: Oxford University Press.

Tsebelis, George (2002). *Veto Players: How Political Institutions Work*. Princeton, NJ: Princeton University Press.

Ueda, Kazuo (2000). "Causes of Japan's Banking Problems in the 1990s." In Takeo Hoshi and Hugh Patrick, eds., *Crisis and Change in the Japanese Financial System*. Norwell, MA: Kluwer Academic Publishers.

van Wolferen, Karel (1989). *The Enigma of Japanese Power: People and Politics in a Stateless Nation*. New York: Knopf.

Vogel, Steven K. (2006). *Japan Remodeled: How Government and Industry Are Reforming Japanese Capitalism*. Ithaca, NY: Cornell University Press.

Yamamura, Kozo, and Yasukichi Yasuba (1987). *The Political Economy of Japan: The Domestic Transformation, Vol. 1*. Stanford, CA: Stanford University Press.

Yuka Hayashi *Wall Street Journal* (2008). "Growing Reliance on Temps Holds Back Japan's Rebound." January 7, p. A1.

World Bank (1993). "The East Asian Miracle." *World Bank Policy Research Report*. New York: Oxford University Press.

Index